FROM HUMAN TO POSTHUMAN

Technology is one of the dominant forces shaping the emerging postmodern world. Indeed the very fabric of daily life is dependent upon various information, communication and transportation technologies. With anticipated advances in biotechnology, artificial intelligence and robotics, that dependence will increase. Yet this growing dependence is accompanied with a deep ambivalence.

For many, technology symbolizes the faith of the postmodern world, but it is an ambivalent faith encapsulating both our hopes and fears for the future. This book examines the religious foundations underlying this troubled faith in technology, as well as critically and constructively engaging particular technological developments from a theological perspective.

Ashgate Science and Religion Series

Series Editors:

Roger Trigg, *Department of Philosophy, University of Warwick, UK*

J. Wentzel van Huyssteen, *James I. McCord Professor of Theology and Science, Princeton Theological Seminary, USA*

Science and religion have often been thought to be at loggerheads but much contemporary work in this flourishing interdisciplinary field suggests this is far from the case. The *Ashgate Science and Religion Series* presents exciting new work to advance interdisciplinary study, research and debate across key themes in science and religion, exploring the philosophical relations between the physical and social sciences on the one hand and religious belief on the other. Contemporary issues in philosophy and theology are debated, as are prevailing cultural assumptions arising from the 'post-modernist' distaste for many forms of reasoning. The series enables leading international authors from a range of different disciplinary perspectives to apply the insights of the various sciences, theology and philosophy and look at the relations between the different disciplines and the rational connections that can be made between them. These accessible, stimulating new contributions to key topics across science and religion will appeal particularly to individual academics and researchers, graduates, postgraduates and upper-undergraduate students.

Other titles published in this series:

Theology and Psychology
Fraser Watts
0 7546 1672 X (hbk)
0 7546 1673 8 (pbk)

Islam and Science
Muzaffar Iqbal
0 7546 0799 2 (hbk)
0 7546 0800 X (pbk)

Science, Theology, and Ethics
Ted Peters
0 7546 0824 7 (hbk)
0 7546 0825 5 (pbk)

Theology and Modern Physics
Peter E. Hodgson
0 7546 3622 4 (hbk)
0 7546 3623 2 (pbk)

From Human to Posthuman

Christian Theology and Technology in a Postmodern World

BRENT WATERS
Garrett-Evangelical Theological Seminary, USA

ASHGATE

Published by
Ashgate Publishing Limited
Gower House
Croft Road
Aldershot
Hampshire GU11 3HR
England

Ashgate Publishing Company
Suite 420
101 Cherry Street
Burlington, VT 05401-4405
USA

Ashgate website: http://www.ashgate.com

British Library Cataloguing in Publication Data
Waters, Brent
  From Human to Posthuman: Christian Theology and Technology in a Postmodern World. – (Ashgate Science and Religion Series)
  1. Christian ethics. 2. Technology – Moral and ethical aspects. 3. Technology – Religious aspects – Christianity. I. Title
  241

US Library of Congress Cataloging in Publication Data
Waters, Brent
  From Human to Posthuman: Christian Theology and Technology in a Postmodern World/Brent Waters
    p. cm. – (Ashgate Science and Religion Series)
  Includes bibliographical references and index.
  1. Postmodernism – Religious aspects – Christianity. 2. Man (Theology). 3. Technology – Religious aspects – Christianity. I. Title. II. Series.
  BR115.P74W38 2005
  261.5'6–dc22

2005014478

ISBN 0 7546 3914 2 (hardback)
ISBN 0 7546 3915 0 (paperback)

This book is printed on acid-free paper.

Printed and bound in Great Britain by Antony Rowe Ltd, Chippenham, Wiltshire

Contents

Acknowledgments

Writing is the result of relationships, and I am blessed with many good friends and colleagues. Donna Techau, Andy Watts and Steve Long read substantial portions of early drafts of the manuscript. They were generous with their time and attention, offering many helpful comments and criticisms. I am grateful for the patience and inquisitiveness of my students in various seminars. Their probing questions helped me to navigate an often bewildering conceptual landscape, and I hope these explorations did not leave them bewildered in return. Periodic conversations with Ben Mitchell, Heidi Campbell and Kevin Seybold helped me to clarify some key concepts, and I am especially grateful for some extended conversations with David Hogue and Ronald Cole-Turner. The book is dedicated to Oliver O'Donovan and Joan Lockwood O'Donovan. I owe both of them intellectual and spiritual debts that can never be fully repaid. My indebtedness to Oliver will be obvious in the pages that follow, for through his writing, lectures and friendship I have learned how to be a theologian. I expect he will not agree with some of my analysis and application of his work, but I hope my efforts nonetheless reflect favorably upon him as a gifted teacher and scholar. My debt to Joan is less obvious but equally important, for she introduced me to the thinking of George Grant. It is through his writings that I acquired a critical tool for assessing the crucial role technology plays in our current twilight of justice. I would also like to thank Wentzel Vanhuyssteen and Roger Trigg for inviting me to write a book in this series on science and religion, and I especially appreciate the kindness and wise counsel of my editor at Ashgate, Sarah Lloyd. Finally, I cannot imagine undertaking this project in the absence of my wife, Diana, and daughter, Erin. As always, they patiently endured my musings and time locked away in study. They are constant reminders that theological discourse does not consist of mere abstractions, but is disciplined and faithful reflection on the bonds of love and affection.

Brent Waters

To Oliver and Joan

Introduction

This is a book about theological ethics, specifically *Christian* theological ethics. As such, it draws upon and interprets the Christian tradition as a resource in pursuing the tasks of moral, social and political ordering. Although my intended audience is predominantly Christian, I hope I have written in a manner such that readers not sharing this faith will nonetheless find the book to be informative and beneficial.

Theological and moral inquiry, however, cannot be conducted in a historical and cultural vacuum. The task I undertake is to critically examine and assess the influence that technology is exerting on the formation of contemporary culture. This task is certainly not unprecedented. Many treatises either defaming or defending the emergence of modern technological civilization have already been written. Moreover, any reflection on cultural formation cannot avoid the question of technology. Any form of human association, however archaic or advanced, is dependent upon underlying technological foundations, however simple or complex they may be. As Victor Ferkiss has observed, 'Civilizations are based on the interplay of technology and human values' (Ferkiss, 1969, p. 49).

Although coming to terms with the relation between technology and culture is a perennial issue, the contemporary world is entering uncharted territory. This is due in part to rapid advances in such areas as information technology, biotechnology and nanotechnology that quicken the pace of cultural change while also magnifying the scope of human power. In this respect, the transition from an industrial to informational society, for instance, is simply another stage in cultural evolution in which humans exert greater mastery over nature and human nature.

What is unique about this transition, however, is the potential to move beyond mastery to transformation. The sheer ubiquity of technology is forming a technoculture populated by technosapiens, for in order to fully utilize the power of the technologies currently being developed and envisioned, humans must strive to transform themselves into posthumans. Herein lies the problem, for the consequences for good or ill of such radical transformation cannot be known in advance. Again, as Ferkiss warned, 'The synthesis of postmodern technology and industrial man could produce a new civilization, or it could mean the end of the human race' (Ferkiss, 1969, p. 56).

The threat is not solely a result of growing technological power. What is more troubling in many respects is the underlying intellectual, moral and religious presuppositions, often more implicit than explicit, shaping this radically transformative vision. As described in the following chapters, this vision may be characterized as cybernetic as opposed to organic or mechanistic. A cybernetic paradigm reduces material reality to underlying information that can, in principle, be infinitely manipulated and reconfigured.

If this is true, then the only thing preventing a radical transformation of nature and human nature is inadequate technology, a problem that can be remedied, again in principle, through research and development. There is no real boundary separating nature and artifice, only patterns or lines of information that can be erased and redrawn; no real limit that cannot be eventually overcome. Thus my principal contention is that when the *postmodern* emphasis on deconstruction and construction is joined with this cybernetic vision, there is no compelling reason why radically *posthuman* transformation should not be pursued. This does not imply that postmoderns inevitably aspire to become posthuman, only that there is nothing inherent to postmodernism that can effectively oppose this prospect other than to assert emotive preferences or objections.

The two words emphasized in the preceding paragraph require some further explanation for how they are used in this inquiry. The term 'postmodern' is invoked frequently in both academic and popular discourse. Yet it seemingly defies any precise or agreed-upon definition. In employing this term I am referring to the works of social theorists, philosophers and theologians who embrace (or who are accused by their critics of embracing) the historicist assumption that reality is an artifact of imaginative, social or political construction. Hence the affinity with the cybernetic vision described above. In addition, I am *not* using postmodern to refer to an emerging historical era or epoch displacing modernity, for to be a postmodernist requires rejecting any epochal notion of history. Moreover, I also use postmodern as a descriptive shorthand to identify a narrow range of themes and authors that are germane to this book as part of a series on science and religion.

The word 'posthuman' is also generating a growing body of literature, but it too resists any common definition. I use the term to refer to a loose confederation of writers and intellectuals who envision a day when humans will virtually merge with their technology, thereby creating a new and superior posthuman species. In this respect, posthuman rhetoric shares many similarities with and is dependent upon postmodern discourse, but is not synonymous with it. A postmodern, for instance, need not be committed to a posthuman future, but posthumanists are by necessity committed postmodernists.

I argue throughout the subsequent chapters that postmodern and posthuman discourse represent emerging dominant forces in contemporary cultural formation. Consequently, the purpose of this book is to help Christians engage an emerging technoculture in a manner that is both critical and constructive. As an initial step in this engagement, I have limited myself to examining and assessing a restricted range of prominent landmarks within the expansive postmodern and posthuman panoramic landscape. I anticipate that this approach will disappoint two groups of potential readers.

First, this book will disappoint readers who are expecting to find in its pages either a sweeping condemnation or defense of either modern or postmodern modes of thought. My reason for such reticence is that I find commendatory and condemnatory elements in both. I share with postmodernists, for instance, a suspicion of modern certainty based exclusively on empirical data, while rejecting their belief that reality is largely what we make of it. Conversely, I share with modernists the conviction that reality is objective, but I part company when the objectively real is reduced to what is material. Moreover, my task as a theologian is not to recast religious beliefs and convictions in terms palatable to either a modern or postmodern audience. Rather, my task is to formulate a counter discourse to either option, one that is genuinely Christian and theological. In this respect, modernity and postmodernism are not forced options that must be either accepted or rejected, but phenomena to be engaged if Christians are to faithfully articulate and enact their faith within contemporary circumstances.

Second, this book will disappoint readers who are anticipating a detailed analysis of ethical issues related to various technologies and their proposed policy solutions. Admittedly, current and anticipated developments, for example, in information technology, biotechnology and nanotechnology require such painstaking attention if a host of troubling evils are to be avoided. But this is not what this book is about. Rather, pursuing the moral, social and political ordering of an emerging technoculture requires, at least initially, a coming to terms with the broad concepts empowering this cultural vision. In this respect, 'technology' does not refer to technical achievement and its accompanying ethical, social and political problems, but represents a late liberal proclivity toward mutating practical moral reasoning into a technological rationale (O'Donovan, 1996, pp. 271–4). Consequently, this book is interpretive rather than analytical; it is not so much a systematic and exhaustive study as a meditation on our present circumstances.

In short, my goal has been to write a book that will assist a process of Christian discourse, deliberation and discernment for living faithfully in an emerging technoculture.[1] Moreover, such a process should not be insular or uninformed, thereby requiring Christian theologians to know something about science and technology, and how these once separate endeavors are collapsing into a singular act. Yet such open and informed inquiry does not require that theology must be deconstructed and reconstructed as dictated by an ascendant technoscience. The challenge is instead to formulate a theological discourse that assists a Christian formation of good, true and faithful lives in light of the rising ascendancy of technoscience as *the* formative cultural factor. Hence the need for a counter discourse that is genuinely Christian and theological. This task need not be premised on the belief that Christians have a corner on truth and goodness, only that whatever they know about these qualities they know as Christians, however partial and imperfect that knowledge may be. Moreover, in telling this story with the vocabulary and grammar of this counter discourse, they may also endeavor to tell it in a way that enables, rather than disables, other quests for the good and the true undertaken by those who do not share their faith.

Note

1   This threefold process of discourse, deliberation and discernment is borrowed from Verhey, 2002.

CHAPTER ONE

The Late Modern Landscape

The word 'postmodern' is invoked frequently by many contemporary intellectuals, but a precise definition proves elusive. A cottage industry has emerged to debate when (or if) postmodernity began, and when (or if) it has supplanted modernity. This lack of precision is admittedly frustrating, but the very ambiguity associated with this term captures the character of our present circumstances. There is a general perception that the beginning of the twenty-first century marks a time of significant cultural change, but little consensus regarding its causes and direction; no agreement over whether we are riding the crest of a new age or caught in the undertow of a receding one. Such semantic imprecision should not be surprising, however, for any attempt to place contemporary events within a larger flow of history is bound to be tentative and speculative.

Although I have no desire to enter the formal disputes over mapping the borders of postmodernity, I argue in this chapter that some inexact placement of the postmodern divide can be achieved by examining two overlapping cultural shifts. The first shift, beginning roughly in the seventeenth century and extending into the twenty-first with diminished momentum, corresponds with science displacing religion as the culturally dominant and formative force. The second shift, beginning roughly in the late nineteenth century and extending into the twenty-first with gathering momentum, corresponds with technology replacing science as the culturally dominant and formative influence. For the purpose of this inquiry, we may conveniently label the first transition as a shift from providence to progress, and the second as the shift from progress to process.

Some clarification of what is meant by the phrase *culturally dominant and formative force* is in order. Following H. Richard Niebuhr, culture is a general phenomenon that 'comprises language, habits, ideas, beliefs, customs, social organization, inherited artifacts, technical processes, and values' (Niebuhr, 1951, pp. 31–2). Although culture is not divorced from nature and in many respects is created to meet natural necessities, it nonetheless consists of activities that are undertaken to achieve uniquely human purposes (Gustafson, 1981, pp. 3–16). A lake, for instance, is natural while a reservoir is cultural; an angry scream is instinctual but cursing an enemy is a cultured act. Particular cultures, however, do not exist in historical vacuums. Consequently, a culture requires what may be described as an interpretive discourse, broadly conceived, that serves to preserve, reform and pass on traditions; order social and political institutions; and project future aspirations. In this respect, theology, science, or technology may serve as public types of discourse for achieving these interpretive purposes.

Two important aspects of these cultural forces need to be noted. First, the type of public discourse enjoying a privileged status changes over time. The interpretive needs and purposes of a culture do not remain static. An alternative mode of discourse may arise which more adequately meets these needs and purposes, thereby gaining an authoritative and formative status at the expense of the predecessor. Although the shift from one form of dominant cultural discourse to another may occur rapidly, the transition tends to be evolutionary rather than revolutionary, even though the cumulative effect may be dramatic (Basalla, 1988; Kuhn, 1970). A scientific culture, for instance, is markedly different to its earlier theological counterpart, but identifying the point in which the former supplanted the latter defies precise determination.

Second, the emergence of a new dominant and formative cultural force does not mean the old one is necessarily eradicated (Ferkiss, 1969, pp. 27–8). A once prevalent form of discourse may continue to be intelligible even though it no longer enjoys a privileged or authoritative status. Theologians, for example, continue to write books in a culture shaped by science even though theology is no longer regarded as a dominant cultural force. In addition, it is indicative that a cultural transition is under way when different types of discourse appeal extensively to what is perceived as the dominant form of public discourse. In the early seventeenth century, for example, scientists appealed frequently to theological doctrines to buttress the validity of their claims, while in the late nineteenth and early twentieth centuries theologians often appealed to science to support their arguments (Brooke, 1991). More tellingly for the purpose of this inquiry, technology was once portrayed by its most eager proponents as an applied science in order to enhance the reputation of lowly engineers and inventors. Now funding of 'pure' scientific research is increasingly justified by its potential to promote technological development.

With these clarifying notes in mind, we may now begin our exploration of the two cultural shifts that will help us place the postmodern divide.

From Providence to Progress

Question 27 of the Heidelberg Catechism asks: 'What do you understand by the providence of God?' To this the prescribed answer is: 'The almighty and ever-present power of God whereby he still upholds, as it were by his own hand, heaven and earth together with all creatures, and rules in such a way that leaves and grass, rain and drought, fruitful and unfruitful years, food and drink, health and sickness, riches and poverty, and everything else, come to us not by chance but by his fatherly hand' (*Heidelberg Catechism*, 1962, pp. 32–3). This brief answer confidently asserts that nothing occurs that is not in accordance with God's will and purpose. The apparent vagaries of natural forces and daily life are not random events, but indications of a creation being governed by its creator. God is the sovereign Lord of nature and history.

The Catechism, however, is not content to merely assert God's power, for the next question asks: 'What advantage comes from acknowledging God's creation and providence?' The given answer is again terse: 'We learn that we are to be patient in adversity, grateful in the midst of blessing, and to trust our faithful God and Father for the future, assured that no creature shall separate from his love, since all creatures are so completely in his hand that without his will they cannot even move' (ibid., p. 34). The seemingly capricious series of events that humans routinely encounter is in fact a method of divine instruction. Through the unwieldy interplay of good and evil we learn the virtues of patience, gratitude and fidelity. It is only in retrospect, in God's own good time, that we will discern the providential and orderly pattern of God's redemptive plan. In the meantime we must remain satisfied with the assurance of God's steadfast love.

It is striking that these sweeping claims are merely asserted instead of argued. There is no suggestion that nature could be studied and better understood in order to ameliorate human toil and misery; no hint that the justice of God's dealings with humans might be probed, much less challenged. There is simply no effort to persuade the catechumen that the teachings are true. What is also striking to the contemporary reader is the seeming ease and credulity with which the doctrine of providence is asserted and presumably accepted. Yet it must be kept in mind that an instructional document is not meant to persuade, but to summarize what is already believed. Although the Heidelberg Catechism was published in 1563 to reconcile differences between Lutherans and Calvinists in the Palatinate, a long cultural heritage stood behind it though now expressed in a distinctly Protestant rather than Catholic dialect.

Augustine is arguably the most influential figure in shaping the principal strands of this heritage. In his *City of God* he offers an expansive account of God's providential governance of creation. God has blessed humans with everything they need to survive and flourish. The utility of nature in general, and the human body in particular, have been ordered by the creator to achieve this very end. Through procreation, for example, humans perpetuate themselves from generation to generation (Augustine, 1984, pp. 1070–71). These divine gifts are not confined to the realm of natural necessity. More importantly, there are the blessings of intellect and ingenuity which make possible the formation of human culture. In effusive language Augustine describes wondrous achievements in such areas as agriculture, architecture, navigation, medicine, art and literature (ibid., pp. 1072–3). Human history has unfolded within the laws of God's providence (ibid., p. 96), and history is itself an educational process teaching a culture about God's enduring care (ibid., p. 392).

But it is a hard education. God's providential care does not mean that humankind enjoys an earthly paradise, for evils originating in nature and culture conspire to form a 'hell on earth'. According to Augustine, it is only Christ's grace that can liberate individuals from this hell, because the source of evil is sin and not a flawed creation (ibid., p. 1068). Since God governs creation with justice, pain and misery is the fitting punishment for Adam's fateful rebellion (ibid., p. 1073). The presence of suffering is a sign that God has not abandoned creation, but continues to be its sovereign Lord. Moreover, God's justice is tempered by mercy. God's goodness pervades creation, showering the world with innumerable blessings.

It is important to note, however, that these blessings are consolations, not rewards. Humans cannot use divine gifts to create a heaven on earth, but must wait for their relief and perfection in God's own good time. A perfect peace is the promised destiny of the elect, but the way leading to this destination is circuitous (ibid., p. 1082). Invoking the Apostle Paul (Romans 11:33), Augustine reminds his readers that the ways of God are untraceable and inscrutable (Augustine, 1984, p. 896). The outlines of providence can be seen, but only vaguely as puzzling reflections in a mirror. The details of God's providential care are mysterious and can never be known with certainty – at least this side of eternity. The perfect peace that awaits the believer is also a perfect rest; the rest of a perpetual Sabbath. It is in this rest that we shall at last embrace perfect virtue and desire, for it is only in the fullness of time that God's blessings are given to reward rather than console. It is only from this vantage point that one can gaze back upon history and recognize the clear pattern of God's governance (ibid., pp. 897–8).

Consequently, the end or *telos* of the elect is an eternal Sabbath rest. From this endpoint Augustine traces the providential history of creation back to its origin. It is a history comprising seven epochs, in which the present age is the sixth (ibid., p. 1091). It is in the impending seventh epoch that the faithful shall find true peace and rest, enjoying with God in their perfected state an eternal eighth day of creation. The destiny of creation is to share eternity with its creator, for as Augustine asks rhetorically, 'what is our end but to reach that kingdom which has no end?' (ibid., p. 1091)

This brief excursion into the *City of God* does not imply that Augustine was the only or even dominant voice forming an emerging Christian culture. His significance waxed and waned among subsequent generations of theologians. But the range and architecture of his thought cast a long and influential shadow over the developing theological, social and political thought of western Christendom (Brown, 1996, pp. 34–53). That influence remained so pronounced and enduring that he served as a convenient lightning rod for the Enlightenment's assault against the church; to assail Augustine was synonymous with refuting a moribund Christianity (Rist, 1994, pp. 290–94). For what Augustine presented in his masterpiece was nothing less than a 'positive and comprehensive philosophy of history, an interpretation of the entire human drama' (Latourette, 1975, pp. 175–6). It was a drama whose beginning and end in God were certain, but the details of the providential storyline in between proved untraceable. Subsequent Catholic and Protestant editors refined and embellished the storyline, but the essentially Augustinian structure of the drama remained unaltered for over a millennium.

It is not surprising that the seemingly credulous teaching on providence could be merely asserted rather than argued in the Heidelberg Catechism. The terse answers were slogans reinforcing what a long theological and cultural tradition propounded, and what the students thereby already took for granted, namely, that although God was in control of the world and its fate, life in the meantime was tough and uncertain, inspiring a fitting response of faithful patience. What is remarkable is how rapidly following the Catechism's publication its teaching on providence was greeted with mounting incredulity, prompting subsequent theological reformulations that would have appeared barely recognizable to its authors.

In the early eighteenth century, for example, Jonathan Edwards pondered the significance of a collapsing balcony in the Northampton church during the Sunday morning worship service.[1] Shortly after the sermon had begun the balcony crashed, covering the worshippers both sitting in and under it with shattered timbers and other heavy debris. Their rescuers feared the worst, expecting 'to find many people dead, and dashed to pieces' (Edwards, 1974, p. 345). To their astonishment, however, no one was killed, and although many were cut and bruised there were no broken bones or other serious injuries. Edwards is quick to attribute this good fortune to divine providence, but what is interesting to note is his detailed description of and conjecture on how the episode occurred. The building had been allowed to fall into disrepair since a new meeting house was currently under construction. The beams supporting the balcony were especially weak, and their decay had been exacerbated by a severe winter followed by an unusually warm spring. In short, the balcony was an accident waiting to happen. Yet it collapsed so quickly and in such a manner that the 'motions of every piece of timber, and the precise place of safety where every one should sit, and fall, when none were in any capacity to care for their own preservation' (Edwards, 1974, pp. 345–6). The event itself disclosed both God's displeasure and protection, inspiring corresponding responses of humility and gratitude. In expounding the 'miraculous' nature of this providential act, Edwards did not appeal to divine intervention which suspended or violated the laws of nature. Why the balcony collapsed and why timber and bodies fell the way they did in avoiding death or injury were explicable in terms of what was known about the nature of decaying wood and the physics of moving objects. What was genuinely miraculous was that God had ordered a series of events to occur in such a way that the collapsing balcony would have the greatest effect upon the faithful of Northampton. Edwards used the best science of his day to explicate the doctrine of providence revealed in this particular incident, and it was an explication that would not have seemed foreign to his Protestant forbears.

This easy recognition, however, faded in the following century. Horace Bushnell, for example, chides phrenology (a respectable science in his day) for its vain attempt to locate the physical situation of various thoughts within the human brain that could then be subsequently mapped. Presumably this mapping would offer insight into the workings of the soul or psyche. Bushnell is confident that the effort will fail because only poetry can lead the way to a true and complete science of humankind (Bushnell, 1849, p. 73). What this curt dismissal reflects is not a keen ability to discern bad science, but hostility directed against science's growing influence on theology. A turn toward science corrupts religious faith, because theology cannot be understood or expressed in scientific terms (ibid., pp. 93–4, 310–13). Doctrine expresses opinions (ibid., pp. 304–5), and the attempt to cloak them in the mantel of science only perpetuates the decline of Christianity (ibid., pp. 321–2). Bushnell, then, is not anti-science but is opposed to dogmatic theologians who turn to science in constructing their stultifying arguments. This is the case because religious faith in general and Christian faith in particular can only be understood through subjective experience, and this experience can only be expressed in poetic or artistic terms (ibid., pp. 203–4). It is dogma masquerading as, or distorted by, science that restricts this subjective encounter and expression. Consequently, Bushnell feels no need to invoke science in promulgating his doctrine of providence, because he simply has no use for any doctrine. Religion is a matter of the heart, not the head.

Bushnell's dismissive attitude toward doctrine, however, is not entirely representative. Many theologians still believed that religion encompassed both head and heart. James McCosh, Bushnell's contemporary, for instance, wrote a systematic treatise on the methods of divine government.[2] The purpose of his treatise was to portray providence and conscience respectively as the external and internal indications of God's governance (McCosh, 1882, p. 16). McCosh asserts that anyone observing nature can and should conclude that it has been designed by a 'higher intelligence' (ibid., p. 3). Science confirms this observation, although revelation is needed to obtain a full knowledge of God; the external signs of providence must be combined with the internal witness of conscience. In explicating his doctrine of providence, McCosh spends a great deal of time discussing the intricacies of the latest scientific theories, especially in the areas of geology and biology. The purported purpose of his lengthy excursions into the realm of science is to confirm God's orderly governance of the natural world, but the tone is defensive and apologetic. McCosh simultaneously tries to refute the atheistic and pantheistic implications of recent discoveries (ibid., pp. 207–13), while also making traditional Christian claims explicable in scientific terms. He employs Taylor's words, for example, in insisting that 'the great miracle of providence' is 'that no miracles are needed to accomplish its purposes' (ibid., p. 178). McCosh's account of providence reflects a great deal of scientific sophistication, but in the end God appears to be more a decorative ornament than a necessary governor. In turning to the conscience, the tone becomes less defensive and more confident, while the references to science are more cursory and oblique. Seemingly, even if science should call into question the evidence of God's governance of the physical world, the province of the soul is a dependable bulwark for exhibiting the moral need for divine involvement in human life.

These succinct summaries may be used to plot an important trajectory that emerged in theological thinking following the promulgation of the Heidelberg Catechism. Edwards could confidently reassert the theological claims under-lying the Catechism's teaching on providence, and used science to explain God's providential care. Presumably this enriched explanation reinforced the religious responses of humility and gratitude. For Bushnell, however, science impedes genuine religious impulses, because they are grounded in experience rather than rationality. Science is not so much bad as it is used badly by theologians to construct doctrines that ignore the experiential basis of faith. Theologians should concentrate on the spiritual dimensions of the human heart which can only be expressed in poetry and art, rather than attempting to explain God's handiwork in rationalistic and scientific terms. Consequently, there is no reason to address whether science confirms or challenges the doctrine of providence, because there is no compelling reason to propound the doctrine in the first place. At first glance it appears that McCosh employs Edwards's strategy in a more sophisticated manner. Yet, unlike Edwards, McCosh must first defend providence against objections raised by new scientific theories. More importantly, the resulting doctrinal account must be couched in categories that are scientifically intelligible. Although McCosh contends that the inward world of faith and morality mirrors that of the external world, and therefore both are subject to divine governance, the former is clearly more secure and superior to the latter. Thus he shares with Bushnell the belief that the heart is the premier source of faith through which God asserts his moral governance. Moreover, McCosh is confident that the workings of the human psyche will remain an opaque mystery, resisting any definitive inquiries that science might launch. More tellingly, his defensive tone intimates that science has already effectively displaced theology as the dominant form of public discourse.

How may we account for this trajectory plotted by these three Protestant theologians? In order to answer this question, we must return to the sixteenth century and the rise of modern science. A new breed of scientists was gaining greater knowledge about the details of nature and history that had remained impenetrable to theologians. A growing body of scientific knowledge not only enriched intellectual pursuits, but was also applied to improving the health and material well-being of the general population. It was not the human lot to endure misery and suffering to the extent presumed by earlier doctrines of providence. Nor was this transition the aftermath of a so-called paradigmatic revolution. Theology was not shaken simply in reaction to the sun replacing the earth as the center of the universe, but as the result of the increasing ability of science to explain the workings of nature and history which had previously seemed beyond comprehension. The idea of progress fuelled by scientific discovery emerged as a more captivating cultural icon than that offered by an inscrutable providence. An exhaustive examination of how science came to displace theology as the dominant intellectual force is beyond the scope of this chapter, but some revealing points can be noted for plotting the course of this shift.

The antecedents of modern science can be conveniently placed with the recovery of Aristotle in the great medieval universities. This recovery enabled natural philosophers to establish themselves within the faculty of arts alongside the more established and prestigious faculties of medicine, law and theology. Although there were inevitable tensions among these faculties, the natural philosophers, emboldened by recent discoveries of extant texts of *the* Greek philosopher, were permitted to pursue their 'scientific' interests unencumbered, so long as they did not espouse any ideas contradicting scripture or church teaching – for example, Aristotle's claim that the earth is eternal rather than created (Grant, 1996).

Over time the arts in general, and natural philosophy in particular, developed greater methodological independence, easing their subservience to theology. This growing intellectual freedom paved the way for the so-called

scientific revolution of the sixteenth and seventeenth centuries. The employment of these refined methodologies, particularly in conjunction with new
observational and experimental techniques, prompted the emergence of a large
corpus of texts that could be called 'scientific' in the modern sense of the term,
especially in such fields as physics, astronomy and optics. It should not be
assumed, however, that this scientific literature contradicted doctrinal teaching.
Galileo's celebrated trial was anomalous (Lindberg and Numbers, 1986,
pp. 114–35), for more often than not the new science went about its business
with little or no interference from ecclesiastical authorities, as witnessed by the
prodigious work of both Protestant and Catholic scientists (ibid., pp. 136–66,
192–217). Most theologians tended to either ignore the new scientific
discoveries, or embrace them as confirmations of Christian doctrine. More
commonly, it was the scientists who invoked theology to bolster the veracity of
their claims. Johannes Kepler, for instance, argued that the physical structure
of a heliocentric cosmos was a reflection of the Trinity (Brooke, 1991, p. 3), and
Robert Boyle believed that his mechanistic portrayal of the universe reinforced
both the notions of God's orderly governance and miraculous interventions
(ibid., pp. 130–35). It was arguably the inherited constraints of Aristotelian
natural philosophy, rather than theology, that presented a greater barrier to
the new science (ibid., pp. 52–81).

By the beginning of the eighteenth century, however, theology was on the
defensive against what appeared to be an ascendant and hostile science. Yet
care must be taken in assessing this relationship, for it is only a partial
consequence of the more complex agenda of the Enlightenment.[3] The self-
styled philosophes were profane cosmopolitans, dedicated to promoting what
they believed was a liberating humanism. Freedom was the cornerstone of their
project, for its goal was to emancipate humankind from the shackles of
ignorance and superstition. All forms of external authority – save that of
unfettered reason – were objects of contempt, resulting in a wide range of
intellectual and religious targets. These targets were often assaulted with crude
but effective force rather than with any surgical precision. The Enlightenment
was not a uniform movement, but a 'volatile mixture of classicism, impiety,
and science; the philosophes, in a phrase, were modern pagans' (Gay, 1969,
p. 7).

As modern pagans, the philosophes were the vanguard in a war to liberate
history from its Augustinian captivity. Following Augustine's lead in the *City
of God*, increasingly elaborate epochal histories had been published up through
the end of the seventeenth century. The philosophes maintained this essentially
Augustinian structure while simplifying its sequence and recasting its content.
In barest outline, the religious fervor of the primeval orient was tamed by
ancient Greece and Rome only to decline under Christianity, but the long era
of deterioration could now be reversed through a modern rebirth of reason.
The midwife was classical antiquity, for the philosophes drew their inspiration
from Epicurus, Lucretius, Cicero and other kindred luminaries in championing
their born-again paganism.[4] It would not be an easy delivery. The birth canal
was blocked by the encrustations of a millennium of Christian superstition,
requiring radical surgery.

Science provided a useful surgical instrument, particularly in removing the tumor of providence. The strategy employed for dismantling this hideous doctrine was straightforward: it was condemned as being intellectually incoherent and morally bankrupt. The central doctrinal claim that the God who created the world also governs it was particularly vulnerable on both flanks. Divine governance purportedly consists of God's willful acts that are not fully comprehensible to any mere mortal. Consequently, whatever good or ill humans encounter is not the result of blind fate, but God's will. The new science, however, was uncovering a universe governed by law rather than fiat. The problem was not that the workings of nature were in principle beyond the limits of human understanding, but that Christian dogma prevented rational examination as witnessed by the dearth of scientific achievements during the dark ages of Christendom. Moreover, the growing body of scientific knowledge was being applied to improving the quality of daily life. The pain, misery and suffering that God presumably inflicted to teach such virtues as patience and fortitude were in reality the result of ignorance. Wherever science prevailed against superstition, improved health, commerce and comfort followed. Humans could fashion a better world for themselves if only science were unleashed from its bondage to religious disingenuousness. If the church, in both its Protestant and Catholic versions, insisted on clinging to an obsolete doctrine of providence, then they were also invoking a God who was either an incompetent or cruel creator. In either case, such a God was certainly not worthy of obedience or worship. The choice presented was stark: Europe could either cast its lot with the history of a moribund Christianity, or forge a new history of a progressive science invigorated by the rebirth of pagan philosophy.

The tactic deployed initially by theologians in defending providence was to seize the surgical instrument away from the adversary. Instead of challenging God's governance of the world, the new science confirmed God's wondrous work of creation; the laws of nature disclosed the orderly manner in which God governed creation. After all, none other than Isaac Newton – the quintessential scientist – insisted that his work did little more than illuminate the providential design of the universe (Brooke, 1991, pp. 144–51). To a limited extent, this was the tactic deployed by Edwards. Scientific evidence was used to blunt the force of philosophical attack by emphasizing the reasonableness of the theological doctrine he was defending.

This tactic was doomed to fail.[5] With the accumulation of greater scientific knowledge, the gaps within a Newtonian framework could be filled without appeal to divine intervention. Newton himself had created the opportunity for this turn of fortune by contending that the universe reflected evidence of divine design, *not* specific acts of God. Since God had presumably not designed an imperfect universe, then there was little reason for God to be an active participant in the daily affairs of creation. Consequently, a number of theologians turned increasingly to nature, instead of revelation, to describe the relationship between God and the world. These natural theologies portrayed a remote and detached creator. William Paley's watchmaker may have been an elegant theological image in light of the best science of his day, but it portrayed a deity who did little more than observe the beauty and precision of its own handiwork (Paley, 1820). The influence of this turn is seen in McCosh, who purportedly attempted to reassert a robust defense of providence, but devoted much of his effort to demonstrating the compatibility of science and religion. His insistence that God was active in every aspect of the world had the practical effect of making God indecipherable from nature. Although the goal of natural theology was to make God intelligible within a scientific age, the deity expounded was a dispassionate creator and not the God of orthodox Christian faith who gave both drought and rain, and punished and consoled sinners.

Such a God could not sustain religious devotion. Deism and rationalistic Christianity claimed few adherents beyond a small cadre of intellectuals. A God intimately involved in human life was needed to nourish the soul. Yet believers could no longer turn to science to disclose a divine presence in either nature or history. Many retreated inwardly to find God in the depth of their psyche, a place which was presumably invulnerable to scientific scrutiny and skepticism. A religion of the heart offered experience as an alternative foundation for belief, but it was a foundation of poetic sentiment rather than empirical knowledge. This withdrawal into personal faith was the tactic employed by Bushnell. The world could be divided between science and religion. The former guided by reason described physical reality, while the latter following the leading of the heart described spiritual reality. Believers could thereby have their faith nourished by a God who could be neither challenged nor proven by science.

Although a religion of the heart preserved a comfortable and comforting niche for God, the price was dear. Religion was now a matter of private belief instead of public explication. By the mid nineteenth century it was widely accepted that science had effectively displaced theology as the dominant source of reliable knowledge. In this respect the philosophes's expectation that 'religious institutions and religious explanations of events' would be 'displaced from the center of life to its periphery' had been met if not exceeded (Gay, 1966, p. 338). The alliance between a reinvigorated paganism and the new science had proven to be both an intellectual and social force to be reckoned with. Yet this shift did not mean that religion disappeared. It lurked along the edges in the hearts of many individuals, including a large number of scientists. These private religious convictions could inspire spiritual and moral insights of public relevance that could not be easily ignored or dismissed, a fact readily admitted by even the most ardent agnostics. Skepticism, agnosticism and even atheism fueled by a burgeoning confidence in science did not lead inevitably to public immorality, but served to amplify the need for a continuing belief in morality itself.

This dichotomy between private belief and public reason, however, was intolerable if humans were to flourish as a humane *civilization*. Although providence had been displaced as a central cultural symbol, some compelling icon must fill the void if humankind was to fully enjoy its liberation from religious superstition. Progress presented itself as the most promising candidate. With their growing knowledge about the workings of nature and history, humans could apply their reason in fashioning a more desirable future.

The inscrutability of providence could be exchanged for greater control over the seemingly capricious flow of natural processes and historical events. An appeal to divine intervention was no longer needed to discern the pattern of God's plan for creation, if indeed such a plan existed.

In many respects, the torpid natural theologies and retreat to personal experience prepared the way for this shift from providence to progress. Yet contrary to Robert Nisbet, progress was not a latent quality whose origin could be traced back through Augustine to classical antiquity (Nisbet, 1980; cf Ferkiss, 1969, pp. 22–3). Although Nisbet is correct that modern progressivism maintained the epochal structure of history inherited from its Christian antecedents, its content differed radically to that inspired by traditional doctrines of providence. The history of the world was not an account of creation being drawn mysteriously to a destiny assigned by its creator, but an unfolding tale of human potential and capability. Moreover, this progressive trajectory could be plotted, and thereby exploited, by invoking an enlightened naturalism and historicism. What was needed to perceive this pattern, and project it into the future, were reliable methods of inquiry and application that were cumulative, empirical, experimental and precise (Turner, 1985, pp. 194–5). Consequently, science, much more than theology, provided a more suitable intellectual and practical framework for charting the course of a culture predicated on inevitable progress.

Although the philosophes understood their task as another round in the death struggle between Christianity and paganism, their program was oriented toward the future rather than the past. They had no nostalgic desire to restore classical antiquity; it was instead a source to inspire humans to shake off the chains of superstition, and take control of their own fate. The intellectual and moral courage of Athens and Rome could be plundered, but no attempt should be made to resurrect (Gay, 1969, pp. 92–8). Judging by the rhetoric of succeeding generations, the Enlightenment exceeded its own expectations if progress can be understood as a culture oriented toward the future, stripped of any providential trappings. By the mid nineteenth century 'progress', as James Turner has observed, 'did not merely describe human history; it functioned as a central value. Anything that put the brakes on progress smacked of evil' (Turner, 1985, p. 217). Yet to appreciate the import of the ascendancy of progress, particularly in terms of its relationship to science, requires that the story be told in anticipation of its impending demise.

From Progress to Process

By the mid nineteenth century the ubiquitous signs of progress were difficult to dispute, at least in terms of popular perception. The volume of scientific data continued to expand exponentially, exposing a natural world governed by dependable laws. Ignorance was everywhere steadily giving way to knowledge. Moreover, although the growth of scientific knowledge was impressive in its own right, its value was not merely esoteric. A growing familiarity with natural laws was enabling a mastery of nature itself for the sake of improving the quality of human life. The toil, drudgery and suffering which had plagued previous generations were no longer taken for granted, but were seen as problems that could be solved. Medicine, for instance, was increasing human longevity, and was now, more often than not, ameliorating instead of inflicting pain on patients as physicians and surgeons adopted scientifically informed practices. But it was the development of new manufacturing and transportation technologies that had the greatest impact. The construction of large factories in tandem with steam-powered locomotives and ships created unprecedented commercial opportunities. Natural resources were now reliably delivered to factories, and manufactured goods were in turn distributed quickly to rapidly expanding markets. The resulting employment opportunities, wealth and prosperity fueled an economic transformation in which rural and aristocratic societies were displaced by urban, and more egalitarian, social structures. To be sure such developments were not without their critics. The transcendentalists and romantics, for example, bemoaned the loss of both natural beauty and the social graces that plagued the new centers of urban blight, but they were little more than eccentrics offering amusing diversions that did little to slow the inexorable pace of progress. It was the Crystal Palace exhibition, not Walden Pond, that captured the public imagination (Kasson, 1976).

More importantly, there was widespread public belief that progress was, at least in principle, limitless and unending. Why? Because it was also believed that the science underlying the dramatic improvements in material comfort and well-being was also, in principle, unlimited in the knowledge it could discover and apply. Although a direct causal relationship between scientific research and resulting technological development was exaggerated (Turner, 1985, pp. 121–2), it is nonetheless arguable that the marriage of Baconian utopian thought and a refined Cartesian methodology was a significant factor in spurring rapid industrialization (Borgmann, 1992, pp. 34–5). Moreover, since science was held in high public esteem, industrialists and inventors eagerly portrayed their work as applied science. The ploy worked, as witnessed by public accolades for newly constructed museums of science and industry and new systems of scientific management and production. Soon research could scarcely be mentioned without referring to an accompanying development. Science-based technology was, in short, the engine driving modern progress. Ironically, the principal imagery of natural theology had proven prophetic: the dominant reality directing and governing human life was mechanistic. But it was not a mechanism designed by a supernatural creator, but the machines of human ingenuity.

Progress was clearly the most prized legacy of the Enlightenment, yet the symbolic weight heaped upon it by its most eager champions proved incautious. The philosophes were in no doubt that reason in general and science in particular would eventually improve the human condition, but progress was neither as inevitable nor as uniform as their descendents proclaimed. Advances in science and technology did not necessarily mean that moral, social and political progress would keep pace. Condorcet, for instance, insisted that the overall pattern of history was progressive, yet progress itself was the result of a dialectical process, often resulting in unexpected consequences – evil begets good and vice versa. History is a story of both human progress *and* suffering, and the blessings of the former are achieved only in uneven spurts. Although Condorcet remained confident that science offered the best road to progress, as witnessed by his utopian predictions, he also acknowledged that it could be used for good or evil purposes. A golden age lay beyond the horizon, but he was not optimistic that the road leading there would be either straight or easy (Gay, 1969, pp. 112–25).

Indeed, there were some who worried that modernity had lost sight of its progressive horizon. The axis of industry, science and technology had admittedly generated unprecedented prosperity. The distribution of wealth, however, was far from even. The cost of industrialization was the emergence of widespread poverty, deplorable working conditions, squalid cities, political corruption and devastated rural communities and landscapes. Mastering nature was a violent conquest, encompassing the collateral damage of appalling numbers of decimated families and communities (Borgmann, 1992, pp. 20–47). Exchanging the pain and misery of an inscrutable providence for that of willful exploitation was proving, for many, to be a bad bargain. The science which had promised to liberate humans from the shackles of superstition and fossilized tradition was instead serving as a cruel, industrial taskmaster. For many, there was little difference between the medieval serfs tied to the estates of their lords, and modern laborers chained to the factories of their employers.

Something had to be done. Social and political stability could not be maintained in the face of mounting public unrest. The most obvious strategy, to put the breaks on industrialization, was never seriously entertained. Doing so would be tantamount to admitting that progress was a false ideal, a demoralizing prospect given the hard-fought victory in capturing public confidence. The problem was not that the idea of progress was inherently flawed, but that it lacked direction; it needed a rudder and compass. Moral progress had failed to keep up with science. It was crucial that the distance be narrowed, and narrowed quickly, in order that scientific knowledge could be applied in a more humane manner.

Ironically, undertaking this moral task required focusing attention on the *psyche*, a mystery presumed to be impregnable to scientific scrutiny. Since there was no science of the soul, however, where to turn for guidance in accomplishing this task? There were two readily available options. One option was religion (Turner, 1985, pp. 82–95). Although theology had been exiled from the public square, religious sentiments remained alive along the periphery in the hearts of believers. Science had surely become the coin of the realm, but religious faith continued to be a strong force in shaping the morality of many individuals. Indeed, one strategy employed by many evangelicals in response to the ethical issues posed by industrialization was to stress self-improvement. It became increasingly apparent, however, that the issues could not be resolved on a person-by-person basis, because they were deeply embedded in economic, social and political structures. Sufficient moral progress could not be attained by changing individual hearts; more systematic reform was needed. This need rekindled millennial expectations. The city of God was, after all, humanity's destiny and salvation. Only this time hope was not placed in the distant future with the descent of a ready-made heavenly city. If believers had learned nothing else from the Enlightenment and its aftermath, it was that the faithful were called to act, not wait patiently. All that was lacking was a noble moral and spiritual purpose which science and technology could serve. In this respect, God's will became virtually synonymous with human welfare. Consequently, God's city would be built firmly on the earth from the ground up, and the creator had wisely outsourced the construction project to local architects and contractors.

The social gospel movement took upon itself the task of overseeing this project.[6] Its most prominent leader was Walter Rauschenbusch, the pastor of a Baptist church in New York's 'Hell's Kitchen', and a faculty member of Rochester Theological Seminary. Rauschenbusch believed that the widespread poverty and social unrest of the late nineteenth and early twentieth centuries presented a propitious moment for Christianity. Theology needed the social gospel to make it pertinent, and scientific and technological progress required a modern theology to steer it in the right direction. The social gospel marked the 'fact that for the first time in history the spirit of Christianity has ... a chance to form a working partnership with real social and psychological science' (Rauschenbusch, 1997, p. 5). In alliance with the new social sciences, Christians could help reform commerce and industry in accordance with more just and democratic principles. The social gospel, therefore, required that Christian leaders be conversant with the best science of the day to ensure that it be applied in ways promoting 'ethical righteousness' (ibid., p. 15), for theology 'ought to be the science of redemption and offer scientific methods for the eradication of sin' (ibid., p. 57). The root of sin is the selfish ego, expressed through antisocial behavior that diminishes the common good. In submitting to God humans also embrace the common good, and their resulting sanctification is embodied in 'useful labor' (ibid., pp. 102–3). In consistently promoting the common good through just social and political structures, sin would eventually be eliminated. In short, the 'social gospel is concerned about a progressive incarnation of God' within the social and political fabric (ibid., pp. 147–8). If 'progress' were to become genuinely progressive, then Christian and democratic forms of cooperation must be implemented as opposed to the unchristian and autocratic principles of capitalism.

The other approach was that of reason. Although there was no empirical foundation for morality, one could nonetheless think clearly about ethics. Immanuel Kant had demonstrated that ethics could be grounded in universal principles from which rational maxims were drawn. Admittedly the result was a rather thin account of morality, virtually devoid of any substantive claims, but the rational procedural framework Kant offered went a long way in providing the lineaments of a social morality promoting economic and political reform. Dry Kantian principles might not change the values of most individuals, but they could ensure the implementation of public procedures that treated everyone fairly and humanely. Moreover, the absence of firm scientific knowledge about the basis of morality did not mean that science was a hindrance in putting progress back on the right track. First, scientific methods involving rigorous observation, experimentation and dispassionate analysis reinforced a rational approach to ethics. The efficacy of reform was aided more by hardheaded instead of softhearted thinking. Second, science provided valuable information that assisted reformers in achieving their goals. Improved living conditions of the poor, for instance, resulted from knowing something about basic sanitation that could be incorporated in more stringent building codes. Third, although science could neither explain nor predict behavioral variation among particular individuals, great strides had been made in identifying trends within larger populations. The emerging social sciences provided useful data that informed new legislation in such areas as education, healthcare and labor. Reasoned ethical discourse in league with science was what was needed to redirect the social and political order toward a progressive horizon.

Although religious and secular reformers often conducted their respective crusades in isolation from each other, they nonetheless shared a number of goals and assumptions. Paramount among these was a belief in morality itself. Both shared a repugnance of suffering, and the conviction that it could be ameliorated through purposeful human action. Where they differed was at the source of their respective moral visions. For religious reformers it was divine righteousness that should permeate society, whereas for their secular counterparts God was not needed to reform the social order. These differing perceptions did not ultimately matter if the end result was human betterment. Thus both believed in progress, and for both it was unimaginable that true progress could be achieved in the absence of an alliance between science and morality. In this respect even the most faithful reformers were forced to admit that science, unlike theology, was in the best *public* position to maintain a progressive momentum. This acknowledgment did not mean that private beliefs had to be jettisoned, but if they were to have any public currency they needed to be expressed and acted upon in moral rather than religious terms. Religion had not been reduced to ethics, but it was through morality that progressive Christianity made its peace with modernity. There was no reason why Christians could not believe that science and technology, guided by fervent moral values, were the key instruments for building God's kingdom on earth, but it would not be the kind of city envisioned by Augustine.

Yet in the midst of all this progressive optimism, new advances in biology and psychology were already corroding the alliance between science and morality. The corrosive effects were nearly imperceptible, because in isolation from each other the scientific findings appeared benign. But their combined implications would eventually present a withering challenge to the very idea of progress. On the one hand, Darwinism was portraying a natural world that was varied, pliable and adaptive. The world was literally seething with life, not in the fixed form of discrete kinds, but in species that changed and adapted over time. Moreover, humans were very much a part of this evolutionary process – their ancestry was grounded firmly in the animal rather than heavenly kingdom. On the other hand, Freudian psychology was disclosing the complex and intricate strands of the human *psyche*. Powerful desires, often expressed in contradictory selfish and altruistic ways, reflected unresolved and largely unconscious tensions emanating from unfulfilled emotional needs. By identifying and confronting these needs one was enabled to resolve or at least control these desires in a manner that did not result in antisocial behavior. Good mental health required a process of coming to terms with a human nature that was more earthy than angelic in character.

As mentioned previously, the central claims of these seemingly discrete sciences were not perceived initially as challenging a progressive agenda, and in some instances were welcomed as useful weapons to be deployed in the struggle. Darwin's world inspired in many a sense of awe and wonder in the natural grandeur of life, and by way of extrapolation moral, social and political change could be achieved in an evolutionary (read orderly) rather than revolutionary (read chaotic) manner. The sheer complexity of Freud's inner world was equally breathtaking, and offered the company of analysts who would assist individuals in coming to terms with the pace of rapidly changing social structures and mores. Although many of the religious blanched at Darwin's agnosticism and Freud's atheism, their lack of faith did not detract from the usefulness of their discoveries. Evolution could be construed as the way God created and governs the world, and sufficiently sanitized variants of Freudian psychology would later dictate the practice of pastoral counseling.

Not everyone, however, was receptive, because doubts were emerging over whether the alliance between morality and science would result in inevitable progress. Huxley, for example, granted that the nature revealed by science might inspire a terrifying awe, but he was quite certain that it offered nothing of value for ethics (Turner, 1985, p. 256). Although morality must guide science, science *per se* could do nothing to identify or purify the source of moral vision. The Darwinian and Freudian investigations corroborated his skepticism, for when combined they opened a small portal on what had been thought to be the opaque human psyche, and what was seen inside was not pretty. The world was indeed filled with diverse forms of life, but the price paid for their variation and survival was exorbitant. Evolution was an account of continuous and violent competition. One species survived because others became extinct, and even within a species the strong and adaptable thrived at the expense of the weak and maladaptive. The drama of evolutionary ascent was predicated on a subplot of death, and the omnipresent threats of pain and misery accompanying it. Moreover, humans were not spared a role in this bloody spectacle, but were shaped by it. As psychoanalysis revealed, humans carried within their subconscious a host of virulent instincts and murderous impulses that the rational mind was hard pressed to keep under control. The line separating barbarous and civilized behavior was, at best, thin and tenuous. Humans, like any other animal, were driven by the overwhelming urge to survive.

Consequently, morality did not capture the noble quality of human nature, but was merely an adaptive tool offering a survival advantage. Cooperation and compassion, for instance, were not valued because they were inherently good or right, but because they gave a particular individual or group an advantage over others in the competition over scarce resources. Individuals learning the conventions of self-control and altruistic acts were ultimately grounded in a self-interested desire to preserve the stability of one's welfare. Morality was little more than a symbolic method of sharpening the tools of survival.

Although the chain coupling morality and science had not been broken, deep chinks were now apparent in its key links. If religious reformers were to square their beliefs with science, then they must return to the Enlightenment's challenge to explain once again how they could base their morality on a God who was either an incompetent or cruel creator. And if secular reformers were to continue arguing for the efficacy of a morally directed science, then they must explain how a dispassionate reason could somehow be invoked by thoroughly self-interested beings. No readily compelling answers were forthcoming, and in their absence the confident assumption that progress would inevitably result from the alliance between morality and science appeared as little more than spurious rhetoric.

Whether the caricatures of nature red in tooth and claw, and the human as tamed savage portrayed accurately the implications of Darwinism and Freudianism, respectively, is highly questionable. Less contentiously, the imagery seized public imagination, and altered the course of progressive reform. Given the violent tendencies of human nature, the competition of the economic arena was perhaps not such a horrible specter after all. Competing for monetary rewards was arguably a preferable channel for sublimating instinctual drives than other, more violent, options. Over time the human species might be better served if it were comprised of rugged individuals, whose survival in a society being shaped increasingly by technological artifacts would depend increasingly on competition conducted over social rewards instead of natural necessities. Even the socially minded Rauschenbusch did not deny the need for personal responsibility and individual initiative, and that these good goals were at least partially achieved through economic incentives and disincentives. The means of achieving human progress might be counter-intuitive, as Condorcet had recognized. More ominously, many individuals, or perhaps even entire groups or races, might be unable to adapt to these changing social, economic and political environments. The net effect would be escalating poverty and crime unless the reproductive capacities of the ill-adaptive were brought under control. Hence the logic of eugenics that encourages the fit to procreate, while discouraging or preventing the unfit from breeding. Even the tender-hearted Bushnell would take his cues from harsh evolutionary lessons in this respect, contending that the kingdom of heaven would be built on earth by Christians 'out-populating' inferior stock (Bushnell, 1960, pp. 165–83). Human progress was in jeopardy unless the inferior genes retarding its momentum were removed.

These attempts to incorporate the dark side of human nature within the progressive agenda distracted attention from a more troubling, underlying issue, namely, that the alliance between morality and science was a bankrupt enterprise. If neither religion nor reason could disclose *the* normative content of morality, then what was to prevent science from serving a destructive ideology posing as morality? The fear would come true in the bloodbaths of the twentieth century in which totalitarian regimes of both the left and right waged wars and genocidal vendettas disguised as moral crusades to cleanse the world of its vermin (Arendt, 1968). Most distressing to true believers in progress was how easily science embraced the task of perfecting tools of war, torture and terror. The mushroom clouds detonated both in anger and to satisfy scientific curiosity also incinerated the locomotive and tracks of progress. Nor could any massive reconstruction project bring them back. Looking back from this vantage point prompted a growing recognition that the preceding battles over the course of history had been waged in vain. There was no progressive trajectory to discern; only a non-directional *process* marking the passage of time. History was not headed toward a golden age, because history was simply not heading in any direction at all. Thus history was also not a story of the ongoing struggle between religious superstition and enlightened reason. The image was at least half right, because much of human history was an account of conflict, but one more akin to Thomas Hobbes's perpetual war of all against all (Hobbes, 1996, Part I, pp. 7–110). The vast plain of this foreboding state of nature stretched endlessly in every direction, and no rejuvenated Athens, much less a new Jerusalem, waited beyond any of the horizons.

Yet as Hobbes also knew, a tolerable and even crudely civil existence could be forged in this wilderness; indeed, any semblance of human life beyond that of bare animal necessity dictated that the effort be undertaken (Hobbes, 1996, Part II, pp. 111–245). But what recourse was available once the certitudes of religion and reason had withered, and the emotive symbols of providence and progress had been smashed? There was still the will, and unlike previous generations humans now possessed the technological power to assert it more effectively. Moreover, if humans were to carve out for themselves a hospitable niche within a purposeless and directionless history, that power would be needed not only to master nature, but also to master, if not transform, human nature. It is with the postmodern project of directing human evolution that technology begins to supplant science (as well as an already eviscerated theology) as the dominant, formative cultural force, a story that is told in greater detail in the next chapter.

Notes

1   Edwards's account of this event appears in a letter dated March 19, 1737, and is included in the 'Preface' to his *A Faithful Narrative of the Surprising Work of God* (Edwards, 1974, pp. 344–6). For further commentary, see Gustafson, 1981, pp. 93–4.

2   Although the text consulted is the twelfth edition published in 1882, the first edition was published in 1850, one year after Bushnell's *God in Christ*.

3   The following discussion on the Enlightenment draws heavily on the works of Peter Gay as noted in the bibliography.

4   Plato and Aristotle are largely absent from their canons. See Gay, 1966, pp. 31–203 regarding the influence of pagan sources in the Enlightenment.

5   The following discussion on the aftermath of the Newtonian revolution in respect to failed theological defenses of providence and subsequent appeals to a religion of the heart is indebted to the work of James Turner as noted in the bibliography.

6 The leaders of the social gospel movement drew much of their inspiration from the English Christian socialism movement led by F. D. Maurice and Charles Kingsley. For a succinct overview, see Douglas F. Ottati's 'Foreword' in Rauschenbusch, 1991.

CHAPTER TWO

A Postmodern World

Twenty years before the end of the second millennium, Robert Nisbet lamented that progress was at bay (Nisbet, 1980, pp. 317–51). A culture of self-confident optimism was being displaced by one of disillusionment and despair. This regrettable circumstance was the result of a series of acidic attacks against tradition, the core values of western civilization, economic growth and the denigration of reason and knowledge. At the close of the twentieth century, the world was shrouded in chronic indifference and rampant credulity. Nisbet, however, refused to abandon hope. He was confident that the fate of progress rested ultimately upon the fortunes of its Judeo-Christian forbears, and such a distinguished lineage embodied the stubborn faith in a world in which a movement 'from the inferior to the superior must seem as real and certain as anything in the laws of nature' (Nisbet, 1980, p. 5). Even in the midst of this pall, Nisbet could detect a gentle breeze of renewed faith foretelling a tidal surge that would enable the ship of progress to continue its voyage. Or to change the metaphor, since progress was the precocious child of providence, it was a reliable object of faith and hope.

Yet if the principal argument of the previous chapter is correct, Nisbet's interpretation of the lineage and fate of progress must be challenged. The optimism of a progressive culture based on science was not crushed because of a failure to realize its latent moral potential. The new sciences unveiled the workings of natural phenomena that were in turn harnessed as various forms of power, a process that was particularly pronounced in the rapid development of industrial and transportation technologies. But science did not discover or disclose anything in nature suggesting how such power should be used in a so-called progressive manner. Science did not take the baton from its reluctant religious parent and then stumble. Rather, an inscrutable divine will was exchanged for an equally ambiguous human will. Belief in progress was therefore as much an act of faith as was belief in providence. Moreover, the Darwinian and Freudian glimpses into the human psyche suggested that any hope for a more reliable object of faith was unlikely. Human behavior did not evolve along any discernible providential or progressive trajectories, but adapted to changing environments. And the ensuing competition was often lethal, especially when combined with powerful technological capabilities as witnessed by the sheer carnage and brutality of the twentieth century. Nisbet's ship of progress was not at bay but was beached and salvaged, and thus a rising tide of faith is irrelevant because the idea of progress cannot be believed back into existence.

Consequently, it would be a grievous error to indict Darwin and Freud as the murderers of modern progress given the principle of *corpus delicti*. Modernity's legacy of unprecedented violence and cruelty is not the result of any so-called Darwinian–Freudian worldview; armies did not march off to war and Gulags were not built because a generation read books on evolution and psychoanalysis. Rather, the inquiries they inspired served as a sobering reminder that human behavior was as much demonic as it was angelic, so any notion of inevitable progress was hopelessly naïve. Darwinian and Freudian principles merely reinforced a plea for setting realistic expectations that had been hinted at in the Enlightenment. Kant, for example, argued that human nature had been ordered in such a way that innate discord would inspire a rational approach to cooperation. One could trace a kind of progressive direction of human history, but it was a chart comprising periodic dips and spikes (Kant, 1991, pp. 87–92).

What cannot be easily explained, however, is the wide variation between the peaks and valleys of late modernity. If recent history is merely the record of a Kantian correction, one shudders at the prospect of a genuine catastrophe. The rapid rise of science and technology alone cannot account for these wild fluctuations. Although humans possess unprecedented technological power, there is no obvious evolutionary reason why they would so frequently use it to such a destructive extent. Moreover, modernity could also be characterized by unparalleled achievements in improving the material well-being of many people. As Colin Gunton has observed, late modernity is a 'paradox' of 'extremes' in which many are 'better fed, housed, educated and provided with medical care', while many more have been 'consigned ... to death by warfare and other modern means of mass destruction' (Gunton, 1993, p. 38). Or to pose the matter as a question: why is late modernity seemingly being forced to choose between its utopian dreams and apocalyptic nightmares? The answer is that the emergence of these diametrically opposed options is endemic to the postmodern shift from a culture of progress and science to that of process and technology (Ferkiss, 1969, pp. 26–7). Yet before this argument can be made, we must first examine an additional landmark from the intellectual landscape of the late nineteenth and early twentieth centuries.

Nietzsche Blinked

To grasp the import of the postmodern shift one must first come to terms with the late modern world, and as George Grant has observed, 'There is no escape from reading Nietzsche if one would understand modernity' (Grant, 1986, p. 89). This is a necessary prerequisite given the extent to which the thought of that troubled philosopher has permeated contemporary philosophical, social and political thought. His influence is particularly striking in regard to his thoroughgoing historicism. More than any other philosopher before or after, Nietzsche pondered the modern world as a place of unrelenting flux. Late moderns perceive time *as* history, and therefore can assign no essence, permanence or purpose to their perpetual becoming. We know that both individually and corporately we 'make ourselves as we go along' (Grant, 1995b, p. 41). His historicist presuppositions are now taken for granted as part of the cultural air we breathe; even people who have never read Nietzsche are nonetheless shaped by him.

In this section Grant's analysis of Nietzsche's historicism is used to draw out some of the more prominent aspects of the postmodern shift. I use Grant's critical assessment for two reasons. First, I find that whenever I encounter Nietzsche for any length of time I suffer intellectual vertigo. To explore the mind of late modernity's greatest seer I need the companionship of a guide who is more familiar with the complex terrain. Second, although Grant's assessment is highly critical it is nonetheless reliable. Moreover, his criticisms provide the basis for more constructive arguments that are developed in subsequent chapters.[1]

Grant uses Nietzsche to 'enucleate' – 'to extract the kernel of a nut, the seed of a tree' (Grant, 1995b, p. 13) – late modernity. Nietzsche offers the most revealing kernel, for his 'words raise to an intensely full light of explicitness what it is to live in this era'. He does not create this era but 'unfolds' it, and in this unfolding we catch a glimpse of our fate as late moderns (ibid., pp. 13–14). This is especially true in respect to Nietzsche's historicism. There are two general meanings of the term *history*. One is a study of the past, while the other connotes a form of existence. In the latter instance, humans are historical beings in that they are shaped by the temporal processes they construct. To be historical in this sense means that past, present and future are collapsed into a single mode of being. Consequently, historicist dogma insists that all human acts and intellectual outlooks depend on a 'particular set of existing experienced circumstances' (Grant, 1986, pp. 83–4).

Again, Nietzsche did not invent this historicist mode of being, but he recognized it as the ethos of the modern era. More importantly, he explicated as baldly as possible the intellectual and moral implications of this ethos. To conceive time as only history is premised on a fundamental rejection of the philosophical and theological traditions inspired by Athens and Jerusalem.[2] On the one hand, the Platonic claim that temporality can only be understood in respect to the eternal is rejected as little more than idle speculation. There are no eternal forms or universal ideals against which human thought and action should strive to conform. Whatever images of so-called truth, beauty and goodness might be said to exist, they are the result of human, not divine, artifice. As history discloses, morality and politics are simply the fabricated and rationalized values of the strong imposed upon the weak. Whatever meaning can be seized from temporal existence is the result of concrete acts of will, not intellectual contemplation.

On the other hand, although Christianity viewed history as a realm of God's revelation, it too was deceived by a false hope in eternity. Christians simply clung to the belief in a creation being drawn toward its eternal creator, and since the creator was graciously involved in its temporal unfolding, its human creatures could cleave to a notion of divine goodness. Science, however, exposed this belief as a fantasy, because no trace of goodness could be found in the so-called created order. If nature and human nature were to be described as somehow 'good', it would require valuing continuous strife and suffering. Consequently, it was ironic that the church had turned to science to bolster its belief in providence, for as Grant notes wryly, the 'very greatness of Christianity was to produce its own grave-diggers' (Grant, 1995b, p. 39). Propagating the lie that God was redeeming the world was simply masking a willful attempt of the weak to take revenge against the strong.

Yet how are western civilization and its values to endure if the rationality of Athens and the faith of Jerusalem are no longer plausible resources to draw upon? There can be no simple or even critical appropriation of the past, because historicism renders mute any so-called wisdom or purpose of history. The historicist perspective compresses past, present and future into a single, non-dimensional mode of existence. Humans can trace a rough chronology of events, but the tracing itself discloses no normative end, nor any particular future course or direction. Consequently, humans know they are temporal beings, but their temporality enfolds them to such an extent that they can only experience themselves as self-made creatures.

The troubling outcome of the historicist captivity is seen in Nietzsche's scathing criticism that philosophy lacks a 'historical sense' (Grant, 1995b, p. 36; O'Donovan, 1984, pp. 119–28). As Darwinism makes clear, there is no fixed human condition given the radical nature of change over time. The fundamental fact of human life is its historicity. Yet philosophy has tried perennially to demonstrate some permanent aspect of human nature. According to Grant, this is precisely the point Nietzsche rejected, insisting that any sense of permanence must be expunged from any vantage point claiming to be modern. History cannot be defined, and therefore no purpose or direction can be forthcoming. 'Put negatively, in the historical sense we admit the absence of any permanence in terms of which change can be measured or limited or defined.' Consequently, we are forced to accept the 'finality of becoming' (Grant, 1995b, p. 37). Any attempt to discover permanence betrays a desperate belief in an enduring essence such as a self or a soul, but the endeavor amounts to little more than the search for a phantom. The result was the feeble efforts of modern theology and moral philosophy to weigh good and evil on the scale of a fictional truth.

This desperation helps to account for the frantic efforts of modern science to impose order on a disorderly nature that its inquiries were disclosing. More importantly, it also helps explain why in appealing to science modern theological and philosophical accounts of progress served as moral sedatives in mitigating the terror of a chaotic nature and human nature. In this respect, the rise of modern science provided a rearguard action against acknowledging the historicist abyss that it was helping to create. As Grant has observed, 'At the beginning of the nineteenth century the consequences to be drawn from the dawning historical sense had been alleviated for many by the belief in progress' (Grant, 1995b, p. 38). What Nietzsche exposed with great clarity was that no moral purpose or progressive trajectory could be gleaned from studying nature. This possibility had once existed in Christian thought, because a sense of permanence and direction were grounded in a divine wisdom that could be discerned and applied through reason. This perspective in either a religious or profane guise, however, was no longer tenable, despite the valiant scientific efforts to preserve rationality by substituting progress as the basis for moral judgment. But as Nietzsche saw, the historical sense led to the inevitable conclusion that belief in even the possibility of morality must be jettisoned. Ironically, modern science could trace its lineage back to both Platonic and Christian origins, and at the heart of both these traditions was the conviction of the existence of a rational and permanent goodness. And science had in turn drawn upon both to develop the surgical precision to remove that heart from both cadavers.

According to Nietzsche, 'great living' could only occur by confronting the chaos bequeathed by the historical sense, and he was fully cognizant that the chaos could only be confronted through historical horizons (Grant, 1995b, pp. 39–40). Yet unlike previous philosophers, Nietzsche knew these horizons were not imposed through some providential or progressive order, but were simply fabrications. No horizon is a statement about what is real or true. 'The historical sense teaches us that horizons are not discoveries about the nature of things; they express the values which our tortured instincts will to create' (ibid., p. 40). We map and traverse a landscape of our own making. Yet Nietzsche also acknowledges that once we know these horizons are fabricated, their ability to sustain moral and intellectual courage is shattered. Thus the power of his well-known aphorism 'God is dead', for the death of God is also the death of all objective horizons. With the predominance of the historical sense we in turn lose history itself, and with that loss the ability to define, and without definition there can be no purpose. Consequently, to say that humans have no 'history and therefore cannot be defined is to say that we can know nothing about what we are fitted for' (ibid., p. 41). We create ourselves in reference to our constructed horizons; we shape ourselves only in reference to our self-made selves. If purpose can be said to exist at all, it is simply to assert the raw, naked will.

It is important to remember that Nietzsche's analysis of modernity occurs at the same time that the idea of progress reached its apex. The second half of the nineteenth century exuded a confidence that the quality of human life had never been better, and would continue its steady improvement into the foreseeable future. Moreover, the problems that continued to plague society would be solved by joining moral improvement with rational, social (and to a more limited extent biological) engineering. The alliance of moral reformers, scientifically trained social workers, physicians and eugenicists were on the brink of ushering in a new golden age. Yet Nietzsche saw (or better, saw through) the progressive values of freedom, rationality and equality as nothing more than hollow rhetoric; poltergeists from the ghost-towns of Athens and Jerusalem that haunt and distract those confronting an indifferent world. For without God or the good there can be no equality and the very rationality used to enlarge the scope of freedom is a poisoned pill.

Accordingly, late modernity produced two classes of people: last men and nihilists. The last men settle for a highly degraded conception of happiness, one devoid of nobility. They are a class of people who are clever, incapable of self-deprecation and therefore cannot rise above a very low bar of a debased sense of pleasure. The last men are driven by the desire to create a world of cozy comfort, and hence their fascination with technologies that produce goods and services that can be readily consumed. Anyone reading Nietzsche should not be surprised by the emergence of a mindless and seemingly insatiable consumerism.[3] In contrast, the nihilists know they are little more than their wills. But unfortunately there is nothing noble for them to will, and in the absence of nobility it is better to will nothing than have nothing to will. Consequently, nihilists are 'resolute in their will to mastery, but they cannot know what that mastery is for' (Grant, 1995b, pp. 45–6). Such resolute but frustrated willing results inevitably in unspeakable violence. Again, anyone paying attention to Nietzsche's prophecies should not be shocked by the carnage of the twentieth century.

The resolute yet directionless willing of late modernity proffers revenge as the most viable motive for constructing history. The last men want revenge against any remnant of nobility, while the nihilists seek vengeance against a world where there is nothing noble to will. Consequently, it also appears that one of two possible fates await late modernity: the last men will have their revenge of equally satiated petty desires, resulting in a social, but comatose, equilibrium, or the nihilists will take their revenge by annihilating a petty world they have grown to hate. Neither option is remotely ennobling.

Nietzsche, however, offers a pale glimmer of hope. Although his sympathies lie with the nihilists – their love of nobility is, after all, admirable – he recognizes that their frustration may very well end in untold destruction. Yet if the nihilists can acknowledge that resolute willing contains no real content, then perhaps they can also rise above the banal happiness of the last men. Where can the inspiration for such tenacious courage be found? Nietzsche points to the classic Greek tragedies, particularly the suffering endured by their principal characters. This does not mean that late moderns should try to recover Greek virtues, for even if such a prospect were desirable any attempt at recovery would be rendered mute by the modern historical sense. What this ancient imagery of tragic suffering *might* inspire is a renewed love of fate (*amor fati*). It is not, however, a love consummated in eternity, but one stubbornly 'willed in a world where there is no possibility of either an infinite or finite transcendence of becoming or willing' (Grant, 1995b, p. 54). Rather, this new love of fate is discovered in 'the eternal recurrence of the identical' (ibid., p. 55), and in this discovery resides the possibility of the *Übermensch*; those renouncing the desire for revenge. The love of fate renders revenge as a futile recurrence grounded in an equally fatuous despair. It is the *Übermensch* who in recognizing the futility of revenge will have the courage to take on the task of constructing a world in which the possibility of joy displaces that of despair. This task requires that all shreds of purpose, progress and teleology be thoroughly expunged if modernity is to be survived, for they are little more than intellectual and moral constructs disguising the instinctual drive for vengeance. Consequently, it is human nature that must be conquered and mastered if the *Übermensch* are to move on to the more pressing task of building a world they are now free to will given their love of fate. Nietzsche admits that the hope he offers is far from certain; it is a desperate hope against hope.[4] Yet what other species of hope is available in a world of radical contingency? What other hope is available when the rationality of Athens and the faith of Jerusalem have been eclipsed, and all that remains is the process of historicist construction?

It must again be emphasized that in the preceding paragraphs we did not encounter Nietzsche directly, but Grant's portrayal as a device for enucleating modernity. Grant chose Nietzsche not because he is the author of modernity, but its 'seer and conscience' (O'Donovan, 1984, p. 119). Although Nietzsche's prophetic utterances are admittedly hyperbolic, they nonetheless report the acute observations of one who stared wide-eyed and unblinkingly into the heart of the modern project. It is a withering gaze that strips away all rational and moral pretensions to expose an empty husk. Following Joan O'Donovan, we may retrace Grant's enucleation of modernity in a more succinct manner in order to chart the flow of Nietzsche's prophetic utterances with greater precision (ibid., pp. 119–28).

The problem modernity faced was its failure to come to terms with the historical sense it had created. The origins of the modern historical sense can be traced back to Platonic philosophy and Christian theology. Both shared a fundamental conviction of an enduring and universal goodness which embraced the temporal world. For the Platonist, this goodness could be known, albeit imperfectly, through contemplating the eternal, while the Christian allowed that the good was also revealed, albeit in often puzzling ways, within the historical unfolding of God's creation. These twin convictions enabled a teleological understanding of history that was expressed initially in the belief in providence, and later in progress. The rise of modern science, however, made these beliefs untenable. There simply was no *telos* or finality of eternal goodness, but only a history of endless becoming. The crisis prompted by the historical sense was the stark reality of its own historicism. Time could not be conceived in relation to eternity, but only *as* history. Nietzsche was painfully aware of the moral consequences of the historical sense. For a world devoid of purpose and permanence was also a world ripe with the possibility for untold aggression and incessant revenge. Consequently, the crisis of the historical sense can only be resolved through emergence of the *Übermensch*, those brave souls who through their love of fate have willingly embraced a life of tragic suffering in order to quench their thirst for vengeance. Last men and nihilists must become something radically other than they are in order to construct a less vicious world. The only real thread of hope that Nietzsche can cling to is that *homo sapiens* is a transitional species that will evolve into the *Übermensch*. This is why he knows that his hope is remote because the history of evolution discloses that extinction is a far more probable fate.

Grant's gaze into late modernity through Nietzsche's eyes helps to explicate its paradox of extremes. Its unprecedented levels of material comfort and mass destruction stem from conflict within and between its two respective classes of people. Late liberals (a more inclusive designation than last men[5]) are driven by a desire for cozy comfort. The accumulation of material goods and services is the road to happiness. Hence the emergence of mass consumerism in a frenetic effort to satisfy wants that prove insatiable. The problem, however, is not unfulfilled wants *per se*, but the fact that some individuals achieve higher levels of comfort than others. Hence the resulting politics of resentment as a kinder, gentler, and therefore less destructive, form of revenge. The ensuing political struggles, and their closely associated cultural bush wars, are played out over the extent to which market mechanisms or governmental regulation should shape production and consumption in an emerging global economy. Although the ill-effects of these struggles are usually confined to localized victims of crime or poverty, the level of violence can escalate to international or intra-national conflict. The eventual outcome is to set shifting borders of expectations between which individuals may pursue their comfort. The struggles prove interminable, however, because the right is committed to expanding the gap while the left is dedicated to its contraction. In short, the conflict between late liberals is over competing utopian dreams, envisioning a world in which everyone has the opportunity to be equally happy or unhappy.

The principal conflict among nihilists is the extent to which they enact their repugnance of late liberalism through either hyperbolic denunciation or oblivious withdrawal. The former represents an anarchic strategy of exposing the moral void of late modernity. Perpetual protests are not so much directed against the late liberal failure to embrace nobility, but its utter incapacity to value, and indeed despise, anything that might bear a shred of noble semblance. These protests are purposely pointless, other than as a medium for venting rage, because any reforms generated are by definition ignoble and therefore not worth pursuing. Consequently, the principal conflict among anarchists is over the volume of volatile energy that should be expended in their admittedly pointless gestures. The latter represents a sectarian strategy of creating an alternative reality. Despite late liberalism's pervasive influence, small, isolated niches can be carved out. Within the borders of these tiny enclaves courageous individuals may live noble lives, while ignoring, as much as possible, the surrounding banality in which they are encased. Again the point is not to reform late liberal social, economic and political structures, but to practice self-referential lives of nobility within them. Consequently, the primary conflict among sectarians is over the extent of permissible contact with outsiders, and the extent to which this contact contaminates one's pure commitments. In contrast to the struggles among late liberals, the conflict between anarchists and sectarians is muted. This is the case because they are not fighting over the future course of a common world. Rather, they share a disgust of late modern mediocrity, but they disagree, often vehemently, over the best means of expressing their revulsion. Or to pose the dilemma as a question: does the love of fate beckon one toward pointless ranting or oblivious withdrawal?

Late liberals and nihilists, however, inevitably collide, but the collateral damage is usually contained. Anarchists are controlled through varying levels of coercive policing, and the spectacle of their protests is exploited as media events. Although sectarians may often prove irksome, they are usually tolerated so long as they do not disturb the peace and pay taxes (or have them involuntarily extracted). Yet there are times when the violence of the collision proves more difficult to contain. Sectarian enclaves invoking self-proclaimed noble ideals may adopt suicidal fates, either through self-inflicted methods or precipitated conflagrations. Or nihilists may raise the level of violence through provocative acts of terror, or in extreme circumstances pose as leaders of corrupt regimes, asserting their fraudulent vision of a noble fate over the masses through conquest and totalitarian brutality.

The prophetic vision of Grant's Nietzsche is a disturbing one, if for no other reason than the unremitting violence of its hyperbole. Yet underlying the exaggeration is an equally disturbing element of truth, if for no other reason than it helps to account for late modernity's wide gyrations between popular perceptions of so-called progress and regression. In this respect, rapid technological development has served liberals well, for it is the principal means of making their dreams come true. Late liberal utopian dreams inspire bursts of technological creativity needed to produce the goods and services craved by ravenous consumers, but unfortunately illiberal means must sometimes be employed to protect this venture from metamorphosing into the apocalyptic nightmares of enraged nihilists. Hence the frantic efforts to promote global consumerism coupled with equally frenetic expenditures of energy in surveillance, policing, anti-terrorism and isolating or even removing rogue nations to ensure that the process of production and consumption is not disrupted to any significant extent. Consequently, late liberals invoke a notion of progress they, in their more sober moments of reflection, admit is vacuous, to justify violating an equally empty concept of freedom in order to pursue the more pressing goals of comfort and security. But is there really any other rational alternative available? Although the victory of late liberal utopians would undoubtedly produce beings incapable of aspiring toward anything more noble than comfort and security, is not this form of extinction preferable to that of a nihilistic holocaust? And even if the utopian dream fails, is not the effort to delay the apocalypse worthwhile, perhaps even buying enough time to allow the evolution of a true love of fate? Ironically, it is the stubborn *ressentiment* of the 'last men', whom Nietzsche despised, that offers the only realistic thread of hope for the emergence of his *Übermensch*.

Through Nietzsche's unblinking gaze, Grant forces us to peer into the heart of late modernity, to see its naked banality and purposelessness. It is neither an edifying nor inspiring sight. Yet there is also something not quite right with the vista we behold, for at a crucial point Nietzsche, almost imperceptibly, blinked. In that momentary inattention, Nietzsche failed to notice that nihilists are linked irrevocably with his last men, for the two classes are actually the ends of a single spectrum. The one presupposes and is dependent upon the other; their existence requires a mutually parasitic relationship. Late liberals presuppose a nihilistic background against which they construct their secure and comfortable utopias. The dream is that the foreground becomes the dominant feature, while the nightmare is that it will be overwhelmed and disappear into the chaotic background. Nihilists presuppose a liberal background of bland security and comfort within which they strive to carve out pockets of nobility. The dream is that these pockets will prove sufficiently disruptive to prevent any enduring homogenization, while the nightmare is an ascendant liberalism with an infinite capacity to absorb and digest. Accordingly, the tactics employed to construct these respective foregrounds are mirror images of each other, and eventually mutate into the likeness of the other. Late liberal regimes, for instance, develop technologies to produce greater comfort, and technology in turn is used illiberally to secure the productive process itself, culminating in the nihilistic threat of mutually assured destruction against any enemy. Nihilists too employ technology to disrupt the comfort of those dependent upon it. The protest itself, however, cannot remain pointless for very long, eventually succumbing to late liberal mechanisms of control, and culminating in the brutality of totalitarian states or libertarian indifference.

In short, the most comfortable liberal is a frustrated nihilist, while the most ardent nihilist is at heart an acutely resentful liberal. The former sublimates a deep-seated grief for a lost nobility in a blessed rage for order, while the latter masquerades a profound envy under a cloak of noble renunciation. Consequently, any remnant of Nietzsche's thin hope in the *Übermensch* is effectively voided. If nihilists are nothing more than very angry last men, then there is no comprehensible reason why they should come to love their fate. The noble suffering they must embrace is incommensurable with their underlying desire for security and comfort that they cannot truly renounce. More importantly, security and comfort are the only remaining objects of desire left in a world that has renounced any possibility of purpose and permanence. The very quality that might inspire the requisite nobility is nothing more than a phantom. At best, a sullen resignation to fate can be achieved, but such sullenness is far more likely to inspire a death wish than joy.

Following Grant's interpretation of Nietzsche, the pervasive materialism and violence of late modernity stems from its inability to embrace fully a world purged of any purpose and permanence, and therefore any resulting providential or progressive trajectories. The rapid development of various technologies merely amplifies the predicament. Yet paradoxically this act of purgation provides a promising horizon, for the resulting void may itself perform a purposeful function. A postmodern *telos* of *no telos* offers modernity a way out of its dilemma: if there is no fate to be loved, then a suitable alternative can be fabricated. Moreover, those constructing this alternative fate are simultaneously reconstructing themselves. To will, rather than love, a fabricated fate is accompanied by a recreation of the one who is willing. There is no need to wait for the *Übermensch* to evolve, for a similar being can be created or engineered. Or more prosaically, to cross the postmodern divide is to enter a malleable terrain that is not only navigated by incessant shaping and reshaping, but in which the navigator too is relentlessly in flux, even merging with and re-emerging from the landscape itself. The radical plasticity of the postmodern orientation is attained because its *telos* is also its *techne*. The future will be largely what we make of it; what it is willed to be. The postmodern *telos* of *no telos* is in fact a *telos* of *techne*.

There are two important elements which the preceding, and admittedly awkward, paragraph attempts to convey. First, the elasticity of the postmodern world is not a result of more powerful or efficient technologies. If this were the case then postmodernity would be little more than a form of hypermodernity. Second, the *telos* of *techne* is not a circuitous route of imposing a resuscitated version of progress. Historicist presumptions are too strong to allow any restorationist strategy to succeed. *Techne* is postmodernity's *telos* because, following Grant, the once discrete acts of knowing and making have been collapsed into a single act of willing (Grant, 1986, pp. 11–34). Or more radically, *techne* became *telos* with the recognition that the world's only underlying and universal feature is information. Since information has no inherent meaning it can be recast, conveyed and interpreted in virtually endless arrays. The fluidity of information means that all borders are temporary, and any definition permeable. Reality is a construct of shifting patterns of information within and through various media. The same pattern holds for those individuals and groups constructing their respective realities. The postmodern reality is being made by self-constructed beings. Moreover, to perceive the world in terms of underlying information is already to think and define oneself as a cyborg (Haraway, 1991, pp. 149–81). Consequently, to cross the postmodern divide is also to enter the posthuman terrain. But this anticipates an argument to be developed in the next chapter, for we must first linger a bit longer within a constellation of emerging postmodern characteristics.

Postmodern Attributes

How is the intellectual, moral and political chaos unveiled by Nietzsche's gaze negotiated? To some extent, the postmodern enterprise can be understood as an attempt to navigate the deteriorating late modern landscape, a difficult and treacherous task since there are no fixed landmarks or horizons. A comprehensive expedition is beyond the scope of this section, but focusing on three prominent characteristics may suffice to indicate some salient features. These characteristics include the changing interests and interpretations of the explorer; the constantly varying terrain explored; and the continual and simultaneous reconstruction of explorer and terrain. Or in programmatic terms, postmodern navigation incorporates and assigns the values of *subjectivity*, *malleability* and *mastery*. It may be objected that these values are more congenial with a progressive modernity than the postmodern world that is supplanting it. Confident, self-motivated explorers survey unknown terrain to assert their mastery over it through willful manipulation. The exploration paves the way for improving the lives of future settlers. These values, in short, reflect an orderly rather than chaotic world. This objection, however, is misplaced for two reasons.

First, modern progress was premised on a notion of discovery and description. The task of the explorer is to understand and describe the terrain in order that this knowledge can be used by subsequent settlers in forming habitable communities. The mastery at issue is one of accurate knowledge, and such accuracy includes discerning given natural limits in order to set reasonable goals and expectations. Although these limits are often tested and revised, it is acknowledged in principle that there are natural limits that cannot be transgressed. The mastery at stake is more a matter of managerial skill than the power to create. Transforming the wilderness into a garden involves the application of natural laws and processes to human interests and purposes, not recreating nature and its creatures. Modern agriculture, for instance, is the result of good management of natural resources, rather than the intentional creation of new plants and animals. Moreover, the exploration does not construct the explorer. A certain constancy and objectivity of the observer is presupposed over against the observed. Scientific methodologies require dispassionate observation to test the veracity of what the observer has discovered. A proper observational distance is needed, thereby requiring that the borders separating the observer from the observed be clearly demarcated. This does not suggest that explorers *per se* are devoid of subjective responses to their explorations, but these are expressed, at least ideally, through the meaning assigned to their findings rather than their exploratory methods. This assigned meaning is properly enacted through moral, social and political ordering of human associations that should be aligned with both the structures of natural limitations and progressive historical trajectories. Although science is discovering that nature and human nature are more plastic than first assumed, neither is assumed to be infinitely malleable. If this were the case then any notion of progress would have to be abandoned. If the borders separating progress from regress are merely temporary constructs imposed by varying subjective preferences, then there are also no objective standards to plot the progressive direction of history. The purpose of modern science is to develop a methodological mastery that discloses, rather than refashions, the world. The progress resulting from this mastery serves to conform human aspirations to a set of realistic goals imposed by an objective reality.

Second, a so-called postmodernity has not supplanted modernity. To speak in postmodern terms requires the complete expurgation of any progressive, or even epochal, understanding of history. There simply is no modern era that is being displaced by a successor. What the shorthand 'modern' designates is a currently privileged account of the way the world is, while the shorthand designation 'postmodern' refers to the contestation of this privilege by insisting that no such account is possible. The world cannot be described by an observer, because both are temporary constructs. To observe and describe is to create, and the creative act in turn fashions the creator. For the postmodern there are no real borders separating the explorer from the terrain being explored; both endlessly shape and form the other. The resulting 'world' is an unguent background out from which momentary descriptions emerge and disappear, providing the texture of a modulating foreground. Explorers can never transcend this flux to describe the process as a whole, for their descriptions form the foreground's texture that draws upon, and is in turn absorbed back into, the background. Consequently, the values of subjectivity, malleability and mastery are both modern and postmodern values, though entailing radically differing connotations. For moderns, subjectivity is enriched through the application of discovery, but the act of discovering *per se* transforms neither the observer nor the observed. Although an objective knowledge of nature and human nature discloses some malleability that aids progressive self-control there are inherent limits to this flexibility. For postmoderns, subjectivity is a textured construct against an infinitely malleable background of fluid information. Both the world and the self are continuously created and recreated rather than discovered and controlled. Mastery therefore entails the power to create (temporarily) a foreground texture, and such creativity marks a pattern of willful (yet temporary) identity, both individually and corporately.

It is neither surprising nor ironic that the values of subjectivity, malleability and mastery can serve simultaneously both modern and postmodern purposes, because as contesters postmoderns have a necessarily parasitic relationship with moderns. Yet this stance begs the question: who or what is the modern host? Given the preceding section, it might be tempting to associate moderns with late liberals, and postmoderns with nihilists. The temptation, however, should be resisted. As was argued above, late liberals and nihilists are *not* two distinct classes, but the opposite ends of a common spectrum. This is one reason why in their intramural disputes and extramural conflicts the rhetoric and programs of one often degenerate into the mirror image of the other. The postmodern stance may be said to infiltrate and disorient the entire range of the spectrum, thereby serving to amplify rather than resolve the inherent tensions as the spectrum itself is subsumed into the *telos* of *techne*. This amplification is endemic given the postmodern commitment to the continual erasure of borders. The disputes among and between late liberals and nihilists are not over the necessity of physical and social borders, but over where they should be placed and how they should be maintained; borders may not be permanent, but they are solid and enduring. Given the postmodern disregard for such solidity and endurance, the erasure of borders inspires conceptions, forms of discourse and social interactions that are often artificial and violent. To willfully create a foreground texture requires the nearly continuous violation of any surrounding boundaries, and in their erasure the other ceases to be other. Yet who or what is this will that creates and asserts itself? And how is this will created and asserted? These are the questions that are addressed in the remainder of this chapter and the next.

Subjectivity

For the postmodern, identity is the outcome of an ongoing process of self-creative and expressive acts; the formation of a textured foreground out from and against a fluid background. A constant flow of novel experience is thereby required to form, interpret and project an evolving identity; otherwise it recedes back into a formless void.

Consequently, the postmodern self is premised on two requisite qualities. First, there must be a sufficient means for obtaining experiential input. This is achieved through the various senses. Hence postmoderns are sensually embodied. Second, there must also be a sufficient means for interpreting, expressing and assigning value to experiential inputs. This is achieved through various cognitive abilities. Hence postmoderns are embodied minds. The mere presence of the first prerequisite, however, does not necessarily result in what may be described as a self. There are some sensually embodied individuals, for instance, that lack the cognitive ability to interpret, express and assign value to experiential inputs. To be a human is not synonymous with being a self.

Although the interdependence between the two prerequisite qualities must be acknowledged, the second transcends and is valued more highly than the first, because it enables the subjective creation and expression of identity. It is the mind that is the dominant source of the self.

It may be objected that what the preceding paragraph describes is the late liberal doctrine of autonomous personhood, which is merely the moral and political instantiation of Cartesian dualism that postmoderns purportedly reject. Late liberal social and political theory has already established the primacy of mind over sensory input. Or more prosaically, it is biography, not biology, that should be ensconced in social mores and legal codes.[6] Postmoderns merely amplify the passion of the struggle against biological essentialists over such controversial issues as abortion, embryonic stem cell research, euthanasia and assisted suicide. In short, the postmodern 'self' described above offers nothing new. We may enucleate this objection, however, to expose the extent to which the postmodern turn has reshaped the terms of late liberal moral discourse that encases and quarantines the principle of autonomous personhood. This exposure also discloses a form of postmodern discourse that although appearing similar to late liberal rhetoric, is nonetheless dedicated to the eventual extinction of autonomous persons.

Late liberalism's autonomous person is a social construct of assigned value based on rough approximations of cognitive abilities. Conceptually, a person is self-aware, and practically this condition is instantiated through the assignment of political rights enabling persons to pursue their respective interests. To be a person one must therefore have the ability to calculate and pursue one's interests. Hence attempts to define personhood invariably appeal to certain cognitive abilities. Admittedly, these attempts have not produced any consensus among late liberal theorists, but for the purpose of this inquiry, we may generalize that a person is an individual who has the ability to express past experiences and aspirations for the future, and is able to assign value to both expressions. Or in more emotive terms, only persons can express an interest in how they want to or should be treated. Given this generalization, at present all persons are human, but not all humans are persons. To designate something as human does not automatically admit it into a realm of moral regard. Yet withholding this admission does not mean that non-persons should be treated in a cavalier or insensitive manner. Since personhood is a conceptual and social construct, non-persons can (and often are) treated, in varying degrees, *as if* they are persons. Fetuses, anencephalic infants and patients in a persistent vegetative state, for example, do not have the ability to express how they want to or should be treated. Yet those exercising custodial care are usually not at liberty to regard them as property to be disposed of as such. Rather, elaborate attempts are undertaken to treat them as if they have certain interests (and in some cases rights) that should be respected. Yet any attempt to discern how a particular fetus, anencephalic infant or patient in a persistent vegetative state might want to be treated is an imaginative exercise. Moreover, it is an exercise conducted within differing social and political contexts, accounting for the wide range of moral practices and laws within various liberal regimes governing such issues as abortion, infanticide and euthanasia.

Autonomous personhood, then, is an assigned status, derived from particular social and political relationships. Hence, in principle the autonomy granted to persons is a spectrum rather than an absolute category, reflecting historical variability and mutability. Late liberal traditions have struggled to determine the boundaries of personhood in which autonomy is bestowed, the rights entailed in that bestowal and under what conditions autonomy may be restricted or withheld. Although these issues have been hotly contested the disputes have not been arbitrary. Rather, the late liberal debates over autonomous personhood have tended to focus on what may be characterized as bodily integrity and mobility. Autonomy is exercised through a freedom of movement, and physical constraints (other than those that are self-imposed) restricting this movement prima facie violate the integrity of one's autonomy. This does not imply that physical mobility is unlimited or there are no legitimate reasons for imposing restrictions, but neither do these strictures imply that the status of autonomous personhood should be removed or withheld entirely, which would serve to legitimate arbitrary violations of bodily integrity. All late liberal regimes, for instance, recognize – to varying degrees – the necessity of restricting the mobility of dependent children, soldiers and prisoners, but these restrictions do not justify abuse or torture as legitimate methods for enforcing these constraints. Late liberal social and political ordering presumes the necessity of protecting the bodily integrity of persons, thereby ensuring their autonomy and mobility to form various relationships and associations.

This premise is enacted through the choices made by autonomous persons. Embodied persons are constrained by geography and time. If interactions can only be conducted through 'face-to-face' encounters, then a person's mobility is also constrained. One must either restrict interactions to other persons in close proximity, or expend the time to travel to distant locations. Geography and time, however, need not restrict the mobility of autonomous persons. An agent, for example, may be sent to a distant location to negotiate, exchange goods or deliver and receive documents. In this respect, the authorized agent signifies the embodied presence of the person being represented. Consequently, restricting the mobility of the agent is also assaulting the integral borders and autonomy of the represented person.

The development of modern transportation and communication technologies enlarged the scope and frequency of these representational interactions, compressing both time and distance. With jet aircraft, for instance, a journey once requiring weeks or months has been reduced to days or hours, and electronic banking has become a more convenient method of depositing or withdrawing money from a banker's vault. With the increasing ubiquity of information technology, especially the Internet and world wide web, communication and transactions are conducted in virtual time as well as real time. The net effect of these technologies is an expansive range of representational interactions, conducted by highly mobile persons at 'locations' that grow more fluid. More importantly, the character of these interactions shifts away from representing an embodied presence to referring to a disembodied will.

Consequently, late liberal accounts of autonomous personhood have become increasingly abstract. This trend is exemplified in John Rawls's 'veil of ignorance' (Rawls, 1972, pp. 136–42). Individuals deliberating on social and political ordering must do so without any knowledge of what their status might be in the systems they construct. Such ignorance ensures the justice of these structures, because one cannot know in advance one's sex, gender, race, and physical health or disability. No rational person would therefore create social and political structures that would affect these conditions adversely, for justice is rendered through fair procedures. One important consequence of this *purely* procedural understanding of justice is that it commits social and political ordering to mitigating the natural inequalities occurring among individuals.[7] Such mitigation is required to ensure that freedom and equal opportunity are honored in practice as well as in theory (ibid., pp. 83–90, 201–3). Hence late liberalism's relatively easy embracing of assisting infertile individuals to reproduce, and ameliorating physical disabilities through a combination of architecture, improved medical treatment and developing sophisticated prosthetics or other compensatory technologies.

This commitment to ameliorating natural inequalities, however, entails a subtle yet significant shift in emphasis, for the actual process of amelioration requires that bodily integrity can no longer be honored. Overcoming infertility, for instance, normally requires recourse to some combination of invasive surgery, donated gametes and surrogate wombs; the reproductive process itself becomes increasingly disembodied. Or ameliorating or preventing disabilities requires, on the one hand, radically invasive surgeries or deployment of sophisticated prosthetics, while on the other hand, prevention entails extensive screening and monitoring in order to detect and destroy 'defective' embryos and fetuses. Bodily boundaries must be traversed if the bedrock values of freedom and equal opportunity are to be fairly dispersed among autonomous persons.[8] This move suggests, however, that autonomy is no longer grounded in preserving bodily integrity, but in enabling the subjective interests of an assertive will. This move is anticipated in Rawls's insistence that a well-ordered society enables rational persons to formulate and follow their respective 'life plans', and these plans are best fulfilled through an array of options or opportunities that persons draw upon in adjusting and implementing their plans (ibid., pp. 404–16). Autonomy demarcates the ability to select a range of subjective experiences entailed in freely pursuing one's plan. What Rawls fails to mention is the ubiquitous role that technology plays in developing and exercising these choices given its ability to compress time and distance. And this compression in turn implies that the human body is a limitation that must be overcome to further expand the range and quality of the subjective will.

Once this move is made, however, there are no liberal grounds upon which objections to *self-enhancement* can be made. Since a fulfilling life plan entails subjective satisfaction, enhancing one's ability to select and partake from a more extensive experiential menu presumably enriches personal satisfaction. Consequently, the technologies used to mitigate natural inequalities can also be employed to enhance personal performance. This enhancement goal is achieved by adopting a two-pronged strategy. First, bodily functions are improved in order to overcome the limits of the body. At its most basic level it is a strategy of qualitatively enriched longevity. Living a long life relatively free of illness and suffering is a rational and satisfying life plan. It is also a plan that persons can fulfill through a combination of improved diet, exercise, healthier lifestyle and better healthcare. More speculatively, advances in genetic technology may slow ageing; stem cell research may lead to more effective therapies for repairing or replacing damaged tissue and organs, and nanomedicine may promise radical advances in diagnostic and therapeutic techniques.

Overcoming bodily limitations initiates the second prong of self-enhancement by transcending the physical and temporal nature of embodiment. Although increasing longevity presumably enhances one's subjectivity, a person nonetheless remains delimited by the location that one's body occupies. Even though various technologies enable a greater range of personal representation by compressing time and location, the embodied limitations of representative agency are muted rather than transcended. Transcending enhanced human bodies requires that borders be frequently pervaded, erased and redrawn. This could be accomplished initially through advances in psychopharmacology (for example, memory enhancement) and prosthetics (for example, optical implants) that enhance both the range and intensity of sensory inputs. More ambitiously, neural implants would enable speedier access to information, and more vivid participation in computer simulations and virtual reality programs. More speculatively, a person's mind could be uploaded into a computer and then downloaded simultaneously into various substrata. The net result is that location and time – and therefore one's body – grow increasingly irrelevant in a person's quest for enriched experience. The person is defined and expressed through self-referential experience that transcends the body in order to maximize the range and quality of one's potential subjectivity.[9]

No compelling objections to technological self-enhancement can be offered on late liberal terms so long as three conditions are met: (1) that competent persons have been fully informed and have freely consented to the enhancement methods employed; (2) that no other persons are intentionally harmed in pursuing these enhancements; and (3) that all persons have a fair opportunity to pursue self-enhancement. Consequently, the idea of bodily enhancement and transcendence *per se* is not peculiarly postmodern. The postmodern move occurs when the principle of self-enhancement is extended to enhancing future generations. Presumably a strong late liberal objection can be raised that enhancing offspring violates the bedrock principle of autonomy, because future generations cannot grant their informed and free consent. Future persons may be harmed because enhancements have been imposed on them that they might not have chosen had they been offered a choice.

Jürgen Habermas, for instance, propounds such an argument in respect to the genetic modification of embryos. With the combination of reproductive and genetic technologies, parents have a growing ability to exert greater control over the characteristics of their children. A 'previously unheard-of relationship arises when a person makes an irreversible decision about the natural traits of another person' (Habermas, 2003, p. 14). This capacity to manipulate offends our moral sensibilities by distorting the symmetry of the parent–child relationship. The advent of preimplantation genetic diagnosis (PGD) in particular signals a steady drift toward what Habermas characterizes as 'liberal eugenics' (ibid., pp. 16–23). Unlike previous eugenic practices which were used to implement racist political policies, this liberal incarnation is driven by the desire of parents to obtain desirable children by utilizing technologies within a global market. Increasingly parents are selecting children in much the same way as they choose other goods or commodities.

How does Habermas defend our injured sensibilities against 'the obscenity of this reifying practice' that is shaping 'a society which is ready to swap sensitivity regarding the normative and natural foundations of its existence for the narcissistic indulgence of our own preferences' (ibid., p. 20)? He contends that the liberal commitment to autonomy offers a solid bulwark. Liberal eugenics is wrong because its operative technology prevents enhanced members of future generations from exercising their autonomous self-realization and self-actualization. Eugenic programming is incompatible with the fundamental liberal conviction that persons should not be forced to pursue lives not of their own choosing. Consequently, a person has a right not to inherit a genetically modified genome. More expansively, so-called liberal eugenics erodes the underlying symmetry of the social relationships constituting civil society. A fundamental equality instantiated in the principle of autonomy is predicated on lifelong socialization rather than engineering individuals. Eugenic enhancement simply cannot be pursued fairly in liberal societies, because it destroys a foundational commitment to equality and autonomy. As Habermas asserts, 'Up to now, only persons born, not made, have participated in social interaction' (ibid., p. 65). This distinction between the born and the made is crucial to protecting the dignity of autonomous persons, for birth signifies 'a natural fact ... constituting a beginning we cannot control' (ibid., p. 58). Attempting to master this uncontrollable beginning denies the embodied character upon which liberal society is predicated.

Habermas is confident that in appealing to autonomy he has formulated an impregnable defense that simultaneously strips liberal eugenics of any plausible justification, while preserving the fundamental liberal principle of freedom. He accomplishes this task by avoiding any plea to the inherent dignity of embryos – a claim that could not be sustained in light of the liberal endorsement of reproductive freedom – while preserving the primacy of personhood. This strategy allows Habermas to undercut what he believes is the only plausible justification for genetically modifying embryos, namely, that it is a more expansive and efficient application of lifelong socialization; that 'there is no great difference between eugenics and education' (ibid., p. 49). In late liberal society embryos may be created to harvest stem cells or assist individuals in obtaining children, but their genes may not be altered to fulfill the desires of narcissistic parents. Such intervention violates the embodied foundation upon which autonomous personhood rests: persons have the right to modify their own bodies, but not those of others who can neither grant nor withhold their consent.

Given the assumed strength of his argument, Habermas is bewildered that most of his prominent critics do not assault his fortress directly, but bypass it altogether (ibid., pp. 75–100). Habermas explains this lack of engagement by contrasting the European philosophical orientation toward metaphysical concerns as opposed to American pragmatic interests. Hence liberal eugenics within the American context is perceived as an extension of reproductive rights. I do not wish to either challenge or affirm the descriptive accuracy of this transatlantic divide (much less speculate where Britain should be placed), but if Grant's contention that North America is the prime exemplar of late modernity (Grant, 1969, pp. 15–40) is correct then the future does not bode well for the embodied foundation of Habermas's late liberal society. What Habermas fails to recognize is that the reason why he need not be engaged directly is because the foundational principle of autonomy is not being eroded by eugenic technologies, for their use is already justified by the prior negation of the foundation he invokes. Habermas is defending a ghost. Embodied personhood is no longer a defining boundary, but an unfortunate limitation on the scope and quality of subjectivity; a limitation which should be overcome, not honored. In emphasizing cognitive and subjective qualities of personhood, late liberal social and political thought also took a postmodern turn exacerbating the problematic status of the body. The so-called natural and normative foundations that are now presumably under assault by liberal eugenics cannot be defended, for they have already been absorbed by the shifting sands of subjectivity in which the body is more a problem than a definitive feature. Many individuals may be offended by the prospect of liberal eugenics, but the offense is emotive rather than rational or normative. What Habermas fails to recognize is that late liberal society is no longer comprised of embodied persons, but populated with persons who happen to have bodies.

One ramification of this postmodern turn is seen in Habermas's failed attempt to demonstrate the immorality of altering the genes of future generations. His argument places a heavy burden on the 'fact' that birth cannot be controlled. This 'fact', however, is more fluid and less stubborn than Habermas admits, for it is being subjected to increasing levels of control. The advent of reproductive technology was accompanied by a social and political formula regarding its use: all persons have the right to pursue their respective reproductive interests, and some persons require technological assistance in exercising that right, thereby transcending their bodily limitations (Robertson, 1994). On strictly liberal grounds few objections can be raised against this formula. Technology simply assists the natural reproductive capabilities of human bodies. Yet the formula contains the latent implication that if persons have the right to obtain children, then they also have the right to obtain *desirable* children. If a person has the right to use technology to obtain a child that satisfies a subjective parental desire, then using technology to control the qualitative outcome can only serve to intensity that satisfaction. In addition, asserting greater qualitative control is driven by an inexorable logic that moves from selecting against undesirable traits to selecting desirable ones, and with future technological development enhancing them. In transforming procreation into a reproductive project, it becomes increasingly difficult to resist an implicit imperative to maximize a favorable outcome in terms of parental desires and expectations (Meilaender, 1995, pp. 61–88 and 1996, pp. 11–25).

The autonomy Habermas prizes has nothing to do with the body, other than as an enabling or disabling means of satisfying subjective desires, and technology plays an increasingly central role in correcting the body's deficiencies or augmenting its performance. The given 'fact' of birth is displaced by a willful reproductive process. Consequently, even Rawls's equalitarian proclivities do not prevent him from suggesting that veiled deliberation on a well-ordered society does not preclude the prospect of improving the genetic endowment of its inhabitants (Rawls, 1972, pp. 107–8).

As a good liberal, Habermas is rightfully offended by the prospect that what was once ' "given" as organic nature, and could at most be "bred," now shifts to the realm of artifacts and their production' (Habermas, 2003, p. 12). But his offense serves to exemplify why his purported bulwark of embodied autonomy can be easily bypassed, for late liberal society made a postmodern shift in which artifice is rapidly displacing nature as the principal metaphor of social and political ordering (Bernstein, 1991). Both the persons *and* associations comprising civil society are malleable constructs. When children are made rather than begotten, then birth is no longer an independent 'fact' but a sign of satiated parental desire. Moreover, the lifelong associations in which persons are socialized are also highly fluid since formative natural and normative foundations have been removed. In short, Habermas fails to see the radical malleability of the postmodern world and its inhabitants, because he fails to take into account the crucial shift from organic to cybernetic modes of discourse.

Malleability

In her book *How We Became Posthuman*, N. Katherine Hayles offers an interpretive account of the rise of cybernetics, and the accompanying social and political implications. The chief lineament of her inquiry incorporates an overview of the three-phase development of cybernetics as an emerging science following the Second World War. The first phase (1945–60) is dominated by the concept of homeostasis (Hayles, 1999, pp. 50–112). Based on the research of Norbert Wiener and his associates, humans, as well as other organisms, were perceived primarily as information-producing entities. Within this schema, autonomy is derived from a series of feedback loops that allow an organism to be self-regulating in response to environmental factors. The same principle applies to machines. On a hot day, for example, a human perspires while a thermostat triggers an air conditioner. In respect to discernible actions, the manner in which organisms and machines process and exchange information mirrors each other, raising the prospect, at least in principle, that the line separating the organic from the mechanistic can be removed, or is at least far more permeable than generally assumed.

The second phase (1960–80) expanded the work of the first with its emphasis on reflexivity (ibid., pp. 131–59). Rather than observing the reactions of organisms and machines to informational stimuli, attention focused on how information itself is organized. Based on research findings in which electrodes were implanted in a frog's visual cortex, Humberto Maturana claimed that a brain constructs rather than perceives reality. In a crude sense, the eye conveys information to the brain that it must process and interpret, but this construction implies there is no objective world to behold. As Hayles has observed, 'Certainly there is something "out there," which for lack of a better term we call "reality." But it comes into existence for us, and for all living creatures, *only through interactive processes determined solely by the organism's own organization*' (ibid., p. 136, emphasis original). The mind constructs perceived unities from the information it processes which in turn couples it to its environments. Consequently, life may be defined as the ability of an organism to maintain its internal organization for processing information over time. Maturana's work implies that no definitive interpretation of an objective reality can be forthcoming, because all that can be produced is an infinite regress of interpretations of interpretations. Moreover, there is also no reason to assume that this ability to process and interpret information is necessarily confined to humans or organisms, but could be replicated in the development of intelligent machines.

Hayles identifies the third phase (from 1980) as virtuality (ibid., pp. 222–46). The underlying goal driving research in this phase is to exert maximum control over the future course of human evolution. This immodest objective is based on the assumption that since the universe consists principally of information, any entity that can code and process data is alive. Information is therefore inherently superior to materiality, altogether erasing, in principle, the line dividing nature and artifice. A posthuman vision arises in this phase, driven by the hope that if humans can become pure information then they can also achieve immortality. The problem to overcome is that information is always embedded in a medium and must be extracted. To become posthuman requires the ability to remove the information constituting a personality from the body and to place it in a superior substratum. This hope is premised on the Platonic assumption that the form of an organism can be separated from its material construction; form defines life. This assumption is also reductionistic, because it reduces the apparent complexity of a material body to informational simplicity. Once this simplicity is identified then life itself can be reduced and defined to an underlying binary code. It is these dualistic and reductionistic assumptions that are driving current developments in robotics, artificial intelligence (AI) and artificial life (AL), especially as reflected in the works of Rodney Brooks, Ray Kurzweil and Hans Moravec.[10] These visionaries conceive a future in which all borders dividing biological from artificial life have been removed. Indeed, they can conceive no other alternative, because in a 'computational universe, the essential function for both intelligent machines and humans is processing information' (Hayles, 1999, p. 239). Since information is the universal feature of both material and immaterial realities then both nature and human nature are also infinitely malleable. This malleability, however, presents a dilemma: the evolution of life is predicated on competition and mutation. Victories go to those life-forms that are most adept at adapting to changing circumstances, and this adaptability reflects a superior computational ability to process and organize information. Humans to date have emerged as the dominant species in this evolutionary competition given their superior computational ability. With the advent of intelligent machines, however, it is only a matter of time before humans will be supplanted by the artifacts of their own creation. The only rational course to take, if any semblance of subjective human experience is to survive, is to merge with these artificial life-forms, thereby creating a new posthuman species.

Hayles's tale is not as bland as the preceding summary suggests. She offers a richly textured portrait of an emerging technoculture by weaving together the interrelated stories of cybernetics, the emergence of the cyborg as cultural icon and how the historically constructed human is becoming posthuman. The third story culminates the preceding ones. The construction of the cyborg requires sophisticated informational linkages between humans and their prosthetic networks. By 'prosthetics' Hayles refers to the various silicon-based technologies that enable individuals to process and organize information within an expanding range of possible patterns. This emerging posthuman vision presupposes that since information is superior to materiality, biological embodiment is an 'accident of history rather than an inevitability of life'. In evolutionary terms, the body is merely the 'original prosthesis' of the mind, so augmenting or replacing the body is a more efficient continuation of this evolutionary trajectory. Consequently, there are no absolute boundaries separating 'bodily existence and computer simulation, cybernetic mechanism and biological organism, robot teleology and human goals' (ibid., pp. 2–3).

Hayles weaves these stories together to explicate her central thesis that the emergence of the posthuman vision is not an outcome of a so-called deterministic technological system. Rather, 'People become posthuman because they *think* they are posthuman' (ibid., p. 6, emphasis added). Hayles exposes the formative power of posthuman discourse by examining selected science fiction texts paralleling the three developmental periods of cybernetics. This genre is particularly revealing because it reflects the strong relationship between late liberal culture and modern science. Most importantly, it is a genre that captures the profound ambivalence of that relationship. The future worlds portrayed by such authors as Bernard Wolfe, Philip K. Dick and William Gibson are both dreamlike and nightmarish. They envision a world in which technology empowers humans to overcome their physical limitations to encounter a wider and deeper range of experiential opportunities. But it is also a world of mutilated and disembodied entities, pursuing ravenous predation, gratuitous exploitation and unspeakable violence. The future is both heaven and hell.

According to Hayles, this simultaneously utopian and dystopian vision of the future reflects an unresolved tension between cybernetic principles and liberal moral and political convictions. The leading figures in phase one, especially Wiener, recognized that their research could potentially challenge the fundamental liberal tenet of individual autonomy. If organisms, such as humans, were essentially self-regulating machines then the feedback loops processing internal and external information that constituted them as such could be subjected to manipulations threatening their autonomous structure. Rather than resolving this tension it was presumed that there were inherent organic limits that would resist infinite manipulation, thereby preserving the requisite definitional borders of autonomous individuals. This assumption allowed the cybernetic pioneers to conduct their research while aggressively championing the central liberal value of autonomy. In the second phase the tension was not revisited, and it was taken for granted that the implications of cybernetic thought were compatible with traditional liberal convictions. Consequently, there is no sign of any tension in the third phase; the future posthuman is an extension of the disembodied pattern of information that has come to define personhood in an uncompromisingly libertarian manner. A person is simply a will that can be inserted within and asserted through a variety of media.

How may we account for this relatively rapid denouement of the body? Hayles contends that the unresolved tension was not a consequence of radically new modes of thought challenging traditional liberal concepts. Rather, what the cybernetic pioneers and their subsequent disciples failed to recognize was that the concept of autonomous personhood was not as robust as they assumed, and had already been severely eroded by late liberal social and political thought. The liberal concept of freedom was based on the notion of self-possession, combined with the absence of external constraints on willful mobility and exchange. With the emergence of expansive markets, however, the myth of self-possession became more difficult to maintain. The market was not so much composed of embodied persons conducting exchanges, as that the exchanges formed constructed persons. Within a market there is no given quality defining what a person is other than the ability to exchange; even corporations are regarded as legal persons. The autonomous person is not a given, but a socially constructed individual with malleable, rather than definitive, borders. Posthuman discourse takes the next logical step by rejecting any sense of a natural or given self that can be possessed. 'The posthuman subject is an amalgam, a collection of heterogeneous components, a material–informational entity whose boundaries undergo continuous construction and reconstruction' (Hayles, 1999, p. 3). For the posthuman, there is no autonomous self that is given, because the self can only be made. Even the subjectivity of technologically unaltered individuals is perceived as an artifact. Late liberals, then, possess bodies but are not themselves self-possessive bodies. Most importantly, since the body is not 'identified with the self' it becomes 'possible to claim for the liberal subject its notorious universality, a claim that depends on erasing markers of bodily difference' (ibid., pp. 4–5). Only in this diminished sense does posthuman discourse perpetuate the liberal tradition.

What does Hayles make of the emerging posthuman world? She is of two minds. She acknowledges that any conceivable human destiny is inevitably one deeply entwined with technology (ibid., pp. 279–82), while also admitting that it is a potentially perilous destiny. The problem, however, is not the prospect of a posthuman future *per se*, but how it will be constructed. 'What is lethal is not the posthuman as such but the grafting of the posthuman onto a liberal humanist view of the self' (ibid., pp. 286–7). Her solution for avoiding this deadly fate is to create posthuman bodies that celebrate 'finitude as a condition of human being', and this condition is in turn necessary for 'our continued survival' (ibid., p. 5). What Hayles shares with her posthuman interlocutors is the assumption that human life is an artifact to be constructed, and the goal at stake is survival. Where she differs is how to achieve the goal. Her strategy is a simple one: we must think as embodied persons rather than disembodied patterns of information. In short, media matter. She implements her strategy by insisting that the metanarrative of the third phase, exemplified by Moravec, must be countered by alternative narratives; embodied narratives rejecting the efficacy of any metanarrative, be it liberal or posthuman. Any attempt to impose teleology, be it progressive or technological, must be resisted by a radical historical contingency. A posthuman world must be fashioned by socially constructed persons, who in turn form their own particular histories and destinies.

The adequacy of Hayles's strategy of countering a metanarrative with a metanarrative of no metanarrative is questionable.[11] What is important to note, in this regard, is her striking confidence that what is at stake is *thought*. Do humans really transform themselves into posthumans through their thinking? If so, then she begs the issue of how *constructed* bodies provide a normative standard for guiding subsequent thought. Most importantly, if thought has such formative power, how is it related to the knowledge and ability to create material objects (or at least arrange their formative patterns of information)? Or to the contrary, has knowing and making already been collapsed into a single act, and to such a significant degree, to render her proposed strategy ineffectual? In order to address these questions, we must turn our attention to mastery as the premier postmodern attribute.

Mastery

This brief section serves as a preface for elucidating the chief postmodern attribute of mastery, a task undertaken in the next chapter. Mastery is the foremost issue at stake, because the overriding goal of *survival* is grounded in the operational principle of controlling one's fate. Hayles shares with her posthuman interlocutors the assumption that the future is ours to construct, so survival is the overriding consideration in order that a future can be constructed. She agrees that whatever future may ensue it will be one designed and populated by posthumans; her quarrel is over how this posthuman fate and its inhabitants shall be formed. For Hayles, such formative power resides in thought. Consequently, the moral challenge at hand is one of imagination: how should we imagine ourselves as posthumans? And how should we enact our imagining in ways that promote our survival?

Hayles's answer is to celebrate finitude as the only means of preventing the disappearance of the body through the toxic joining of liberal autonomy and posthuman construction. The appeal to finitude suggests that Hayles could make some normative claims about the limits of modifying human bodies. She makes no such claim, however, for doing so would presumably require asserting a counter-metanarrative, a tactic she dismisses as equally destructive. Yet in the absence of such normative claims, it is difficult to envision how finitude *per se* can make any substantive difference in forming the posthuman vision, since the enterprise is dedicated to overcoming finite limits inherent to embodied existence. Is there really a substantial difference between imagining oneself as a finite or infinite cyborg? Moreover, the emerging posthuman is not simply the outcome of thought. Rather, the posthuman is the product of mastery; the ability to manipulate and reshape material and organic objects in line with particular goals. Hayles is partly right in insisting that the task before us is an imaginative one, but it is an imagination more akin to engineering than science or other forms of thought; it is an imagination in which *theoria* and *techne* are collapsed into a single act of will. No matter how much we may think of ourselves *as if* we are cyborgs, we do not become such creatures until the border separating flesh and machine is indivisible.

Consequently, grafting liberal humanism onto the posthuman is not as deadly as Hayles asserts, for she fails to recognize that the notion of constructing a posthuman – a notion she embraces – is not a foreign object to be added, but the budding of a nascent feature. It is not so much the case that cybernetics and liberal humanism represent incompatible modes of thought whose combination results in extinction. Rather, the former represents the logical unfolding of the underlying rationale of the latter. As Grant saw clearly, the advent of modern liberalism was predicated on the mastery of nature and human nature (Grant, 1969, pp. 13–40). The freedom such mastery engenders is the ability to make happen what humans want to happen. As a result nature, as well as human nature, is a raw resource to be transformed in accordance with what is willed (Grant, 1986, pp. 30–31). The moral platitudes of progress accompanying the rise of modern liberalism disguised an insatiable will of mastery and transformation. Late liberalism is inexplicable if separated from its earlier marriage with technology, for the term itself denotes the 'idea that modern civilisation is distinguished from all previous civilisations because our activities of knowing and making have been brought together in a way which does not allow the once-clear distinguishing of them'. Moreover, the marriage always implied that 'we have brought the sciences and the arts into a new unity in our will to be masters of the earth and beyond' (ibid., p. 12).

If Grant's analysis is correct, then Hayles's appeal to finitude offers no moral guidance in constructing the posthuman, for finitude has been the enemy that liberalism, through its technology, has sought to master. Consequently, her objections can simply be bypassed in much the same way as Habermas's objections to genetic engineering, for she is asserting an emotive preference rather than appealing to a normative claim. When offered the choice between a posthuman future that is finite or immortal, her proposed resistance may very well prove futile. Yet we cannot think ourselves into being immortal, and thus we must turn our attention to the technological feasibility of actually achieving such a goal.

Notes

1 Chapters five and six.
2 Grant offers a concise overview of these two traditions in his essay 'Two Theological Languages' (Grant, 2002, pp. 49–65).

3 Cf Grant's earlier analysis of consumerism (Grant, 1995a), in which Nietzsche is conspicuously absent.
4 As Joan O'Donovan notes, in respect to hope, Nietzsche echoes themes which are similar to those propounded by Christians (O'Donovan, 1984, pp. 123–4).
5 Following Joan O'Donovan, equating last men with late liberals is a descriptive rather than pejorative designation.
6 See, for example, John Rawls's account of justice (Rawls, 1972 and 1996).
7 For critiques of Rawls's account of justice that are especially pertinent to this inquiry, see Grant, 1985 and Song, 1997, pp. 97–119.
8 For a more detailed account of these issues, see Waters, 2001.
9 A more extensive discussion of technological self-enhancement is undertaken in chapter three.
10 See Brooks, 2002, Kurzweil, 2000 and Moravec, 1988 and 1999.
11 Hayles revisits this issue in her essay 'Flesh and Metal: Reconfiguring the mindbody [sic] in virtual environments', in Mitchell and Thurtle, 2004.

Postmodern Technologies

Modern technologies may be characterized as systematic attempts to master nature and human nature. The rise of the useful and mechanical arts in medieval Europe improved the comfort and quality of daily life, as well as promoting exploration and commerce (Noble, 1999, pp. 9–20). The Renaissance and Reformation amplified the central role of human ingenuity, and the Enlightenment enhanced the trustworthy and progressive character of technological development by linking it with scientific principles (Lasch, 1991; Passmore, 1970, pp. 190–211). The ensuing industrialization of the nineteenth and twentieth centuries in turn generated unprecedented advances in transportation, communication, medicine and weaponry. Initial developments in biotechnology, nanotechnology, information technology (IT), artificial intelligence (AI) and robotics have augmented a perception of science-based technology as the most reliable, if not sole, source of human flourishing. It is arguable that the new *technoscience* has created a *technoculture* of machines and artifacts, becoming the 'natural' environment for many of the world's inhabitants. The mastery of nature is seemingly so complete that wilderness has become a garden to be preserved and protected, rather than a malevolent threat menacing the borders of civilization.

This characterization of modern technology is admittedly a generalization, and like most generalizations it conceals as much as it reveals. It nonetheless offers a promising starting-point for ascribing an emerging postmodern technoculture for two reasons.

First, the generalization serves as a reminder that the modern mastery of nature was driven by an ameliorative rather than transformative goal. Nature had to be tamed if humans were to flourish, and technology was a useful instrument for creating cultural spaces in which this flourishing could occur (Brunner, 1949, pp. 1–15). Human cultures defined and asserted their identities over and against nature, but the objective was to enable its inhabitants to flourish and not to radically transform nature and human nature in the process. Industrial and transportation technologies made daily life more comfortable by producing a wide range of consumer goods and enabling speedier transport; the printing press, telegraph and telephone expanded the scope and speed of communicating and disseminating information; advances in agriculture, sanitation and medicine enabled dramatic advances in healthcare and longevity. Modern technology applies nature's laws and secrets as disclosed by science to promote human welfare, but the intent is not to transform either nature or human nature. Modern mastery is more akin to perfecting the riding skills of a broncobuster in domesticating a wild horse than changing either into a new creature. Initial developments in biotechnology, information technology and robotics generally honored this limited purpose.

It may be objected that the mastery described above inevitably alters both nature and human nature. A wheat field is not the same landscape as a prairie; a racehorse is not the same creature as a wild mustang; an investor in commodities has little in common with her hunting–gathering forbears. In short, technology changes the nature of a landscape, a horse, or a human being. Granted, but these changes are the results, not the goals, of constructing cultures that invariably necessitate the modification of natural environments and evolutionary patterns. Moreover, these changes have been incremental rather than revolutionary. Increased wheat production is the result of cross-fertilization, improved fertilizers and pest control; racehorses are the fruition of generations of selected breeding; commodity traders enable the production and consumption of food through expanding markets. Although these changes may be described as radical over time, the pace was gradual and cumulative. Even in instances of more intentional interventions into the biological processes of an organism, the purpose, for moderns, is to augment rather than alter natural functions. Developing pest-resistant strands of wheat, using artificial insemination to breed racehorses, and inoculating children against disease reflect a mastery of nature, not its negation or that of its masters.

Postmodern mastery attempts to transform nature and human nature in accordance with human goals and desires. Plants and animals, for example, are genetically modified to deliver medication when eaten. These changes are the result of purposeful interventions whose desired results are accomplished in a highly condensed timeframe; mastery is exerted in a revolutionary instead of evolutionary manner. In this respect, postmodern mastery appears to be little more than an amplified version of its modern counterpart. There is, however, a significant difference in perspective. Moderns assume they are encountering natural environments and processes composed of delineated objects and organisms. Consequently, technological development and application encounter a range of given functional purposes, and violating the functional purposes of various objects or organisms to achieve certain objectives often requires a moral, as well as engineering, decision. Does harvesting stem cells, for instance, justify the creation, cloning and destruction of human embryos? Answering this question requires a determination of what an embryo is (person or mass of cells) and whether its use for non-reproductive purposes is warranted. In contrast, postmoderns encounter natural environments and processes that represent underlying patterns of information that can be reorganized with various technologies. The perceived boundaries of various objects and organisms are not definitive but highly malleable, and may be erased and redrawn in accordance with human objectives and desires. Human DNA, for example, may be inserted to create hairy cacti, thereby creating a novel pattern of information.[1] Manipulating information, however, does not relieve the manipulator of moral responsibility, but the perceptual context of moral deliberation has been radically altered. It is one thing to destroy a human embryo in order to harvest its stem cells, and quite another matter of applying the DNA they contain to achieve a therapeutic objective.

A postmodern technoculture is still a distinctly human artifact created over and against nature, but it is a malleable nature whose underlying and formative data are progressively subject to human manipulation. Culture in turn also comprises patterns of information that evolve through purposeful human acts rather than natural selection. Consequently, the line separating nature from artifice is permeable and temporary, and with the development of greater technological sophistication and precision the two become merged into a single pattern that both reflects and is subject to the human will. In principle there is no objective reality against which human identity is shaped and measured, but only information to be interpreted and configured. Moreover, humans as the masters of nature and the builders of culture are themselves patterns of the same malleable information, and therefore subject to their own manipulation. There are no given borders or boundaries that determine what it means to be human. That determination lies squarely and solely in what humans will themselves to be. The mastery of nature and human nature will only be complete, only be perfected, through human self-transformation. But transformed into what? There is no single answer to this question, for postmoderns know that any horizon toward which they might aspire is nothing more than a projection of their own historicist imaginations. Yet to be postmodern requires that they must nonetheless will their own transformation in order to be the masters of their own destiny. They must will themselves to become something other than they are, though they cannot know what that something will be in advance. They are driven by the desire to become something other than human, to become posthuman.

The principal tool for achieving this self-transformation is an expanding cache of technologies enabling greater manipulation of the information comprising nature and culture, and thereby human nature. It is broaching the relationship between postmodernity and posthumanism that prompts the second line of inquiry: what are the mythical and religious themes driving this self-transformation? As Michael Heim has observed, 'Behind the development of every major technology lies a vision' (Heim, 1993, p. 118). It will be no different with the technologies used by postmoderns to transform themselves into posthumans. Critically examining these mythical and religious themes helps to explain why postmodernity is not displacing modernity as a historical era, but is subsuming and transforming it within a thoroughgoing historicist vision. Postmodernity is simultaneously the affirmation *and* negation of modernity. Following David F. Noble, despite the Enlightenment's apparent victory of displacing theology with science as the dominant force of cultural formation, religious motivations were never eliminated but only muted (Noble, 1999, pp. 3–6). Rapid technological development was often praised in profane, progressive and scientific terms, but it was 'driven also by distant dreams, spiritual yearnings for supernatural redemption' (ibid., p. 3). Indeed, 'modern technology and religion have evolved together, and as a result the technological enterprise has been and remains suffused with religious belief' (ibid., p. 5). Consequently, it is not surprising that religious themes continue to inform the development of postmodern technologies, for postmodernity is modernity's prodigal child. Yet since postmodernity is also the negation of modernity, its religious themes are radically reinterpreted and redirected. Modern millennial expectations for an Edenic and Adamic recovery, for instance, were reinforced by advances in modern science and technology. Humankind, it was believed, was entering a golden age when it would faithfully exercise its divinely mandated dominion over creation, and, more importantly, would obtain the state of perfection humans enjoyed prior to the fall (ibid., pp. 21–100; Passmore, 1970, pp. 116–327). The postmodern turn is to insist that such a restorationist program is too confined. Complete mastery over nature, and derivatively human nature, cannot be achieved until humans perfect themselves by becoming a superior species. If the modern project is to make humans better, then the postmodern goal is to make creatures that are better than human.

What exactly is a posthuman? The question is impossible to answer definitively because no such creature yet exists, and there is little consensus among those who speculate on its emergence. Despite this ambiguity the prospect of a posthuman future is generating a growing body of literature.[2] In order to gain some clarity, we may focus briefly on a movement dedicated to transforming humans into posthumans. Transhumanism is a multifaceted and ill-defined movement.[3] What holds its varying and contentious proponents together is an unwavering belief that the current state of the human condition is deplorable, and the only effective way to remedy this plight is for humans to use various technologies to radically enhance and transcend their innate and latent capabilities. The condition of humans is wretched because they are finite and mortal creatures. Consequently, the overriding goal is to overcome these limitations through a series of progressive transformations. The most immediate challenge is to increase longevity. The first step is being taken through a combination of improved healthcare, diet and performance-enhancing drugs. Regenerative medicine represents a significant second step, especially when stem cell research and cloning are combined with the introduction of sophisticated prosthetics, mechanical organs and artificial tissue. As these technological innovations improve, human capabilities will also be greatly enhanced, culminating in greatly expanded life-spans. Simply extending longevity, however, is not enough, for further development, both as individuals and as a species, is limited by morbidity and mortality. Consequently, the eventual goal is to achieve virtual immortality, through either extensive genetic engineering (de Grey, 2004), or uploading the mind which can then be downloaded into various robotic or electronic media (Moravec, 1988, pp. 108–24).

Transhumanism is a transitional movement dedicated to transforming humans into posthumans. This goal is based on two underlying assumptions: first, the essence of human identity is lodged exclusively in the mind, and second, the evolution of mind is an open-ended and malleable process. It is a highly developed mind that makes humans the currently dominant species. Through rational and imaginative thought in tandem with an assertive will, humans achieve their goals and satiate their desires. Indeed, it is the mind that enabled humans to develop as a culture formed and forming species. Moreover, it is the mind that allows a human being to be a unique individual. In this respect, the transhumanist agenda is informed by the humanistic and liberal traditions with their emphases on autonomy and freedom. Unfortunately, further development of free and autonomous minds is severely limited by the finite constraints of fragile and mortal bodies. Fortunately, these constraints can be overcome by mastering future evolutionary development. As Nick Bostrom asserts, we should 'view human nature as a work-in-progress, a half-baked beginning that we can learn to remold in desirable ways' (Bostrom, n.d.). The immediate problem is that natural evolution does not provide adequate baking time; hence the imperative to extend longevity as far as possible. More extensively, Bostrom presumes that both the mind and the biological medium in which it is currently lodged both comprise raw data. In principle, there is no limit to the amount of information that could comprise a mind. The challenge is to overcome the physical and temporal limitations of the mind so it may expand endlessly by accumulating more information. Although this challenge is admittedly formidable it can be surmounted, because the media in which mind is contained and through which it is expressed also comprise malleable information that, again in principle, can be manipulated infinitely into more enduring and desirable patterns. In this respect, transhumanism takes a postmodern turn away from its humanistic and liberal forbearers by insisting that no fate can be loved other than one that is self-created. The only fate that humans can genuinely love is a posthuman destiny of their own making.

The remainder of this chapter examines how anticipated technological developments may be used in constructing a posthuman future as propounded by various transhumanist proponents. The examination also discloses how postmodern applications of these technologies do not so much supplant modern, progressive values and modes of discourse, but subsume and radically reinterpret them. Hence the posthuman vision incorporates seminal mythical imagery and religious themes that are critiqued in greater detail in the following chapter.

Technology and Identity

Since, as transhumanists claim, the essence of human identity resides in the mind, it is imperative that cognitive performance be enhanced, and the scope of experiential opportunities expanded in order to construct a posthuman future. A number of therapeutic advances are being undertaken that may prove promising in achieving these more ambitious objectives. A new generation of psychopharmacological drugs is treating various behavioral disorders and related diseases. Ritalin, for example, is used widely to control hyperactivity in children, and Modafinil is employed in treating narcolepsy. The same drugs, however, can also be used to augment performance. Many high school and college students use Ritalin prior to examinations to focus their attention, and some athletes have admitted taking Modafinil to enhance their mental preparation (Lamb, 2004). More widely, Modafinil is being used to ward off doziness or avoid sleeping for extended periods of time to increase productivity (O'Connor, 2004; Begley, 2004). In addition, transcranial magnetic stimulation, used for treating depression, enhances the problem-solving abilities of healthy individuals.

Given rapid advances in brain research, it is anticipated that even more effective treatments will soon be developed. It is expected, for instance, that improved imaging techniques could be used to locate and map memories stored in the brain. Traumatic memories could then be removed. The same technique could be used, however, to remove merely unpleasant memories, and augment or create more pleasant ones in their stead (LaFee, 2004; Stein, 2004). More expansively, clinical trials of new drugs to treat Alzheimer's disease have shown promising initial results. Furthermore, it is hoped that stem cell research will lead to more effective therapies for treating strokes, brain injuries and a widening range of neural disorders and diseases. These therapies could also, in principle, enhance such cognitive abilities as improved calculative speed and memory recall.[4]

The net effect of such therapies and enhancements will presumably improve the quality of life for many individuals, making them happier and more productive. Moreover, given greater longevity promised by anticipated advances in regenerative medicine paralleling these developments, it is crucial that mental capabilities be preserved in an aging population. Yet enhancing the mind faces the stubborn constraints of the physical brain and its dependency on biochemical processes. There is presumably an outside limit to how much information can be stored in the brain, as well as the speed of organizing, accessing and interpreting it. This limit, however, can be overcome through neural implants that would enlarge memory capacity and enhance computational speed. The twin effects of psychopharmacological and biotechnological enhancements will not only maximize natural capabilities, but also transcend them through the introduction of electronic devices. The prospect of enhancing the mind, however, faces an even more daunting challenge: it remains dependent on a brain (albeit an enhanced one) that is constrained by its physical location in the body. The physical and temporal handicaps of that location thereby deprive the mind of a wider range of informational input that it now has the capacity to process, store and utilize.

The first step in solving this problem has been taken with the advent of virtual reality. To enter virtual reality is to cross a threshold where physical and temporal limits are suspended. It is therefore a world of potentially limitless experiential opportunities. One can see pigs fly or sparrows swim; pilot a jet aircraft or soar like an eagle. It is a world whose laws and boundaries are subject only to those imposed by the imagination, and the ever-advancing capabilities of the technological milieu. It is not merely a realm of high-tech fantasy fulfillment, for the user becomes part of, and one with, the total virtual experience. A person can be engrossed in a movie or lost in a book, but one becomes immersed in and absorbed by virtual reality. It is a reality in which the cybernetic principles of organizing and reconfiguring information reign dominant. Hence the neologism *cyberspace* to designate a fluid realm where every border and any boundary is erased and redrawn at will. This fluidity is exemplified by the ease with which multiple virtual identities are constructed. It is not necessarily the same person who participates in various virtual reality or simulation programs, and more broadly wanders and encounters other virtual personalities in cyberspace. Data are manipulated to disguise or fabricate such factors as age, gender, nationality, ethnicity, sexual preference or career. The motivations for such plastic identities range from harmless playfulness to vicious predation; from naïve trust to malicious fraud. It is one thing for a mother to pretend to be a young girl while instant-messaging her daughter, and quite another matter for a pedophile to disguise his intentions to lure a young boy to a rendezvous; one can provide credit card information to purchase a book online, and one can also hack the information to steal from its holder. The mere advent of cyberspace does not cancel a need for ethics, but the nature of moral agency and conduct requires redefinition. Are there common moral principles, values and rules that cut across all virtual identities and realities? Or do such principles, values and rules vary widely within the varying regions of cyberspace? More extensively, do moral principles, values and rules make much sense within a realm of temporary borders and fluid boundaries? (See Houston, 1998; Pullinger, 2001; Schultze, 2002.)

As humans enhance their minds they may choose to take up greater residency in cyberspace, since it will offer a vaster range and intensity of experiential opportunities. Virtual reality may become a more emotionally satisfying and mentally challenging locale than so-called real reality; a superior venue to construct and assert one's identity. If predictions regarding the pace of computational speed prove true, then within a few decades neural implants may be required to take full advantage of new super-fast computers (Kurzweil, 2000, pp. 220–21). What was envisioned originally as a useful tool becomes a necessary prosthetic to compensate the natural limitations of the brain. Taking this fateful step toward becoming a cyborg exacerbates the ethical questions posed above. If, for example, traumatic or unpleasant memories can be removed, why not replace them with more wholesome and pleasant ones? Would not virtual memories of happy childhoods, loving relationships and splendid consensual sex produce healthy and well-adjusted personalities? It may be objected that constructing one's identity from virtual experiences is inherently deceitful and fraudulent. By definition a mentally healthy and well-adjusted individual is one who has learned to come to terms with traumatic or unpleasant experiences. What is at stake is truthful and accurate recall, not fabricated memories. What this virtual identity offers is little more than fantasy, denial and escapism.

The objection is unconvincing, however, because it fails to acknowledge the cybernetic character of postmodern identity. Identity is a narrative construct. The mind does not simply recall past experiences as objective events, but rather, constructs interpretive memories. Identity is, in short, storytelling (Hogue, 2003). What brain enhancement and virtual reality technologies offer in tandem are potentially more powerful and effective storytelling tools, because of the greater range of experience and qualitative control they afford. The plot and storyline of narrative identities is now subject to willful control rather than capricious events. In many respects these technological enhancements enable a more honest approach to identity construction, because they remedy the suffering entailed by traumatic and unpleasant memories (through their removal and replacement) instead of treating symptoms (psychotherapy and drugs). The ability to remove, create and interpret a broader range of experience is an improvement over the conventional lies, deceit and rationalizations inherent in constructing identities over time. It is therefore imperative that brain enhancement technologies be developed rapidly and utilized widely since identity is grounded in mind. What is at stake is not the so-called nature of real experience, but the sources and interpretive control of information; the postmodern *I* is an ongoing and emergent process of patterned information, governed by a subjective will that is also undergoing perpetual change. Consequently, since the mind is the essence of what it means to be human, there is no compelling reason to privilege experiences of so-called real reality over its virtual counterpart as a resource for constructing narrative identities. The line separating these realms is, after all, also made up of permeable and temporary patterns of information, which with increasing technological capability *can and should* be erased and redrawn.

In order to appreciate the imperative behind collapsing real and virtual realities within a common spectrum, we must pause to ponder the cyber metaphysic prompting a drive for greater mastery. According to Heim, 'With its virtual environments and simulated worlds, cyberspace is a metaphysical laboratory, a tool for examining our very sense of reality' (Heim, 1993, p. 83). It is only in coming to terms with the ontological structure of cyberspace that we may understand and assess its internal, albeit fluid, structure. According to Heim, it is a metaphysical exploration that begins with Plato and ends with Leibniz (Heim, 1993, p. 84). Plato's ontology is premised on a fundamental division of body and soul. Although this separation does not necessarily entail disparaging the body, the soul is clearly superior because it is eternal rather than temporal. Indeed, perfect release from pain and suffering can occur only when the body, as the prison of the soul, is destroyed in death. This theme of the immortal soul was subsequently adopted by orthodox Christian theology, though muted with its accompanying doctrine of the resurrection of the body. Consequently this dualistic ontology confined finite and temporal existence to the realm of necessity, separated from an eternal realm of truth and goodness.

Much of the modern project may be characterized as a series of clumsy attempts to either fill in or bridge this chasm. Materialistic moderns encounter an even more daunting challenge than their Platonic and Christian forbearers, however, for they maintain a dualistic framework in which the mind is exchanged for the soul. Unfortunately, the mind is lost with the death of the brain, so there was no eternal aspect of human ontology. Unlike Platonists and Christians, moderns cannot anticipate or take consolation in the prospect of a liberated soul or resurrected body. The only viable recourse is to transform necessity into goodness. Technology plays a central role in this endeavor, for the progressive mastery of nature amplifies the extent and quality of the life of the mind. This mastery not only frees many individuals from physical toil and drudgery, but technology itself becomes a mechanism and symbol of asserting a willfully created identity over and against natural limits. Since there is no eternal good to be had, there is at least the supreme temporal good of an expanding range of enriched experience enabled by the development of various technologies. If necessity cannot be conquered it can at least be tamed. Contrary to the popular, but vacuous, accolades that technology is used simply to improve the quality of human life, its purpose, following Hannah Arendt, is to transform the life and lives of humans into artifacts of the will (Arendt, 1998, pp. 144–53).

The desire to construct a culture of artifice leads Heim to contend that the late modern fascination with technology is more aesthetic than utilitarian. This artistic bent is portrayed in the ubiquitous embracing of information technology (IT) that he likens to an erotic marriage, since computers augment both our senses and power (Heim, 1993, pp. 84–6). IT symbolizes an expansive process of fabricating, possessing and consuming the objects of individual and corporate desire. With the aid of various technologies we 'seek to extend ourselves and to heighten the intensity of our lives in general through Eros'. More dramatically, it is 'a drive to extend our finite being, to prolong something of our physical selves beyond our mortal existence' (ibid., p. 87). Cyberspace is therefore a means of satisfying an erotic drive. It is important to note, however, that its internal structure embraces simultaneously modern and postmodern tendencies. As Heim contends, mathematics transformed science from an act of observation to that of manipulation (ibid., p. 92), but in cyberspace the manipulation of physical objects and organisms is displaced by the manipulation of information; data comprising both the manipulated and the manipulator. In addition, virtual realities populated by cyber personalities try to maintain a modern sense of autonomous identity in an environment where the physical borders defining such an identity have been rendered porous and pliable.

This uneasy tension leads to a resolution suggested by Leibniz's monadic metaphysics. A monad refers to a self-contained and secluded entity. It is a non-material substance with no spatial or physical properties that are derived from its mental activities. There is no external world to encounter, no widespread vision to behold, only projections of its self-generated desires and vistas. 'The monad exists as an independent point of vital willpower, a surging drive to achieve its own goals according to its own internal dictates' (ibid., p. 97). Hence monads have no need for windows. But as Heim insists, they do have terminals. 'The mental life of the monad – and the monad has no other life – is a procession of internal representations' (ibid., p. 97). Although a monad is solitary it nevertheless interacts with other monads, otherwise it would have no inputs to process and project. Monads do not exist ethereally, but within networks. Networked interactions, however, do not include encounters with any so-called objective realities. Monads interface with various representations or interpretations; experiences that can be easily stored, simulated, manipulated and disposed of. The monad is a composite of surrogate experiences based on sensual perceptions that must be interpreted, reconstructed and projected back. Strictly speaking, there is no physical contact among monads, for physicality as such is also a projected construct, and thereby illusory. Consequently, there is nothing but perception on the rapidly changing monadic landscape.

Yet Heim insists that although monads are solitary, they nonetheless 'belong to a single world' (ibid., p. 98). The interpretive activities and willful exploits of autonomous monads are coordinated and harmonized by a 'Central Infinite

Monad, traditionally known as God' (ibid., p. 99). This god is analogous to a central nervous system in a complex organism, enabling each monad to pursue 'its separate life according to the dictates of its own willful nature while still harmonizing with all the other monads on line' (ibid., p. 99). Each monad is a microcosm of the macrocosmic network. The underlying pantheism of Leibniz's metaphysics prevents cyberspace from degenerating into a realm of sheer anarchy.

This pantheistic faith allows Heim to commend the bright side of cyberspace and its virtual realities. More broadly, IT permits a bracketing of spatial and temporal limits – *not* their erasure or removal – thereby countering the loneliness and anomie of late modern society (ibid., pp. 99–101). The emergence of virtual realities and cyber communities need not corrode virtuous lives. Yet Heim admits that this bright side cannot be achieved on cybernetic terms alone. Rather, lives that are genuinely human must remain anchored to reality, for in its absence moral values and virtues have no content. Consequently, the significance of cyberspace and its virtual realities resides in its instrumental ability to 'redeem our awareness of reality' (ibid., p. 124). The power of virtual reality stems from its potential to elicit strong emotions and feelings, thereby enabling the construction of more humane cultures; it is an artistic and imaginative tool to reorder and augment but not to create reality. To anchor cyberspace to reality, three of its crucial existential 'features' must be brought into cyberspace, but then transformed 'beyond immediate recognition' (ibid., p. 136).

First, mortality and natality are givens that affirm humans as finite and fragile creatures. Birth and death demarcate an individual's life, and without these constraints one's grounding in formative kinships and sense of place in equally finite and fragile ecosystems is not possible. Second, reality is by definition temporal, thereby providing continuity between past and future. Since the future is emergent, the past cannot be simply erased or reconstructed, otherwise the passage of time is little more than a series of unrelated and fleeting fantasies. Third, since 'biological life-forms' are finite and temporal, 'a sense of fragility or precariousness pervades our real world, frequently making suffering a default value' (ibid., p. 136). We care for ourselves and others, because necessity dictates that fragile and mortal creatures must be careful to avoid harm's way.

How will virtual reality transform these existential features? Heim insists that simply evicting 'finite constraints might disqualify virtuality from having any degree of reality whatsoever' (ibid., p. 137). Yet imposing these constraints upon cyberspace would merely duplicate rather than reshape and enhance reality. Virtual reality should instead inspire the imaginative creation of many alternative worlds, and more importantly, alternative values and modes of thought emerging from their creation. Time can also not be exiled from cyberspace, but it can be reckoned in ways that avoid the 'deadliness of the real world' (ibid., p. 137). The chief virtue of virtual reality is the leisurely and gracious setting it affords for concentrated mental and experiential pursuits by suspending temporal restraints. Most importantly, virtual reality also suspends and ultimately ameliorates the existential threats of the reality it seeks to transform. The necessity to care will always be endemic to the human condition, 'but with the help of intelligent software agents, cares will weigh on us more lightly' (ibid., p. 137).

For Heim, virtual reality is ultimately an act of intense philosophical contemplation. It is entering a realm in which finite perceptions are dissolved by an infinite array of imaginative possibilities. Consequently, it is also a place where we may lift anchor from spatial and temporal constraints, not then to drift aimlessly but to explore unknown regions, eventually finding a safer harbor to again drop anchor. Such philosophical exploration is by far the most significant opportunity afforded by virtual reality, and failing to take advantage of this opportunity presents its most crucial challenge. As Heim admits, if the anchor when once lifted is never dropped again – or worse, the chain is willfully broken – then the dark side of cyberspace will come to the fore. Instead of offering a safe haven, it will become a Gnostic and Manichean inferno whose inhabitants loathe the very existential features that anchor humans to the real world. Rather than enabling the creation of a better reality, it will revert back to a Hobbesian state of nature, or better cyber-nature. It will be a state populated by cyborgs, who, in loathing the finitude and frailty of the body see it as rancid meat to be discarded, are becoming their prostheses. But its disposal will entail the loss of the defining human capacity of care.

Heim's anchor to reality is an illusory hope, for the finitude, temporality and caring he champions – even in their radically transformed versions – lack any normative content. He offers no suggestions regarding how mortality and natality, for example, and past and future are grounded in nature, and thereby define human nature. Consequently, he also has little moral guidance to offer regarding how care is exhibited within these constraints. More tellingly, he offers no clue whatsoever what the morality (or immorality) of withholding care might mean. This is seen in his portrayal of virtual reality as a sanctuary in which one is temporarily released from the cares of the real world. In effect, the best that virtual reality can proffer is a temporary sojourn in a world devoid of suffering. Yet to accomplish this goal, it must be a world equally devoid of mortality and natality; a world in which past and future also have no real meaning. It is revealing in this regard that transhumanists, the vociferous proponents of mind enhancement, have virtually nothing to say about Heim's defining characteristics. Natality has been lost in ceaseless discussions on the value of germline modifications of offspring, or more commonly whether sexual pleasure should be enhanced or sublimated. And finitude and temporality more broadly have been subsumed into a mantra against the evils of mortality and subsequent quest for immortality.[5] Heim's anchor cannot hold, because it lacks sufficient substance, and is cast in a sea without any solid bottom. The finitude, temporality and caring he affirms are not in themselves realities, but indications of a greater defining reality that he is either unwilling or unable to designate and explicate. It is difficult, if not impossible, to imagine what a transformed understanding of caring might mean in a realm dedicated to relieving, if not eliminating, the heavy burdens of finitude and temporality. The goal is not to enhance care, but to eliminate the conditions that make it necessary.

In addition, the kind of philosophical contemplation afforded by virtual reality that Heim envisions is untenable given the technology's purpose and rationale. His case is built on the modern presupposition that thought precedes action. An act is the concrete application of thought. Virtual reality is a laboratory where different thought experiments may be conducted without the risk of any real consequences. What Heim fails to recognize is that such a safe laboratory cannot exist for very long within postmodern cyberspace. Following George Grant, in the late modern project of mastering nature and human nature, the once discrete realms of knowing and making have already been thoroughly interpenetrated, and thereby increasingly indiscernible (Grant, 1986, pp. 11–34). Science and technology can scarcely be conceived in isolation from each other. The postmodern move is to culminate this momentum by collapsing knowing and making into a single act of will, implemented through an emerging technoscience. This move necessarily enfolds its users into its own unfolding destiny. Technoscience purportedly enhances willful freedom by offering an ever-expanding supermarket of options from which customers freely pick and choose, but what is occluded is that the notion of freedom as choice is transformed by the destiny accompanying an unfolding technoscience. The freedom to pick and choose is part of a larger package deal. Consequently, virtual reality is not a contemplative laboratory where ideas are created, and then taken to the factory of the real world to construct a better anchor. Rather, it is a domain that individuals with enhanced minds use as a means of generating a broader and richer range of personal experiences. Hence the momentum of the endeavor is not to suspend finitude and temporality, thereby easing the cares of the world, but to abolish the limits altogether, thereby eradicating the need to care. Contrary to Heim, the destiny of postmodern cyberspace is not to build a better anchor, but to eliminate the need for one whatsoever.

Heim is correct in contending that the crucial existential features he identifies will be radically transformed in cyberspace. It is a transformation, however, entailing the loss of any given and discernible values as they erode and evaporate into the morass of malleable information used in shaping and asserting an array of changing identities. The enveloping power of this destiny of the ascendant mind is seen in the cyborg's iconic status in postmodern and posthuman thought. As N. Katherine Hayles contends, it is only through the emergence of something like a cyborg that humans can simultaneously liberate themselves from the tyranny of a so-called nature and human nature, and construct for themselves a more hospitable posthuman future. For it is only such a creature that will have the power to erase and redraw the 'natural' boundaries that have been used for oppressive purposes; genuine freedom can only be achieved by a purposive melding of humans with their technology. The value of virtual reality is not to provide a safe haven of intellectual contemplation, but to provide an experiential tool in constructing a posthuman world. The goal is not to provide a sanctuary from reality in order to imagine a better one, but to deconstruct and reconstruct what is real. The posthuman does not need an anchor to any 'reality'. Indeed, the anchor, the ship it anchors and the sea bottom upon which it rests are nothing more than temporary patterns of information that can and should be rearranged. Contrary to Heim, whether or not the cyborg represents the dark or light side of cyberspace is nothing more than a matter of perspective and preference.

As was discussed in the previous chapter, Hayles is not disturbed by the image of the cyborg. The humanity of this new creature need not be sacrificed by its creators. So long as finitude and embodiment are celebrated, and liberal autonomy resisted, the posthuman will be an improved version of its predecessor. She is guardedly optimistic that a humane posthuman can be constructed, because we already think of ourselves as being posthuman. Developments in neuro-enhancement and information technology are thereby not formative, but instrumental in embodying a posthuman vision. This posthuman vision can in turn be used as a control mechanism for picking and choosing among various technological applications in fashioning finite, postliberal cyborgs. With the aid of such good will, the emerging cyborg need not represent the dark side of cyberspace that Heim fears.

Hayles's sanguine vision of a posthuman future is perplexing. As was also discussed in the previous chapter, it is difficult to imagine what a finite and embodied cyborg might entail, particularly when she is unwilling or unable to explicate any normative claims regarding which aspects of human nature need to be transformed, and which should be maintained in constructing ourselves as cyborgs. More telling, is her naïve confidence in the ability of the will to control the process of technological enhancement. Presumably the power to control this process can only stem from its subservience to a formative metanarrative. Yet she rejects the imposition of any such narrative; indeed, the emergence of the cyborg is celebrated, because such a creature denies and destroys the possibility of any metanarrative. Her bravado, however, hides her failure to come to terms with technology as a formative as well as instrumental force. If Grant is correct that knowing and making have been collapsed into a single act of will, then the issue at stake is not one solely of imaginative identity but also engineering. Humans are not becoming posthuman simply because they imagine themselves as such. It is through a wide range of technological enhancements that humans will physically and mentally alter themselves into posthumans. Consequently, the will Hayles extols cannot provide the guidance she wishes, for, again following Grant, the will is itself being recast by the unfolding and enfolding destiny of the technological potential she has already embraced for the purpose of reconfiguring natural borders and boundaries. In the absence of any normative claims about aspects of a human nature she wishes to selectively enhance, correct or expunge, there is no compelling reason within the cybernetic rationale, from which she is deeply partaking, to celebrate finitude. Hayles's embodiment and Heim's anchor are little more than rearguard tactics.

Enriching the experiential life of the mind through tandem developments in neuro-enhancement and IT serves as an ultimately frustrating first step in becoming posthuman. Alas, the enhanced and enriched mind must leave the limitless domain of cyberspace, and return to the finite and mortal limits of embodied existence. Yet there is no reason why one must or should straddle the two domains, for in principle the boundary separating them can also be removed. Pushing back the finite limits of embodiment is merely the first skirmish in transcending the confines of time and space.

Technology and Finitude

In order to create a more satisfying range of experiential opportunities, humans must transcend their finitude, and by implication their mortality as well. Attempts to enhance the mind through biochemistry and IT demarcate initial steps in overcoming spatial and temporal limits that constrain the scope and quality of human experience. Consequently, these tentative steps need to be placed within a more ambitious agenda of transforming humans into posthumans, as exemplified through recent and anticipated developments in such areas as biotechnology, nanotechnology, artificial intelligence (AI) and robotics.

These technologies are routinely employed within various agricultural and industrial processes. Biotechnology, for instance, has been used to produce pest-resistant plants and enhance the selected breeding of livestock. A growing range of new or improved consumer goods has been produced through various applications of nanotechnology. Robotic technology and increasingly AI are used extensively in manufacturing, and consumer gadgets and household items. Most of these initial applications are deployed in a manner that can be characterized as late modern; as part of a larger project of humans asserting their mastery over nature. If human nature is somehow changed in the process, it is a secondary consequence resulting from the benefits of transforming organic and inorganic resources into artifacts, goods and services. Human behavior is admittedly altered, for good or ill, by the availability of abundant and cheap food, stain-resistant clothing and efficient machines. Presumably the purpose for producing these items is to satisfy (as well as create) the desires of consumers, and not to directly or substantially change the nature of their being.

In contrast, a postmodern application of these technologies may be characterized as the simultaneous attempt to create a novel array of consumer goods and services, *and* transform the nature or being of the producers and consumers as well. Someday biotechnology may routinely produce chimeras or new bacteria; with nanotechnology we might be able to transform inert matter into food or a virulent virus; the AI assistant of the future will put a contemporary PDA (and its user) to shame. All of these possibilities raise important issues in such areas as environmental ethics, cultural formation, and social and political ordering. For the purpose of this inquiry, however, the remainder of this chapter focuses on the transformative part of the postmodern agenda. Recent and anticipated developments in regenerative medicine offer a revealing perspective on the practical import of what this transformation entails.

Genetics is the basic science underlying regenerative medicine.[6] Recombinant DNA technology, for instance, is used to produce human-protein drugs to treat diabetes, and promote the formation of red blood cells. It is also anticipated that genes can be used to stimulate the growth of new tissue, and create antibodies to either suppress or enhance the immune system in treating such diseases as rheumatoid arthritis and various cancers. The principal advantage of this approach is that unlike chemically based drugs, which merely support failing or damaged organs or tissue, these treatments cure disease and repair damage while having less toxic side effects.

Cellular biology also plays a major role in regenerative medicine. Human cells are used to manufacture artificial skin and grow blood vessels. Stem cells offer even more promising treatments. It is anticipated that adult stem cells can be harvested, cultured and reinserted to heal damaged or worn-out tissue, bones, nerves and organs, producing highly prized therapies for those suffering brain and spinal injures, and more generally aging populations. Adult stem cells, however, often prove difficult to locate and activate, and may be ineffective in treating a number of diseases and injuries given their limited flexibility. Alternatively, embryonic stem cells may provide a resource that is easier to obtain, and their plasticity offers potentially greater therapeutic benefits. A major hurdle to be overcome is that inserting adult or embryonic stem cells into a host that is not genetically matched might trigger an immune reaction. One way to overcome this difficulty is to clone embryos that are created from the patient's cell sample.

Prosthetics is another instrument in regenerative medicine's tool chest. Fabricated hip joints, heart valves, blood vessels and cochleas are already being employed. Recent experiments suggest the feasibility of curing blindness with artificial retinas, or overcoming paralysis with neural implants. Nanotechnology is enabling the creation of more effective stints, and more speculatively, holds the promise of continuous diagnostic monitoring, augmenting immune systems, and repairing tissue and organs without invasive surgery. Neural implants may someday amplify memory and cognitive abilities, as well as providing a direct connection with external computer networks.[7]

The benefits of regenerative medicine are obvious. Greater diagnostic precision enables earlier and more effective medical interventions. Exploring the intricacies of the map produced by the Human Genome Project and nearly ubiquitous monitoring will allow medicine to react to the early onset of debilitating and life-threatening diseases. More effective therapies improve the quality of many patients' lives. Diseased or damaged organs, for instance, will be repaired or replaced, thereby restoring one's health entirely. Genetically or artificially enhanced immune systems will replace cumbersome inoculations, and improved screening of pre-implanted embryos can help prevent the birth of children with severe disabilities. In addition, physical and cognitive performance can be enhanced, and therapies redeployed to augment a variety of functions. Drugs, for example, might be used to improve memory, or optical implants employed to provide telescopic or night vision. In short, the singular benefit of regenerative medicine is that many individuals will live longer, healthier and more productive lives.

The benefit, however, is accompanied by a host of vexing issues such as the moral status of the embryo, research funding, and policies governing access and delivery of healthcare. These are admittedly important issues, but there is also the larger question of the social, political, moral and religious visions driving the development of regenerative medicine. Toward what end are current and anticipated developments in regenerative medicine being directed? And how should the desirability of that end be assessed? The remainder of this chapter offers a response to these questions.

If the principal benefit of regenerative medicine is improved health, then the beneficiaries will presumably live longer lives. The development of superior diagnostic, therapeutic, preventive and enhancement techniques are bound to raise the statistical norm for average life expectancy. Yet if three-score-and-ten becomes obsolete, what measure should replace it? One hundred, one hundred and fifty, five hundred years or more, perhaps many more? At present, science cannot offer a definitive answer of what the outside limit might be. If embryonic stem cells, for instance, prove to be as totipotent as hoped, then the possibility of infinite tissue and organ rejuvenation cannot be ruled out. Moreover, if attempts at cellular manipulation encounter stubborn obstacles, sophisticated prosthetics can be used to achieve similar results.

The prospect of increased longevity does not suggest that regenerative medicine is merely a high-tech version of Ponce de Leon's quest for youthful immortality. Yet extended longevity has been a highly visible factor in creating public interest and investment in the fledging biotechnology industry. The names of such companies as Geron and Osiris, and announced discoveries of 'immortality' and 'fountain of youth' genes, have captured the attention of elderly venture capitalists and aging baby boomers (Hall, 2003). Such hyperbole only serves to skew and disappoint public expectations, but there is nonetheless a growing perception, in both the industrial and medical literature, that aging is akin to a disease that can be treated. In the absence of any known outside limit regarding longevity, however, what constitutes effective treatment? Without a given limit it would appear that regenerative medicine is the first step in a struggle against growing old. But if medical technologies are developed and deployed for this purpose, does this not raise a rather awkward question: is aging a disease that can be cured? The question helps disclose the heart of the matter, because the chief benefit of regenerative medicine is its ability to cure rather than merely treat disease or injury. It is through rejuvenating the functions of tissue and organs that longevity is extended. Consequently, to cure aging is not to contend against the passage of time *per se*, but the accompanying cellular degeneration and resulting morbidity.

If aging is a disease to be cured, however, does this not suggest that the advent of regenerative medicine also signals a declaration of war against the old enemy death? Presumably the answer must be 'yes', for the end result of degeneration and morbidity is mortality. Yet what would victory against this old foe mean, and what would be the cost? Total victory would be immortality, and if this ambitious goal proves elusive – at least initially – greatly expanded longevity would represent a partial but nonetheless significant triumph. The cost of winning this war would entail the radical transformation of medicine as a practice *and* the patients it in turn transforms. To wage war against death requires that medicine forsake its traditional emphasis on caring in favor of curing.[8] The chief medical practice would no longer be to offer care and comfort to patients suffering the ravages of illness and deteriorating bodies, but to eliminate the organic causes or sources of their suffering. The role of medicine would not be one of assisting patients to come to terms with their mortal state, but to enable them to vanquish mortality or at least keep degeneration and morbidity at bay for as long as possible. Moreover, waging an effective war against death requires medicine to transform its patients. The move from caring to curing entails blurring, if not erasing, the line separating therapy and enhancement. This is particularly the case at the cellular level in which a combination of bio- and nanotechnologies is deployed to overcome the Hayflick limit, effectively reengineering the patient. Consequently, the patient is simultaneously the beneficiary and artifact of such transformative healthcare. Medicine is no longer dedicated to relieving the human condition, but radically changing it.

If regenerative medicine is the first step in curing aging, and the first salvo in a war against death, then a provocative issue is forced upon us, namely, should humans use their technology to become something other than human? It would seem that some such aspiration is at play if the goal is to use technology to overcome or extend the mortal limits programmed into the human biology bequeathed by evolution. Yet if these limits are overcome or greatly extended then mortality is no longer a definitive feature of human life. Yet in the absence of this definitive feature, what are humans aspiring to become as artifacts of their own engineering? Or, to pose the same question more starkly: should humans aspire to become posthuman?

We have already encountered Hayles's ambivalent and the transhumanists' enthusiastic endorsement of this aspiration. The modifications envisioned by regenerative medicine surveyed above, however, represent relatively modest interventions. The convergence of biotechnology, nanotechnology and sophisticated prosthetics will purportedly extend longevity, but achieving this goal will only serve to enhance human performance rather than transform humans into a new and superior species. Consequently, a much more extensive round of technological transformation is required if spatial and temporal constraints on the breadth and depth of formative experiential opportunities are to be effectively transcended. It is in attempting to overcome finitude that Hayles and the transhumanists part company. What prompts their unhappy separation is a fundamental ontological disagreement, particularly in respect to the relation between mind and body. Before parsing out the import of this dispute, however, we must first examine in greater detail the posthuman future envisioned by transhumanists, particularly in respect to the means they propose to use in pursuing their transformative agenda.

What kind of technological process will be required to transform humans into a superior species, and what might the emergent posthuman be like? As noted above, no definitive reply can be forthcoming, but Ray Kurzweil and Hans Moravec have offered some speculative answers. In accordance with Moore's law, computers will match the memory capacity and computing capability of the human brain by 2020. Since computational speed will continue to grow exponentially, it is only a matter of time until machines become intelligent and conscious as they surpass the computational performance of the human brain. This new form of artificial life (AL) will not be confined to antiquated desktop and laptop computers. With parallel developments in nanotechnology and electronic technologies, AL will exist in highly mobile and dexterous robotic machines, exhibiting a rapidly growing capacity for adaptive learning. By the mid twenty-first century emergent characteristics will enable AL to enjoy a range of experiential opportunities that cannot be entertained or even comprehended by the human mind.

The emergence of AL is not surprising given preceding evolutionary trajectories. Life evolved from inert matter, and in turn became sentient culminating in the intelligent human animal. AL represents the only effective strategy for preventing this trajectory from running into an evolutionary dead-end given inherent biological limits. The dead-end can be avoided, however, because there is no reason why the mind, as the essence of identity, need remain dependent upon the brain, for the issue at stake is the speed and efficiency of processing information. Machines offer a superior substratum for the mind to more fully develop its processing capabilities. If life *as* mind is to be significantly enriched, then evolution dictates that the original biological prosthesis of a brain confined to a body must be replaced by a superior medium. Reality is, after all, merely the selection, interpretation and manipulation of pertinent information. In this respect an inefficient natural selection is displaced by a purposive and willful selection.

There is, of course, a sobering side to this evolutionary tale. When an old species is forced to compete with a new superior one, the former must either adapt or become extinct. Humans will soon face the same junction with AL. It might be argued that one way of avoiding this unhappy dilemma would be to prohibit technological development before it is too late (Joy, 2000), but Kurzweil and Moravec contend that an irreversible momentum is already established (Kurzweil, 2000, pp. 40–88; Moravec, 1988, pp. 6–50). Consequently, the only viable survival option is for the creators of AL to merge with their creations. This rather clever, albeit parasitic, adaptive strategy is made possible by the mind's digital basis. The data constituting one's mind will be scanned, copied and uploaded into a computer (Kurzweil, 2000, pp. 101–31; Moravec, 1988, pp. 100–124). The information constituting the mind may then be downloaded into various biologically engineered, robotic or virtual substrata, resulting in virtually immortal personalities processing an infinite array of experiential inputs. What were once called humans will survive by becoming, in Kurzweil's terms, software rather than hardware, or in Moravec's more evocative imagery, by casting off the poor jelly in which the mind was once encased. In short, spatial and temporal constraints will not just be transcended but eliminated.

The price for this radical transformation is the disappearance of humans as embodied creatures. The price, however, is not exorbitant given the return. One's mind will be projected simultaneously in multiple locations. Personalities can be merged or novel identities formed. Perhaps a universal consciousness will emerge, limited only by the borders of the universe itself. Although Moravec is less sanguine than Kurzweil about the utopian prospects for the future, he is nonetheless confident that the eventual outcome will entail the emergence of a super intelligence enabling a range of experience of unimaginable breadth and richness. With the advent of AL, mind will create its own destiny; the future rests with artificial mind children, not biological offspring. To contemplate the death of the human in favor of the posthuman, then, is not to grieve but to anticipate and celebrate. Eventually artificial life will evolve into pure thought, transforming the universe into an expanding cyberspace of mind (Moravec, 1999, pp. 163–89). Once the 'Omega Point' of universal mind has been reached (ibid., pp. 201–2), the resulting posthuman life will be far removed from its human ancestry – indeed, unrecognizable and incomprehensible from our current vantage point – but the subjective experiences of our primitive past need not be lost, because '[w]holesale resurrection may be possible through the use of immense simulators' (Moravec, 1988, p. 123). Although the process of taking on this 'new form of existence' will require 'human personalities' to mutate in unrecognizable directions, 'these future machines' are 'our progeny, "mind children" built in our image and likeness, ourselves in more potent form', thereby offering humankind its 'best chance for a long-term future' (Moravec, 1999, pp. 11–13).

It can be objected that the posthuman future envisioned by Kurzweil and Moravec is more an idle fantasy than a realistic proposal. Many, if not most, of the technologies they anticipate may prove infeasible. Recent studies in neurology, for example, suggest that the mind simply cannot be separated from the brain or more broadly from biological embodiment. The medium, alas, does matter (Jeeves, 2004; MacKay, 1991). Yet the prospect of a posthuman future is for some so menacing, that the relatively modest interventions being undertaken by a nascent regenerative medicine should be prohibited. Even minor enhancements should be resisted, because they launch humans down a road whose toll is too dear to pay – the loss of their dignity.[9]

In reply to the question of whether or not humans should aspire to become posthuman, Leon Kass, for instance, offers a resounding *no*. For the chairman of the President's Council on Bioethics, the very idea that humans would willingly aspire to become posthuman should prompt a response of repugnance: 'No friend of humanity cheers for a posthuman future' (Kass, 2002, p. 6). A quest for immortality or greatly extended life-spans necessarily imperils the very mortality and finitude from which meaning and virtue are derived (Kass, 1985, pp. 299–317). It is in coming to terms with their finite limits, and the inherent pain and suffering entailed in those limits, that humans embody the nobility of spirit that is supremely expressed in procreation, for the future is properly shaped through progeny rather than extending the lives of the progenitors. 'Nothing humanly fine, let alone great, will come out of a society that is willing to sacrifice all other goods to keep the present generation alive and intact. Nothing humanly fine, let alone great, will come from the desire to pursue bodily immortality for ourselves' (Kass, 2002, p. 20). In short, being and remaining human requires that humans cling tenaciously to their finitude.

Kass is deeply suspicious of the science and philosophy underlying any flirtation with a posthuman future. Following Hans Jonas, he insists that late modern science is driven by a relentless desire for mastery and manipulation,

exerting maximum control over nature and human nature. Presumably this
control will result in greater human freedom, but ironically humans become
increasingly enslaved to the tasks required in such mastery, exchanging a
capricious nature for fickle engineering (Kass, 1985, pp. 25–40). Moreover,
there are few moral brakes to be applied to slow this momentum, for late
moderns are largely convinced that there are no normative concepts defining
what it means to be human and therefore no normative ends to be pursued in
preserving their dignity. For Kass, unlike Hayles, the great fear of the future 'is
not tyranny but voluntary dehumanization' (ibid., p. 71).

Francis Fukuyama also offers a forceful but more muted *no* to the prospect
of becoming posthuman. He shares with Kass the worry that regenerative
medicine represents the first step in engineering humans toward an inhumane
future. Augmenting the performance of the human mind and body means that
human nature is also being transformed, and he believes that a strong
philosophical argument can be offered against this transformation. The gist of
his argument can be captured by summarizing two substantive claims. First,
any meaningful discourse on human rights must be grounded in human nature
which is defined as 'the sum of the behavior and characteristics that are typical
of the human species, arising from genetic rather than environmental factors'
(Fukuyama, 2002, p. 130). Individuals, societies and political structures are not
created *ex nihilo*, but are derived from innate behavioral characteristics. The
instinct for parental care and affection, for example, helps to account for the
institutions of marriage and family that pervade all cultures. Moreover, a
natural moral sense has evolved over time as demonstrated in a range of
emotive responses that is 'species-typical' (ibid., pp. 140–43).

The second substantive claim is that dignity is not an abstract concept, but a
natural quality derived from a genetic endowment that is uniquely human. It is
also an endowment promoting emergent, rather than reductive, forms of
behavior among individuals and groups, and any attempt to separate the parts
from the whole would disfigure a nature that is uniquely human. Altering
genes, albeit for therapeutic reasons, is nonetheless also an alteration of human
nature. Tinkering with the human genetic endowment could very well negate
the civil and political rights of liberal democracy which seek to instantiate the
very dignity that is being unwittingly assaulted. Consequently, any prospect of
a posthuman future should be resisted because 'we want to protect the full
range of our complex, evolved natures against attempts at self-modification.
We do not want to disrupt either the unity or the continuity of human nature,
and thereby the human rights that are based on it' (ibid., p. 173).

Fukuyama can only offer a subdued rejection of a posthuman future,
however, because he admits that if biotechnology were solely a menace to human
dignity then it should be prohibited. Yet he cannot bring himself to make this
recommendation, for he also acknowledges that potentially beneficial therapies
can be developed despite the threat. Biotechnology is a 'devil's bargain' in which
'obvious benefits' are mixed 'with subtle harms in one seamless package' (ibid.,
pp. 7–8). Can the benefits be separated from the harms? Fukuyama believes they
can by using '*the power of the state to regulate*' (ibid., p. 10, emphasis original).
He proposes a series of policies that would assess proposed research and

technological applications in light of the philosophical standard of human dignity he espouses (ibid., pp. 121–218). Moreover, since the standard of assessment is also the moral norm to be protected, such research should proceed slowly and cautiously. As a member of the President's Council on Bioethics, Fukuyama's voting record on embryonic stem cell research and cloning demonstrates that the pace should indeed be very deliberate.

In their defense of human dignity, neither Kass nor Fukuyama appeals to religious arguments.[10] Kass makes several religious allusions but does not develop them further, and Fukuyama admits that his account of dignity could be argued on theological grounds, but rejects this option as an unnecessary strategy. This casual dismissal, however, renders their respective arguments ineffectual. At best they can merely assert the likelihood that a posthuman future is a dangerous one, and based on the risks and benefits at stake it is a future that should be avoided. Consequently, the dignity they invoke is a rhetorical device rather than a substantive claim. On their own philosophical terms they cannot offer a normative account of human dignity that is sufficient to expose the prospect of a posthuman future as an immoral endeavor in its own right, and not solely in terms of its possible outcomes. A theological argument would prove more effective, because those advocating and pursuing a posthuman future are drawing heavily on implicit religious convictions that need to be exposed and dealt with as such. The following chapter examines these religious convictions, particularly in respect to their derivation from selected Christian theological themes underlying the posthuman vision, and more broadly the emerging postmodern technoculture.

Notes

1 See Laura Cinti's 'Cactus Project' as an expression of transgenic art at http://www. lauracinti.com/
2 See, for example, Fukuyama, 2002, Graham, 2002 and Kass, 2002, pp. 141–73.
3 The two principal transhumanist organizations are the Extropy Institute (http://www. extropy.org/) and the World Transhumanist Association (http://www.transhumanism. org/index.php/WTA/index/). See also the websites 'Nick Bostrom's home page' (http://www.nickbostrom.com/ethics/values.html) and 'Betterhumans' (http://www. betterhumans.com/).
4 For an overview of current research and anticipated advances in various therapies and enhancements, see President's Council on Bioethics, 2003.
5 For examples of transhumanist literature on the topics alluded to, visit the websites referenced in note 3 above.
6 The following discussion on regenerative medicine is adapted from a paper, 'Extending Human Life: to what end?', I delivered at an international symposium on 'Ethical Reflections on Regenerative Medicine', Centre for Applied Ethics, Hong Kong Baptist University, 6–7 May 2004. Publication of the proceedings is forthcoming.
7 For a concise overview of recent and anticipated developments in regenerative medicine, see Haseltine, 2003, pp. 38–43.
8 This shift has already occurred to a significant extent. See, for example, Engelhardt, 1996, Kass, 1985, McKenny, 1997 and Ramsey, 1970, pp. 113–64.

9   The following discussion on human dignity in relation to the prospect of a posthuman future is again adapted from the paper referenced in note 6 above.
10 In a recent article, Kass appeals more directly to religious principles in analyzing the moral status of the human embryo (Kass, 2004/2005).

CHAPTER FOUR

Postmodern Theology

The objection to a posthuman future that it imperils human dignity is not effective, because it asserts a religious claim on strictly philosophical grounds. Consequently, the objection lacks sufficient descriptive clarity and normative weight to demonstrate why the prospect of transforming humans into posthumans is an immoral proposition. It remains unclear what the dignity is that is being threatened, and why it is paramount that, whatever it is, it should be protected against extensive transformation. Equally important, however, proponents of a posthuman future fail to make a convincing case, because they also assert a religious claim on philosophical and ideological grounds. Consequently, their proposal lacks conceptual clarity and teleological precision to demonstrate why transforming humans into posthumans constitutes a moral imperative, or is at least a worthwhile goal that should be pursued. It is far from clear what a posthuman future might be like, and what normative, social and political objectives would be pursued in the process.

These respective failures can be better explicated by turning our attention away from the question of whether or not humans should aspire to become posthumans as addressed in the previous chapter, and toward a more revealing, though largely occluded, issue of the relation between necessity and goodness. This shift is needed, for, as was also noted in the previous chapter, it is virtually impossible to answer the question with much precision. It is not clear if the *posthuman* lionized by proponents and vilified by critics is the same creature. It cannot be otherwise, for how could such a being, possessing unimaginable capabilities, command a descriptive consensus? The transhumanists are at a loss to describe a virtually immortal creature, while N. Katherine Hayles refuses to speculate on what the constructed, yet finite, posthuman body might be like; it remains a mystery what exactly Francis Fukuyama wants to preserve through regulation, and what Leon Kass wishes to prohibit. Why do these varying prognostications span the gamut from utopian dream to apocalyptic nightmare? It is in addressing this underlying question that the value of speculating about a posthuman future is disclosed, for the expressed hopes and fears reveal what is preoccupying the prognosticators. Hence the following section examines how each of the preceding answers to the question of becoming posthuman comes to terms with the more immediate relationship between the necessary and the good.

Necessity and Goodness[1]

For the purpose of this inquiry, necessity may be defined as the use, acquisition or consumption of things which are needed to sustain the life of an organism over time. In regard to humans these things include air, water, food, exercise, rest, shelter, reproduction and the like. None of these things is either inherently good or evil, and each is assigned a relative value by those using, acquiring or consuming it. We do not normally ponder breathing as a moral dilemma, and I may value eating over resting while you prefer to exercise. Necessity is thereby a formative feature of culture, particularly in respect to the tasks of moral, social and political ordering. These cooperative tasks enable individuals and associations to acquire necessary items in a relatively efficient manner, while also mitigating the more destructive consequences resulting from their competitive acquisition. Culture allows humans to escape the constant bloodletting of Hobbes's notorious state of nature. Although useful distinctions may be maintained among such categories as natural, historical and moral necessities, they are each ultimately grounded in the effort of creatures to survive and propagate over time.

Necessity, however, poses two problems, at least for creatures, such as humans, who have the ability to contemplate their fate. First, necessary things sustain the lives of creatures, but these creatures cannot be sustained indefinitely. Humans are finite and temporal: they are born, grow old and die. Moreover, it appears that this fatal pattern for individual human beings is necessary to promote the survival of the species over time. Natural selection has pieced together a human organism that is efficient at breeding but little else. Consequently, they need to produce and raise their offspring, and then get out of the way to allow the next wave of breeding to run its fateful and fatal course. Once individuals have passed their reproductive potential, evolution has absolutely no interest in how much longer they survive. Second, there is the problem of how necessary things are acquired, used or consumed. These items are apparently scarce, and therefore tend to be acquired, used and consumed in a competitive manner. This competition is both inter and intra species. *Homo sapiens*, for instance, presumably acquired the requisite skills to eliminate their Neanderthal competitors, and among humans some individuals are better equipped than others in competing for scarce resources, resulting in a stronger species over time by culling weaker genes from the pool. Hence the need for moral, social and political structures regulating the extent to which violent methods may be employed in this competition.

The preceding summary is admittedly a generalization, but it nevertheless serves to demonstrate why the necessary and the good are not synonymous or even complementary concepts. Survival, for instance, necessarily entails pain, suffering and morbidity associated with mortality. Although the death of an elderly and infirm parent may benefit offspring directly, and the welfare of the species generally, it is nonetheless perverse to designate the parent's fate as being good. Even Christians ardently longing for a new life in Christ over the old life in sin nonetheless identify death as the final enemy. Moreover, competitive violence has been amplified to nearly unspeakable levels with the growth of late modern societies and political regimes. Although poverty or war may prove to benefit some at the expense of others, it would again be perverse to claim that war and poverty are good. In short, it cannot simply be asserted that because something is necessary it is good, much less, that something is good because it is necessary.

Many philosophical attempts have been made to relieve this stark tension between necessity and goodness. The Hegelian and Marxist solution, for example, is that history settles the issue, or more correctly, those who write and enact history. The Hegelians tried to transform the necessary into the good through a self-realized freedom that overcomes necessity. This freedom would be achieved through progressive historical acts, culminating in the absolute state that had mastered nature, and fulfilled human nature. Consequently, there are no categorical moral constraints on human acts which strive to realize this perfected freedom. Marxists took a similar path, but the goal was to achieve a classless society as the epitome of perfect freedom. The objective at stake was social rather than political. In both cases, the resulting pain and suffering in achieving the goal is justified, because it is necessary for obtaining the greater good of the absolute state or classless society. Concentration camps and gulags are the brutal prerequisites for transforming necessity, in its myriad forms, into goodness (Arendt, 1968 and 1998, pp. 79–174).

The weakness of this approach is that it exchanges natural necessity for historical necessity, thereby amplifying the scope of suffering and misery entailed in perfecting human freedom. The move virtually justifies force as a redemptive tool in which goodness and necessity become the fabric of attenuated notions of progress. This move results in a cavalier attitude toward evil, for acts of cruelty and violence are justified by historical necessity. Yet it invokes a denuded understanding of justice, for it is the good of the powerful that is achieved at the expense of the weak. As George Grant has written, 'The screams of the tortured child can be justified by the achievements of history. How pleasant for the achievers, but how meaningless for the child' (Grant, 2000, p. 100). The hope that human action can achieve goodness by replacing natural necessity with historical necessity is delusional. Grant goes on to assert that any appeal to historical progress 'is blasphemy if it rests on any easy identification of necessity and good' (ibid.).

In opposing this blasphemy, Grant offers an alternative Platonic–Christian understanding of the relation between goodness and necessity. Following Simone Weil, Grant contends that the creator withdraws from creation, in order to give its creatures genuine freedom as an act of absolute love. The creation and its creatures become something truly other than God, and therefore a proper object of God's love. This withdrawal, however, subjects the creatures to the harsh dictates of necessity, thereby constraining their freedom. Necessity distributes misery, violence and disease 'in accordance with its own proper mechanism' (Springsted, 1998, p. 73). An infinite chasm separates the necessary from the good which cannot be bridged by any human action. Humans cannot erase or redeem their tragic history on their own terms. In Weil's beguiling words, 'God's absence is the most marvelous testimony of perfect love, and that's why pure necessity, the necessity which is manifestly so different from good, is so beautiful' (ibid.). How do we come to terms with a necessity whose beauty is devoid of goodness? According to Grant, we must learn to love our fate, and consent to the limits it imposes.[2] This love does not result in sullen resolve, but opens us to the love that makes necessity beautiful. Although the necessary and the good can never be joined, the chasm separating them has been bridged by the suffering of Christ as the incarnate mediator (Grant, 2002, pp. 483–9). We consent to necessity in obedience to God, and the resulting love of fate enables a love of our neighbor, expressed in the recognition of fundamental equality and indifferent compassion. According to Grant, this is the best that can be achieved on this beautiful side of the chasm, for the good can only embrace us on the other, eternal side. In the meantime, this eschatological hope is best expressed, following Martin Luther, in affirming a theology of the cross that consents to necessity, instead of a theology of glory that tries vainly to transform it into goodness (ibid., p. 490; Athanasiadis, 2001).

Kass seemingly favors Grant's Platonic–Christian account over the Hegelian–Marxist option – up to a point, and it is a significant point of departure. If becoming posthuman is driven by a quest for extending longevity or virtual immortality, then it represents little more than another vain attempt to transform necessity into goodness. Exchanging natural necessity with technological necessity can have no good effect, because it corrupts medicine as an art which should help individuals to struggle with, rather than eliminate, finite limits. If medicine dedicates itself to waging war against death, then it must also come to hate the very human body it allegedly serves, for finitude and mortality prevent any final victory. Medical therapies should properly be limited to assisting patients to come to terms with lineage, parenthood and embodiment, as finite endeavors entailing suffering and eventual death (Kass, 2002, pp. 96–102). In this respect, medicine is properly an intergenerational institution preserving human dignity by assisting a morally integral process of biological and social reproduction.[3] Any attempt to become posthuman is thereby a hubristic effort to remove the necessary limits that provide the moral foundation of human dignity.

Although Kass acknowledges the beauty of necessity, as conveyed by Grant and Weil, his consent is only partial. Necessity's beauty does not confer to nature absolute sovereignty over the course of human life. Kass readily admits that there are no pre-technological good old days to recover, and there is nothing wrong with medicine helping people live long lives, surrounded by loving children and grandchildren. The biblical three-score-and-ten is a flexible rule of thumb, not a rigid limit, serving to remind us of our mortality, and hence the pressing need of natality. Yet this flexibility presents a dilemma: at what point does medicine cross the line, becoming a hubristic attempt to transform necessity into goodness? Kass is hard pressed to draw this line at any particular location, for he also argues that there is nothing wrong in developing more effective therapies and preventive techniques. Yet if the research underlying regenerative medicine is prohibited, then is not the resulting suffering that could have been prevented justified by the necessity of an inarticulate moral restraint? Seemingly the misery of the few is justified in preserving the dignity of the many. In addition, his objection to regenerative medicine is not with its therapeutic and preventive goals *per se*, but with the production and cloning of embryos to harvest their stem cells. But if the same results could be achieved through extracting adult stem cells, then he would find it difficult to object because greater longevity would be a secondary effect, rather than the primary goal, of better therapeutic and preventive measures. So long as the willful destruction of embryos is avoided, cannot humans have much longer and healthier lives with their dignity intact?

Moreover, the object of Kass's hope for the future is offspring, both in terms of perpetuating the species and protecting human dignity. This means, however, that the chasm separating necessity and goodness can neither be reconciled nor bridged. Procreation and children are instead asserted as goods in their own right, albeit in a diminished form, because such a strategy can only fail in embracing an eternal good that lies beyond a chasm that has never been, and can never be, traversed. Each new generation embodies a hope against hope; a desire that can never be fully satisfied. Through lineage humans may achieve a sense of immortality, but will never encounter eternity. Although any grand scheme for transforming the necessary into the good should be rejected, lesser, temporary niches of goodness can be carved out through the bonds of lineage, kinship and descent. This is perhaps the best Kass can offer because, as Gerald McKenny has observed, he lacks a clear understanding of medicine's moral authority, and therefore can offer only a narrow and prudent vision of the good it purports to be pursuing (McKenny, 1997, pp. 143–6).

When the question is switched from becoming posthuman to that of necessity and goodness, it is, surprisingly, Hayles who shares the greatest affinity with Kass. This claim is admittedly counter-intuitive, for it would seem that her ambiguous *yes* and his resounding *no* to the prospect of becoming posthuman would place them in diametrically opposed camps. Yet Hayles shares with Kass an unflinching opposition to any program attempting to negate embodiment and finitude. Although Hayles is unwilling to invoke or protect a normative value such as dignity, she is nonetheless prepared to resist any effort threatening the survival of embodied persons. Presumably, at some point, then, she is also prepared to draw a line specifying the extent to which the technological transformation of humans may proceed but must not pass, even though she is unwilling to specify in advance where that line might be drawn. Where Hayles differs from Kass is that the great enemy to be resisted is neither Hegel nor Marx and their respective myths of the absolute state and classless society, but a more pernicious liberal humanism, and its myth of autonomy as exemplified by the transhumanists. The small niches of goodness which are to be carved out within a realm of necessity involves the construction of posthumans that have preserved the value of finite embodiment, rather than preserving a so-called dignity derived from lineage and kinship. Consequently, for Hayles the pressing task at hand is not biological and social reproduction, but constructing a social and political order that genuinely promotes the survival and flourishing of its inhabitants.

Since the issue for Hayles is not whether a posthuman future will emerge, but what kind of posthuman future should be constructed, she is ambivalent about the initial steps toward enhancing human performance as currently being undertaken in regenerative medicine. Given the constructive task at hand, the development of embryonic stem cell research, cloning and prosthetic devices is neither inherently moral nor immoral. The concern at stake is one of application: the development of technologies that will either assist or impede the construction of finite and embodied posthumans, with the resulting challenge to discern the difference between the two applications. It is this assumption of instrumental neutrality, however, that imperils Hayles's program. Since she is unwilling to specify in advance any normative value of embodied finitude, early forays into regenerative medicine may trigger an unwanted momentum that cannot be effectively resisted, much less stopped, down the road. As Grant argues, technology is not a neutral set of instruments from which we may pick and choose. Rather, it is a way of life that enfolds its users in its own destiny, thereby transforming or disfiguring what the very meaning of goodness comes to be. To partake of technology generally, and medical technologies in particular, entails a package deal in which any so-called freedom that picking and choosing purportedly affords is illusory (Grant, 1986, pp. 11–34). Technology shapes humans in its image, not vice versa. In partaking of regenerative medicine's early fruits to construct her posthuman future, Hayles may be starting down a road whose inevitable destination is the very transhumanist vision she wishes to resist.

Transhumanists are dedicated to transforming humans into posthumans, because they can discern no aesthetic qualities in the necessary. There is nothing beautiful at all about mortality. This is not a fate to be loved, but one to be resisted and conquered at all costs. To do otherwise is to succumb to a death wish; to consent to extinction. Correspondingly, transhumanists also have no interest in natality, for the birth of a child only serves as a reminder of necessity's death and decay. The task at hand is neither Kass's biological and social reproduction, nor Hayles's social and political construction, but frenetic self-transformation, and projecting oneself as far as possible, or better endlessly, into the future. Since evolution has not equipped humans to undertake this task, they must take its future course into their own hands. Consequently, a relentless war should be waged against death. Therefore, the advent of regenerative medicine is to be welcomed and encouraged as the initial salvo against this mortal foe. The current and anticipated fruits of merging biotechnology and nanotechnology, for instance, should be neither forbidden nor eaten selectively, but consumed voraciously in order to strengthen humankind for the battles lying ahead. Those seeking to prohibit or restrict the requisite research and experimentation should be regarded as the true enemies of humanity, for in trying to preserve a so-called dignity or finitude they are conspiring with the enemy. In this respect, transhumanists have raised the ante on Hegel and Marx: the genuine good of freedom cannot be attained in either the absolute state or classless society, but only in the virtually immortal posthuman. It is only when mortality has been vanquished that we can be truly free. Thus whatever scientific and political means are required to wage an effective war against death are justified by the historical necessity of achieving this perfect freedom.

In appealing to immortality, however, the transhumanists tip their hand. Despite their rhetoric, they cannot really claim a humanistic pedigree. No humanist would willingly consent to transforming humankind to the extent that it ceases to be human, for this would destroy both the measure and the goal of the very moral enterprise undertaken, namely, to be fully and therefore *only* human. Transhumanists also harbor a death wish of transforming *Homo sapiens* into extinction in order that the posthuman can emerge. But it is far from clear if creatures dedicated to the suicide of the species can think any more rationally about the moral, social and political implications of regenerative medicine, and the larger prospect of technological transformation, than those who have consented to eventual extinction through natural selection.

Moreover, the immortality transhumanists seek will not grant the kind of mastery they desire. Even within Greek mythology the immortals are not eternal, and therefore remain subject to a fate they cannot control. Rather than bridging the chasm separating necessity and goodness, transhumanists are committed to digging it deeper and wider. Consequently, they have not raised the ante on Hegel and Marx, but swept both aside in favor of Nietzsche. His hope of the *Übermensch* is now possible with the advent and anticipated development of various enhancement technologies. Their adulation, however, is limited, for unlike Nietzsche the prerequisite for the emergence of this new being is not a love of fate, but rather, the outcome of an engineering project designed to negate fate. The transhumanists have bet everything on technological potential. But how will these high-tech survivalists respond if our initial forays into regenerative medicine propel us toward a destination that can only disappoint? Specifically, what happens if death proves an unconquerable enemy and a race of enhanced creatures are left with a necessity that remains a fate they cannot love? In Grant's words, they 'will be resolute in their will to mastery, but they cannot know what that mastery is for' (Grant, 1995b, pp. 45–6). Given the technological power at their disposal, one shudders to think what might occur if the more ardent transhumanists conclude that it is better to will nothing when there is nothing good to will.

It is such an apocalyptic specter that Fukuyama wants to avoid by regulating the research underlying regenerative medicine. His rationale is straightforward: natural selection has produced humans as a species capable of developing and sustaining liberal democratic societies. This is no small blessing since these societies go a long way in softening the sharp edges of natural and historical necessity. In this respect, we may perceive aspects of beauty within the realms of necessity, but these perceptions should prompt us neither to love nor despise fate. Although Fukuyama makes no attempt to bridge the chasm separating the necessary from the good, we do catch glimpses of universal goods through natural law, which should in turn be incorporated in moral, social and political ordering. Our understanding and ordering of these goods have emerged from our natural evolution as a species, so we should be wary of unwittingly unraveling an evolutionary process which to date has served us well and should not be casually disregarded. The therapies and enhancements envisioned by proponents of regenerative medicine, for instance, will alter the human species over time. Consequently, we should only use such interventions in a highly judicious manner so that the natural foundations of liberal democracy are not inadvertently undermined. Such caution may very well consign some individuals to pain and suffering, but their fate is justified by the necessity of preserving the greater good of civil society. In short, necessity dictates prudence to preserve the temporal goods that we have already obtained.

At first glance it appears that Fukuyama has all but slammed the door shut on any posthuman future. By opting for regulating instead of prohibiting research, however, he has left open a crack, and in examining that small space, we discover an unexpected affinity with transhumanists. Fukuyama favors regulation over prohibition because he recognizes that some aspects of regenerative medicine may prove to be beneficial. In facing what he characterizes as a 'devil's bargain' (Fukuyama, 2002, p. 8) he leaves open the possibility that humans may be able to outfox this crafty adversary with a slow and cautious approach. But if the devil can be outfoxed, then what separates Fukuyama from transhumanists is not any normative claim to human dignity, but the pace of transforming humans into posthumans. This is where his confidence in natural selection betrays his normative rhetoric. The goods which natural law purportedly discloses are not given, but emerge from the evolutionary process itself. These goods are self-referential rather than revelatory of any transcendent or eternal source. The evolution of *Homo sapiens* is also open-ended and indeterminate. One cannot specify a particular point of evolutionary development and proclaim 'this far but no farther', for change or mutation is precisely what enables a species to flourish and avoid extinction. As humans evolve over time, then so too do the emergent goods disclosed in natural law, because these goods are also derived from the underlying evolutionary process. Consequently, a posthuman future cannot be foreclosed in advance on Fukuyama's own evolutionary terms. As judicious interventions are introduced through carefully regulated therapies and enhancements, they will still have a cumulative effect over time, thereby effectively transforming humans. If these interventions prove to be no threat to the so-called natural foundations of liberal democracy, then Fukuyama would be hard pressed to argue for the superiority of natural selection over purposively directed evolution. The goods revealed by his emergent natural law may in fact evolve to a point where they dictate the necessity of humans exerting greater control over their evolutionary fate. Fukuyama must be open to this prospect, for unlike Kass, such things as procreation, lineage and embodiment are not the foundations of human dignity, but the *currently* necessary means of perpetuating liberal democratic societies which in turn bestow dignity to their citizens. If initial forays into the technological transformation of humans should prove no threat to the social and political sources of this dignity, then Fukuyama cannot foreclose the possibility and desirability of a posthuman future, especially if it is populated by more proficient democrats.[4] In short, the necessity of evolution dictates that *Homo sapiens* will become something other than human, and presumably this change can occur through unhurried natural selection or hasty technological transformation. Fukuyama prefers the former, but is also hedging that preference by not foreclosing the possibility of the latter.

This brief excursion into the relation between the necessary and the good discloses that an appeal to human dignity offers no substantive objection to the prospect of a posthuman future. Kass's chief contention is that the attempt to overcome natural or finite limits imperils an inherent human dignity. Natality and mortality are the primary factors shaping the social and intergenerational contours of human life. If the war against ageing is won, then the principal factors defining and delineating what it means to be human will also be lost, thereby having a corrosive effect on the social institutions, such as marriage and family, in and through which humans derive meaning and value. This claim, however, is difficult to reconcile with Kass's equally impassioned dedication to improving healthcare that presumably requires greater technological intervention, and therefore entails some degree of transformation over time. The issue at stake, then, is not transformation *per se*, but the extent envisioned; a line can be crossed in the future when a fragile dignity is lost. Thus the need for vigilance early on, before it is too late. This is an arguable position, but not on Kass's terms. In order to draw *in advance* the line that should not be crossed requires a much thicker normative account of human life, particularly in respect to natality and mortality, than he is willing or able to provide. In the absence of such an account, finitude alone cannot bear the weight of the dignity Kass has hoisted upon it. Humans do not have dignity because they are finite, but they consent to their finite limits in more or less dignified ways. This consent is itself an act of religious faith or conviction in the goodness of eternity that sustains human dignity in the face of necessity. Without this religious framework, the dignity Kass purports to champion is an elusive, moving target, for it is embedded solely in the realm of necessity which mutates over time. Consequently, as Fukuyama demonstrates, the best one can do is regulate how technology will be used in constructing a posthuman future, for what is at stake is not dignity *per se*, but the emergence of democratic societies that promote and sustain it. Since the values represented by the concept of dignity are emergent features of the evolutionary process which make democratic institutions possible in the first place, the possibility of transformation can never be ruled out in principle, but such change should be managed in a prudent manner. Yet again in the absence of substantive religious convictions regarding the *telos* and normative structure of human life, there are no substantive guidelines dictating the prudent course this transformation should take other than procedural rules. In short, the line protecting dignity cannot be crossed, because there is no stable ground on which it can be drawn.

More telling is the refusal of advocates of a posthuman future to admit the religious convictions underlying their vision. This refusal is most apparent in the transhumanist movement. Their principal goal is straightforward: humans should use various technologies to transform themselves into superior beings. Such a being will enjoy greatly extended longevity, if not virtual immortality, and greatly enhanced cognitive and computational abilities. The posthuman will be a creature of mind that has overcome the fetters of finitude, and therefore commands an unimaginable range of experiential opportunities and self-fulfilling potential. Although the details of a posthuman future cannot be described in detail, its lineage can be traced to a humanistic origin. Through reason (read science) and skill (read technology), humans can take control of their own evolutionary fate. Amplifying the voices of the Enlightenment philosophes as its forbears, humankind is destined to perfect itself in an image and likeness of its own choosing. Moreover, it will be a utopian destiny, for its social and political ordering will inculcate the overriding principle of freedom. The posthuman future will be a non-coercive world, inhabited by beings blessed with unlimited possibilities for personal and corporate enrichment, but with their autonomy intact.

In appealing to a humanistic pedigree, transhumanists betray the hidden religious convictions shaping their agenda, for the humanistic tradition they claim as their own cannot bear the heavy, transformative burden they place upon it. At a number of crucial junctures they must reject or ignore the central presuppositions of the humanistic tradition in order to justify their goal of transforming humans into posthumans. Transhumanists share with their humanist ancestors a thoroughgoing anthropocentric outlook. Earlier humanists made substantive and normative claims concerning human nature as discerned through reason. If human good is the measure, however, then it is inconceivable – on humanistic grounds – that we should aspire to become anything other than human. Aspiring to become posthuman is tautological, because it seeks to annihilate both the measure and what is measured. If it is good for humankind to become posthuman, then it follows that it is bad if humans remain human, and any anthropocentric standard is rendered meaningless. To assert that humans should become posthuman requires the invocation of a higher or transcendent good that trumps the anthropocentric standard. What remains unclear in transhumanist literature is the source of this transcendent good that humans should pursue, for as their neologism indicates humans constitute a transitional species. Or, posed as a question: what is the source of the 'trans' that justifies its affixation to 'humanist'?

Furthermore, it is curious, if not contradictory, that transhumanists have so readily embraced late liberal rhetoric to express their principal arguments.[5] As Hayles has demonstrated, the requisite means of becoming posthuman are not readily compatible with operative liberal principles. The concepts of autonomy, freedom, interests and rights presuppose delineated and enduring borders that define and differentiate one individual from another. This is especially the case in respect to one's embodied identity. Becoming posthuman requires that these borders be treated as shifting and temporary boundaries that can be violated, reconfigured and eventually rendered irrelevant. Indeed, cybernetics – the principal science upon which transhumanists place their hope in technological transformation – presumes that all borders are infinitely malleable since they represent organized patterns of information within organisms and systems. Such patterned information can, at least in principle, be reorganized without sacrificing an individual's subjectivity. This is a peculiar claim. What exactly is this subjectivity that endures as an individual enhances her physical and mental capabilities; joins with machines through sophisticated prosthetics and neural networks; uploads her mind; and creates new multiple identifies which may eventually merge into a single consciousness? Within this scheme the posthuman is not simply a highly augmented autonomous liberal. Rather, to become posthuman requires destroying the very cornerstones of autonomy and freedom that define liberal, humanistic agency. What transhumanists are in effect offering is an alternative understanding of agency or personality, but their literature does not explicitly indicate what constitutes this option or what its source might be. Or, again posed as a question: what exactly is this envisioned 'post' that is being affixed to 'human'?

Proponents of a posthuman future address these questions by offering implicitly religious answers. This turn perhaps accounts for both the shrill denunciation of traditional religion and fervent evangelism on behalf of technoscience, as well as their eagerness to wrap themselves in the mantels of profane humanism and late liberalism as a means of demonstrating their irreligion. This move, however, is not a deceptive strategy disguising a hidden agenda. The strident rhetoric and urgent desire to be coupled with liberal humanism may signify an unacknowledged unease with the leap of faith that transhumanists are undertaking. It is a discomfort exacerbated by Hayles's intuition that any decent posthuman world should be populated by embodied and finite creatures. Yet her refusal or inability to make any normative claims about the human body and finitude perhaps reflects her own surprise or disgust that such an effort would require invoking the kind of religious metanarrative she abhors.

The prospect of becoming posthuman is *not* a profane, postmodern alternative to a modern paradigm, mired and encumbered by primitive and un-exorcized religious beliefs. Rather, posthuman discourse represents idiosyncratic religious sentiments that have been forged in postmodern and historicist rhetoric which retains, albeit in a highly eclectic structure, a providential and progressive grammar. Posthumanism is *not* a postmodern alternative to lingering religious beliefs, but is itself a contending postmodern religion. When the situation is posed in these terms, it is easy to see why Kass's and Fukuyama's appeals to dignity fail, for both are unwilling to invoke alternative theological claims which would give their arguments sufficient strength and substance. The task of developing such an alternative theological framework is undertaken in chapter five, but in order to cast the contrast in a stark light the remainder of this chapter examines the implicit theological foundations of posthuman discourse.

Virtual Theology

A few preliminary remarks may serve to clarify the purpose of the following section by dispelling some preconceived notions of what a 'religious' critique of posthuman discourse might entail. First, this section is *not* a theological defense of late liberal social and political thought. Although the preceding discussion demonstrated that posthuman discourse, despite its rhetoric, is committed to an illiberal agenda, this does not imply that religious objections should therefore be construed as championing late liberal ideologies. The social and political teachings of various religions have changed, often dramatically, over time. There is no reason to assume that theological objections to posthuman discourse should be couched in liberal categories. Conversely, religious critiques of liberalism that simply encase posthuman discourse within this larger criticism are misguided. Posthuman discourse represents a uniquely postmodern *religious* movement from which its illiberal social and political principles are derived.

Second, portraying transhumanism as a religious movement is not intended to discredit it in the eyes of a so-called secular world. To the contrary, it is precisely its religious trappings that make it a force to be taken seriously by theologians. Yet is it fair to characterize transhumanism as a religious movement given its apparent anti-religious rhetoric? Admittedly, transhumanism does not incorporate the kind of formal beliefs, worship and piety often associated with traditional religions. Yet following Martin Luther, whatever one's heart clings to is necessarily one's god, or more broadly one's object of faith (Niebuhr, 1960, pp. 119–22). The belief that humans can transform themselves into superior posthumans may be said to serve as such an object of faith, thereby justifying the rapid development and widespread availability of transformative technologies. The transhumanists' frequent appeals to unfettered reason, rejection of all dogma, and atheistic materialism do not make their faith-based movement any less religious.

Third, theological inquiry should not, indeed cannot, be generic. A generic approach quickly devolves into a vague spirituality that many transhumanists purportedly embrace, rendering subsequent critique vacuous. Rather, genuinely critical and constructive scrutiny occurs from the vantage of a particular religious tradition. Thus the remainder of this chapter is written from a perspective embedded in the Christian theological tradition.

At the outset, it may be admitted that posthuman discourse is not entirely antagonistic to some key strands within Christian theology. Posthumanists and Christians agree, for instance, that the current state of the human condition is far from ideal. For the former, humans have fallen short of realizing their true potential, while for the latter, humans have not yet become the kind of creatures God intends them to be. In response, both agree that humans require release from their current condition. For posthumanists, this is achieved through technological transformation, while Christians are transformed by their life in Christ. Both agree that death is the final enemy. One conquers this foe by achieving virtual immortality, while the other is resurrected into the eternal life of God. Consequently, both also place their hope in a future that at present appears as little more than a puzzling reflection in a mirror. One can only guess what life will be like for posthumans or inhabitants of a new heaven and earth.

More expansively, it is also arguable that some key strands of posthuman discourse draw their inspiration from postmodern interpretations of selected themes in Christian theology. Pierre Teilhard de Chardin's vision of human evolution culminating in the universal consciousness of the Noosphere is compatible with the emergence of a posthuman collective mind (Teilhard de Chardin, 1964 and 1965), a point not lost on transhumanists through their easy inclusion of his 'Omega Point' in their lexicon.[6] Moreover, the speculation that subjective experience will be recovered and preserved through complex simulations is not altogether incompatible with panentheistic claims that human experience is preserved within God's eternal life (Suchocki, 1988, pp. 81–96). Theologians portraying humans as God's co-creators agree that they need to take control of their own evolution as a species (Hefner, 1993), in which technology plays a pivotal role, inspiring Philip Hefner to assert that humans have already become cyborgs (Hefner, 2003, pp. 73–88).

The formative influence of these postmodern theological interpretations can be seen, and then used to critically and constructively to engage posthuman discourse,[7] by concentrating on three topics:

- Open and contingent future (emergence)
- Imposing evolutionary order (culture)
- Humans as co-creators (self-constructed artifacts)

It should be noted that the purpose of this inquiry is not to contend that these postmodern theological interpretations provide the basis of a posthuman manifesto, but rather, they tend to unwittingly underwrite the posthuman agenda.

Open and Contingent Future (Emergence)

Evolution, specifically human evolution, plays a foundational role in posthuman discourse. Through the interplay of chance and necessity *Homo sapiens* has emerged as the dominant species. This status is the result of contingent factors produced through natural selection, implying that the universe is devoid of any inherent purpose or governing force. Humans emerged through a fortuitous series of random events, and there is no reason to believe they will continue to enjoy their dominant status indefinitely. They must, in short, come to terms with a radically open and contingent, and thereby unknown and uncertain, future.

Arthur Peacocke attempts to reinterpret the Christian doctrine of creation in light of this presumably incontestable evolutionary principle. He assumes that the emergence of human life is an unnecessary and contingent event, thereby necessitating an open and contingent future. 'The world is still being made and, on the surface of the earth, at least, man has emerged from biological life and his history is still developing' (Peacocke, 1979, p. 80; see also Peacocke, 1993, pp. 72–80). This process, however, is not entirely blind. God may be said to use chance and necessity to fashion the universe; it is through their interplay that a law-like order emerges out of seeming chaos (Peacocke, 1986, pp. 87–102; Peacocke, 1993, pp. 135–83). The dynamic relationship between law and chance produces an ongoing creativity in which the emergence of life is inevitable, but also indeterminate. Although there is no general purpose in the universe despite the presence of life, God has initiated and participates in an ongoing and changing creation (*creatio continua*). Peacocke likens this creative participation to God's composing a fugue (Peacocke, 1979, pp. 105–6) or partnering in a spontaneous dance (ibid., pp. 106–8). What might sound initially as cacophonous noise or appear as awkward stumbling may eventually evolve into harmonious music or an elegant ballet. This creative ordering is one possible option for the future of creation, but it is only one among many other contingent possibilities.

Peacocke's evolutionary account of creation begs a series of closely related questions that are pertinent to this inquiry. Who or what is this God that uses chance and necessity to fashion creation? Why did or does God create a creation capable of producing creatures that have the potential to be in a relationship with God? Who or what are these creatures that God intends to emerge out of the evolutionary process? Evidently we are dealing with a God who loves and who desires to be loved. This requires a being other than God who is both recipient and responder if such love is to be genuine, and if God's desire to be loved is to be genuinely fulfilled. The only way that a creature with such capabilities could emerge – a creature we call 'human' – is through a lengthy and complex interplay among necessity, law and chance. In order to produce a human creature that may freely receive and reciprocate God's love requires evolutionary development that is not predetermined but open-ended. Otherwise the emergent human creature is not genuinely something other than God that God can love and be loved by in return. God, then, takes a risk in creating a creation. The fugue and dance God intends may not be played and danced, because the emergent human creature might prove to be an incompetent musician and dancer.

Peacocke's portrayal of divine creativity raises two pertinent issues. First, if God is an active participant in the ongoing process of fashioning a creation, then what does it mean to claim that *Homo sapiens* emerged as a creature other than God? If, as Peacocke insists, God is ' "in, with, and under" ' creation (ibid., p. 298), then how can it be said that its emergent creatures are something other than God? Are not humans little more than divinely fashioned artifacts? Peacocke's solution is to insist that God is simultaneously a transcendent and imminent creator (ibid., pp. 138–9). Utilizing a panentheistic model, it can be said that the world and its creatures are fully within God, and that God is also beyond the created world. God is present in creation in order to be in relationship with its creatures, but is also sufficiently distant in order for the creatures to be genuinely free. In this respect, God can be thought of as the composer of the fugue and choreographer of the dance, but it is humans who must conduct the orchestra and perform the dance. And it must be remembered that the composing and choreography are being continuously revised in the midst of the performances. Humans are part of a creation that is to date an unfinished work.

Second, since a creative interplay among necessity, law and chance is required to eventually produce a creature with sufficient capabilities to satisfy God's desire to love fully and be fully loved, then there is no guarantee that the competent director and dancer God intends will emerge, given the contingent and open-ended nature of the evolutionary process. God has certainly taken a risk, but is it a reckless risk given the subsequent pain, suffering and misery that is also inherent to an evolutionary process capable of producing genuinely free creatures? Peacocke admits that this is a thorny issue. Within the evolutionary process the emergence of new species is predicated on the extinction of old ones, and the flourishing of a particular species also requires the death of individuals within it. Complex beings in particular are necessarily 'fragile and vulnerable'. Consequently, 'death, pain, and the risk of suffering are intimately connected with the possibilities of new life, in general, and of the emergence of conscious, and especially human, life, in particular' (ibid., p. 165). Suffering, in short, is the prerequisite of freedom. Yet it is difficult, to say the least, to play music or dance with much creative joy and enthusiasm in a world predicated on the ubiquity of pain, misery and death.

Peacocke believes, however, that he can formulate an adequate solution to this problem. Humans must first look to the evolutionary process itself to gain important clues about who or what God is, and what God's intentions for creation and its creatures might be. The cost of developing genuinely free beings is admittedly high, but worth the sacrifice given the quality of the outcome. In their freedom humans also have the capacity for self-transcendence, and thereby the ability to come to terms with their own inherent paradox and tragedy. In transcending themselves, humans have the ability to assign meaning and purpose to their individual and corporate lives, and in doing so encounter the transcendent and immanent creator. More importantly, they must also look to themselves to discern God's desire and intentions for the future of creation. Humankind is not merely the highest animal, but has evolved into a new kind of animal; an animal capable of constructing a self-reflective and meaningful life, and determining its own destiny. Cultural evolution is displacing biological evolution as the most prominent feature in human development over time. 'In other words, evolution is on the verge of becoming internalized, conscious and self-directing' (ibid., p. 169; see also Peacocke, 1993, pp. 242–8). Natural selection is giving way to purposive action and imposition.

It is through human culture that evolution is becoming internalized, conscious and self-directing. Specifically, humans have the potential to achieve purposive goals given creation's open and indeterminate future. Unfortunately, humans often fail to fulfill this potential, and more importantly are aware of their failure. This awareness is the root of sin which is falling short of one's potential and aspirations. What the Bible refers to as the so-called 'fall' is really the emergence of human self-consciousness. Given the findings of modern science, especially evolutionary biology, the traditional doctrine of the fall as the corruption of an original perfection has no real meaning. What has been traditionally called 'original sin' is simply the emergence of human self-consciousness and its accompanying freedom. It is because of this freedom that humans realize they fail to be the kind of creatures God intends them to be, and this realization presents them with a stark choice. 'Not to choose what God intends is, for man, the failure to realize potentiality, to attain the divine image' (Peacocke, 1979, p. 193; see also Peacocke, 1993, pp. 219–23, 248–54). Failing to achieve one's potential is also to fail God. The principal cause of this failure is self-centeredness. A selfish orientation, which is explicable given the nature of evolution, prevents humans from realizing their potential to become the kind of creatures God intends them to be. Seemingly, the evolutionary process which makes possible the necessary prerequisite of self-consciousness and freedom also works against humans from achieving their potential.

Is there a way out of this predicament? Peacocke contends that God wants to express God's intentions to humans, indeed needs to do so if humans are to become the creatures capable of receiving and responding to God's love. Given the radically open and incomplete nature of creation these intentions can be discerned, admittedly in a difficult and incomplete manner, by looking for what God is doing in the world. In transcending ourselves we catch indications of God both as transcendent creator and immanent participant in creation, a creation, it needs to be emphasized, that is in process and far from complete. These indications, however, are more often than not maddeningly vague and imprecise, providing little practical guidance for the concrete actions required to fulfill human potential. Recognizing the dilemma, Peacocke asks, 'might it not be possible for a man so to reflect God, to be so wholly open to God, that God's presence was clearly unveiled to other men in a new, emergent, and unexpected manner?' (Peacocke, 1979, p. 213) In answer to his own question, Peacocke replies that this is precisely what Jesus accomplished. Jesus' relationship with God was unique in a qualitatively open way, and is therefore able to communicate God's intentions for humans in a clear and compelling manner. The life, death and resurrection of Jesus represent the 'paradigm, and paragon, of the potential unity of the created with the Creator' (ibid., p. 229; see also Peacocke, 1993, pp. 255–311). Jesus thereby also enables God to bear the pain and suffering entailed by the evolutionary process imposed by God to bring the creation and its creatures into being.

This does not mean, however, that Jesus is the Christ who redeems creation and its creatures. He is not a divine agent of creation, but mediates its divine meaning to humans. What differentiates Jesus from other humans is not any so-called divine essence or nature, but his uniquely personal relationship with God, whom he called 'father'. Jesus manifests the open-ended quality of creation, becoming *the* model of creativity itself. He signifies a 'new departure point in the creative process, a new beginning in human life, allowing new potentialities to be anticipated and actualized in those who are willing to share in *his human* open response to God' (Peacocke, 1979, p. 232, emphasis original). Consequently, what Christian theology calls the 'incarnation' does not involve any kenotic descent from God, but refers to Jesus' openness to God. Jesus exhibits the possibility of a highly evolved creature's relationship with God, a possibility that any other human being might achieve. In turn, Jesus' resurrection from the dead, however it might be interpreted, is a sign of new possibilities that in itself has no redemptive significance. Jesus' openness to God offers a model of possible fulfillment, but not perfection given the incomplete and open-ended character of an evolving creation. 'Therein Jesus is the supreme exemplar and original archetype of the way God can bring all human beings to actualize that potentiality which all share – the ability to respond to, to be opened to, the God who is our Creator and calls us into *his* future' (ibid., p. 249, emphasis original; see also Peacocke, 1993, pp. 312–37). Since Jesus is a model of our own inherent potential, it is fitting that we follow him in attempting to deify ourselves.

In following Jesus in this way we become co-creators, co-workers and co-explorers with God. We accept, so to speak, our calling to lead the 'orchestra of creation in the performance which is God's continuing composition' (Peacocke, 1979, p. 305). We are free to embrace or reject this calling, but in accepting we fulfill our potential while avoiding a self-centered hubris. In creating, working and exploring with God we impose a divinely inspired evolutionary order, not through biology but, more significantly, through culture.

Imposing Evolutionary Order (Culture)

Given God's panentheistic relationship to creation, Peacocke insists that humans should treat nature in the same way that they do their own bodies, namely, to promote its flourishing and well-being. In other words, we should respond to a creation which God is in, with and under. This being the case, the biblical images of humans as the vicegerents, stewards and managers of creation are to be rejected, because they portray humans as removed from or standing over and against nature, and therefore removed from or standing over and against God. The more constructive images of humans as co-creators, co-workers and co-explorers command greater respect and reverence for creation, which in turn provides a more adequate and sacramental foundation for a Christian ethic of nature (Peacocke, 1979, pp. 297–308).

As Peacocke argues, if the doctrine of *creatio continua* is to be taken seriously, then the interplay among necessity, chance and law must be taken with equal seriousness. If humans are to fulfill their potential, then they must readily embrace a future that is radically open and contingent. This does not mean, however, that they are utterly dependent upon a process of random and blind chance. Humans are free to cooperate with God in creating a more harmonious and humane world, and in Jesus they have a reliable model of the values that are needed to complete this task, for Jesus fulfilled his own potential by devoting himself to God and neighbor. Practically, science and technology provide the principal and most reliable means for completing this task, and coextensively fulfilling personal and social aspirations. 'In other words, when we as persons are most creative – whether in the arts, science, and literature, or in intellectual reflection, or in our work, or in personal and social relations, in general, our distinctively human activities – then we are fulfilling those human potentialities that were unveiled in Jesus uniquely and seminally as the continuous creative work of God in man' (ibid., p. 307). It is through cultures that respect and revere creation (read nature) that humans both encounter God as creator and work with God in fashioning themselves into becoming the kind of creatures God intends them to be. Consequently, humans may celebrate their own fulfillment, as modeled by Jesus, as the foundation of a genuine Christian humanism, and derivatively a genuinely humane culture.

Although Peacocke has reservations regarding the adequacy of the science underlying Pierre Teilhard de Chardin's expansive vision, they nonetheless show some striking affinities. According to Teilhard, the emergence of culture is the most significant event that has occurred in human evolution. Through culture, humans have a cumulative, common memory or 'social heredity' that is passed on from generation to generation (Teilhard de Chardin, 1964, pp. 25–9). In this respect, cultural evolution is more Lamarckian than Darwinian in character. Since acquired traits are cumulative and passed on, each generation benefits from a quantitatively and qualitatively superior cultural inheritance than enjoyed by previous generations. Consequently, cultural evolution is inherently and irresistibly progressive. This does not imply that the history of humankind is free from episodic regressions, but the overall trend is a steady improvement in the quality of human life. Humans have every right to claim unashamedly that they are 'children of progress' (ibid., pp. 67–8). More importantly, there is every reason to assume that this progressive trajectory extends endlessly into the future; we will most certainly spawn grandchildren of greater progress. With the emergence of human culture evolution has become self-conscious, and is therefore poised to make an unprecedented leap; the crossing of an evolutionary boundary resulting from purposeful intent rather than random chance. There are three pertinent implications that may be drawn from this premise.

First, coextensively with the emergence of culture, human history also emerges as the dominant evolutionary factor. It is within a historicist horizon that nature is defined and delineated. Nothing is comprehensible outside of history, so nature is in turn becoming an artifact. To a significant extent the success of evolution now depends on human flourishing. This does not suggest that nature simply comprises infinitely malleable material. Rather, it discloses with stark clarity an evolutionary process oriented toward the gradual coalescence of matter into consciousness. Humankind, particularly in virtue of its emergent cultures, is the apex and defining feature of this evolutionary trajectory. Humans have assumed this definitive role because they emerged as the most complex and conscious coalition of inert molecules, but qualitatively different from any other coalitions. Humankind is simply the final phase of the evolution of life. The fate of the world literally rests in the ability of humans to take charge and direct the future course of cultural evolution.

Second, with the emergence of life there is an accompanying evolutionary tendency toward complex organization. This tendency is present at both the organic and social levels. Plants, for instance, are more complex than bacteria, and chimpanzees have a more complex social structure than rabbits. Human culture incorporates both the most complex organisms and social structures that have evolved to date. These complex organizations are convergent and mutually reinforcing; human biological and social reproduction is mediated through, and directed by, culture. Collectively, it is now almost exclusively in and through culture that humans evolve. Thus the single most important evolutionary process, and therefore historical process as well, that has emerged is the uniquely human capacity for socialization. This capacity promotes an emerging unity of 'super-organized matter', which is unleashing new psychic and spiritual powers. Through both biological and cultural evolution, humankind is constructing a composite mind (ibid., pp. 177–8).

According to Teilhard, there is theological warrant for explaining this orientation toward complex organization. Christ, through the incarnation, is both the history and *telos* of the universe. Over time, the church becomes what might be likened to the 'Christian organism' whose purpose is to direct creation toward its destiny in Christ. The evolution of human culture and Christianity are parts of a single evolutionary trajectory heading toward a convergence of knowledge and love (ibid., pp. 33–5). In summarizing this movement, Teilhard claims that humans represent the highest form of reflective life, their social life marks an advance of this higher life, and Christianity is the axis for socializing this reflective capacity in a manner that will spur even greater evolutionary development. The only remaining evolutionary task is for humankind to achieve its spiritual potential. Christ is therefore the apex and end of creation, because he embodies the moral primacy of charity. Christ's cross in particular, as the supreme act of love, is also the supreme symbol of evolutionary progress, for the reign of God cannot be achieved until humans attain evolutionary maturity. Consequently, the potential for complex organization and socialization will remain unfulfilled unless humans transform themselves in the image of Christ.

Third, convergence is *the* driving force *and* goal of the evolution of life. For Teilhard, evolution will fail if it produces a universe that is a plurality rather than a unity. He contends that the universe is inherently convergent, heading toward a center, for it does not comprise isolated or autonomous conglomerates, but interrelated associations within a greater, integral whole. In this respect, evolution is an emergent force that seeks to overcome and unify creation's initial divergence, forging a cosmos out of chaos. If Christ's cross, as the supreme act of charity, spurs humankind to pursue its evolutionary maturity, then Christ's *parousia* signifies its evolutionary perfection of complete and total unity. Christ is literally the end of creation, for Christ will be in all, and all things will be in Christ. This credo, however, is not a baseless religious assertion, but is, according to Teilhard, grounded in a scientific explication of the evolution of life and its future trajectory. With the convergence of biological and cultural evolution, future advances will occur along novel psychical and spiritual avenues. Or, posed as a question: how will humans evolve beyond the emergence of thought?

In answering this question we encounter Teilhard in his most speculative mood, but his speculations are germane to this inquiry and may be noted briefly. If human evolution is to advance any further, then humans must merge into a larger collective. The most pressing cultural task, particularly in respect to its relation to nature, is not to find a single truth, but to become a single being. The human species must evolve to the point where it becomes the soul of the earth. More expansively, through the evolution of the human species, earth will become a single organism with its own spirit. Over time, the biosphere will become conscious, thereby transforming itself into the 'Noosphere' (ibid., pp. 124–39; Teilhard de Chardin, 1965, pp. 191–212). This is, admittedly, one of Teilhard's most controversial claims, due largely to both its vast scope and vague quality. What he evidently has in mind is the emergence of a collective or global consciousness that he likens to a 'stupendous thinking machine' (Teilhard de Chardin, 1964, pp. 172–3). This evolutionary leap is a result of an emerging global civilization; a 'planetisation' (ibid., pp. 124–39, 174–81) in which humankind is 'trans-humanising' (ibid., p. 241) itself into a species of 'ultra-humans' (ibid., pp. 261–3, 286–7). It is, most importantly, a fateful leap, for the emergence of the Noosphere is literally the first step in a universal movement; humanity's global consciousness is destined to become cosmic. As humans explore and colonize outer space, they will bring with them their highly evolved 'super-love' (ibid., pp. 286–7), which in turn permeates and draws the entire universe toward its 'Omega Point' (Teilhard de Chardin, 1965, pp. 254–72). The emergence of the Noosphere is thereby an initial foray into 'Christogenesis' (Teilhard de Chardin, 1964, pp. 224–5) in which, through the means of an evolving collective consciousness, God is shaping the universe into a single, hyper-conscious being. Consequently, the boundary separating nature and culture must be removed.

Although the ethereal character of Teilhard's breathtaking vision leaves much to be desired, the essential lineaments – at least for the purpose of this inquiry – can be sketched out in more concrete terms. Emergence and convergence are the two inherent principles that characterize and direct, respectively, the evolution of life. A divergent universe is destined to become a unified creation; nature and artifice are destined to become one. It is through human cultural evolution that sufficient evolutionary order is gained to attain this end. Humans thereby carry a heavy burden if they are to cooperate with God in fashioning the universe into the kind of creation God intends it to be. Teilhard is adamant that technology is the principal engine driving this cosmically creative enterprise: 'We are today witnessing a truly explosive growth of technology and research, bringing an increasing mastery, both theoretical and practical, of the secrets and sources of cosmic energy at every level and in every form' (ibid., p. 275). Technology amplifies a broad range of capabilities, inspiring innovative social and political structures that are drawing humankind together in a totalizing manner. As humans edge against the limits of their nature, they find that evolution enfolding upon itself, and in this enfolding they find their salvation in taking command of the future course of their evolution as a culturally constructed species. Even when the research Teilhard championed produces highly destructive devices, evolution's irresistibly and inevitably progressive course remains unchallenged. His singular reaction to the explosion of the first atomic bomb was that it was a great scientific accomplishment. The material world made up of atoms could now be subjected to human purposes. Moreover, the cooperation required in the bomb's construction and detonation served as a precursor of greater human self-organization, for a team of scientists had in fact become 'a single organism' (ibid., pp. 142–3). Humans were now embarking on the process of perfecting themselves, and the atomic bomb merely symbolized the power at their disposal for this transformative project. In short, the significance of the atomic bomb is not its power to destroy, but its potency as a supremely creative act.

Teilhard acknowledges that the proper ordering of cultural evolution requires humans to undertake the enterprise of 'trans-humanising' themselves so that they become the 'ultra-humans' God intends them to be. But who are these creatures, and what exactly are they aspiring to become?

Co-creators (Self-made Artifacts)

Although Teilhard insists that through cultural evolution humans will transform themselves, he offers few clues regarding what these ultra-humans, as well as the interceding beings, might be like other than that they will exemplify Christ's self-sacrificial love. Similarly, Peacocke assumes that culture will exert the greatest influence over the course of future human evolution, though his vision of what this might entail is less grandiose. He nonetheless presumes, however, that if humans cooperate with God they will create for themselves, and all creation, a preferable future outcome. In enumerating this cooperation, Peacocke offers a number of images, but the image of the co-creator carries the greatest weight. In accepting their responsibility for shaping the future, albeit in partnership with God, humans may fulfill their potential in the same manner that Jesus did. Again, however, we are offered few details on how co-creators will accomplish this goal.

Phillip Hefner employs the image of the co-creator as the centerpiece of his theological anthropology. He contends that contemporary theological accounts of what being human might mean must acknowledge the dominant role culture now plays in human evolution. The chief question prompting his inquiry is 'who are we human beings and what are we here for?' (Hefner, 1993, p. 4) Hefner insists that any rational answer to this question must take into account the radically open-ended character of both human biological evolution *and* history. Consequently, theological claims about the meaning and destiny of *Homo sapiens* must be shaped in categories that are scientifically intelligible, for science provides the most reliable source of knowledge. Although theology is not a formal scientific discipline, its chief tenets must nonetheless be presented as proposals that can be assessed through a combination of empirical observation, rational argument and fruitful outcomes (ibid., p. 17–19).

Hefner's central premise is that given the formative power of cultural evolution, any line separating nature from history, and the natural from artifice, is arbitrary, permeable and no longer tenable. This premise incorporates the extent to which these once discrete categories have become thoroughly interpenetrated. Although human culture is the product of a natural, genetic inheritance, the future course of that legacy is being shaped by purposeful human acts. Although humans are asserting greater control over their own fate, they remain dependent upon natural processes and ecosystems for their continuing survival. Rather than speaking of humans as both biological and historical beings, they are more accurately 'biocultural' creatures, or 'biologically formed culture creators' (ibid., pp. 19–20). Human genes and cultures have co-evolved and co-adapted into a symbiotic relation-ship. The creature emerging from this symbiosis is the *created* co-creator. The appended adjective denotes the conditioned nature of being human, while also acknowledging the freedom emerging from this conditional state. The values emerging from this freedom serve, in turn, as a *telos* to guide the moral ordering of the evolving bioculture. This does not imply a natural teleology, but rather, that these emergent values serve a 'teleonomic' function (ibid., pp. 36–40). The created co-creator works with God in pursuing its self-fulfillment (and presumably God's as well) in a manner that protects the world's life-sustaining ecosystems upon which human survival and flourishing depend. It is therefore imperative that created co-creators direct the evolution of their bioculture toward the inseparably joined goals of expanding freedom into novel forms of expression, while taking care to preserve its genetic 'substrate'. The fate of creation rests on the outcomes of cultural evolution in which technology is the 'natural and plausible consequence of the basic nature of *homo sapiens* as a creature constituted both by genes and culture' (ibid., pp. 45–50).

True to his own proposed methodology, Hefner attempts to test and explicate this premise through an elaborate scheme of proposals, theorems, hypotheses and axioms. For the purposes of this inquiry, however, the remaining summary concentrates on the following proposal, three theorems and hypothesis.

Proposal: 'Human beings are God's created co-creators whose purpose is to be the agency, acting in freedom, to birth the future that is most wholesome for the nature that has birthed us – the nature that is not only our own genetic heritage, but also the entire human community and the evolutionary and ecological reality in which we belong. Exercising this agency is said to be God's will for humans' (ibid., p. 27).

Three theorems:

1   The human being is created by God to be a co-creator in the creation that God has brought into being and for which God has purposes.
2   The conditioning matrix that has produced the human being – the evolutionary process – is God's process of bringing into being a creature that represents the creation's zone of a new stage of freedom and therefore is crucial for the emergence of a free creation.
3   The freedom that marks the created co-creator in its culture is an instrumentality of God for enabling the creation (consisting of the evolutionary past of genetic and cultural inheritance as well as the contemporary ecosystem) to participate in the intentional fulfillment of God's purposes (ibid., p. 32).

Hypothesis: 'We now live in a condition that may be termed technological civilization. This condition is characterized by the fact that human decision has conditioned virtually all of the planetary physico-biogenetic systems, so that human decision is the critical factor in the continued functioning of the planet's systems' (ibid., p. 49).

According to Hefner, nature is *the* inescapable matrix in which humans live, and move, and have their being. As a species they owe their birth and continuing sustenance to natural and evolutionary processes from which they can never extricate themselves. Humans, then, are not the stewards of nature, but share with it kinship. In this respect, culture is determined by its natural, particularly genetic, antecedents and ongoing dependency. The fact that humans are creators of culture, however, indicates that they also possess a freedom to transcend this natural determinism. They interpret the meaning of their existence, establish norms and pursue goals and projects through elaborate social structures, rituals and artistic expressions which require reordering natural processes to accomplish these objectives. Cultural evolution, then, discloses that freedom is the determined human condition (ibid., pp. 97–101). Moreover, it is through this dialectic between determinism and freedom that God and humans encounter each other, together co-creating a creation that simultaneously accomplishes God's purposes while promoting human flourishing. Consequently, nature is 'God's great project' in which human and divine 'resources' are invested for the sake of its preservation, continuing evolution and 'redemption' (ibid., pp. 72–5), for it is through the natural processes that God created, that God also bestows grace (ibid., pp. 61–2).

How are created co-creators to manage these resources wisely and faithfully? Hefner insists that science provides the best guide, because it affords a conceptual, contextual and experiential clarity that is superior to any other option. Unlike theology, for instance, science is grounded in empirical data, thereby offering a more reliable and concrete foundation for subsequent moral interpretations and action. Scientific knowledge is *the* prerequisite for both preserving nature *and* directing it further toward novel configurations of freedom. Science enables this distinctly '*postmodern*' move, because 'it means that this kind of interaction between the nature of things and our knowing the nature of things is inevitable, inescapable, and indeed conditions the manner in which life and its possibilities open up for us' (ibid., p. 100, emphasis original). Technology is the practical means of applying this knowledge, for it is the most effective instrument available for redirecting natural processes along a trajectory of greater freedom. Science and technology are the driving forces that have created the contemporary world; cultural evolution, and its attendant freedom, is unimaginable in their absence. Moreover, technology is not merely a collection of instruments, but denotes a set of formative perspectives, values and convictions that are internalized, and through which we 'shape our self-images' that are 'determinative for our lives' (ibid., pp. 104–6). Stated baldly, 'we *are* technology', and 'techno-nature is, in a real sense, the only nature that now exists on our planet' (ibid., pp. 152–5, emphasis original). The created co-creator is also an emerging technosapien.

Hefner is aware, however, that technological civilization is not an unqualified blessing. Although cultural evolution is required if creation is to be free, and technology in turn is needed if such freedom is to evolve, this advance is accompanied by great peril. Simply stated, technology can be used just as easily to destroy as to create. This power has become so great that the ecosystem is now at the mercy of human actions. Indeed, the fate of creation rests in the hands of its created co-creators. How should we respond to this seemingly threatening prospect? Hefner's hope rests on our ability to construct 'worthwhile, desirable, or good' values which are expressed in effective moral rules and codes (ibid., p. 177). These values are derived from an emergent altruistic love – a love promoting beneficent behavior – and the challenge is to instantiate this love within subsequent cultural evolution in more substantive ways. Hefner acknowledges that this is a daunting task, and a happy ending is not guaranteed given the radically contingent and open-ended nature of biocultural evolution. Although the emergence of altruism can be explained scientifically in terms of trans-kinship providing *Homo sapiens* with a survival advantage, no 'ought' can be extracted from this 'is'. Science alone simply lacks the capacity to construct a compelling mythical narrative that is suitable to ensure the survival of creation and its created co-creators.

Consequently, we must return to religion, for religious beliefs, rituals and practices provide a mythical structure that can compel the necessary moral actions. Hefner insists, however, that religious faith must be explicated in terms that are pertinent to an evolving technoculture. In respect to Christian faith, this requires that many, if not all, of its traditional doctrines must be subjected to a thoroughgoing deconstruction and comprehensive reinterpretation in light of scientific knowledge and technological power. The doctrine of *creatio ex nihilo*, for example, is a symbolic referent to the world's ongoing dependence on God, thereby serving as a reminder of the moral regard humans owe to preserving the integrity of natural processes and ecosystems upon which they are dependent.

It is Christology, however, which is the greatest beneficiary of Hefner's revisions. Humans may be said to bear the *imago dei*, yet this symbol does not refer to any innate human attribute, but embodies a divine image in their status as free creators of meaning. Any notion of a 'fall' is therefore rejected, because sin is a consequence of freedom that is necessarily grounded in vulnerability, and our self-interested response to this necessity distorts our freedom. The possibility of overcoming this distortion is exhibited in the symbol of the incarnation. Jesus indicates that nature is a suitable vessel of God's grace, and that grace is, in turn, the foundation, preservation and fulfillment of nature. Christ does not take away the sins of the world; any notion of the 'atonement is to be interpreted as God's statement that God has never been alienated from us and that our lives, modeled in the form of Jesus, are suitable for God's work' (ibid., p. 274). To bear the *imago dei* 'implies that humans can be the vehicle of grace toward the creation, in a way that is somehow reminiscent of God's graciousness' (ibid., p. 238). Since Christ is a wholesome model of this suggestive recollection, his exemplary life and ministry point toward the values humans require in fashioning a worthwhile, desirable and good technoculture. It is in Christ that humans fulfill themselves as created co-creators, displaying the 'potential to actualize a radically new phase of evolution' (ibid., p. 248). This potential is the theological meaning of Christ as the new Adam, and the new Adam is also what humans will become as the result of their co-creative efforts. Consequently, God and the created co-creators are in partnership to move creation toward its 'fulfillment according to God's purposes, a fulfillment that requires our self-giving for the creation, even as Jesus gave himself' (ibid., p. 253). This is a grand and hazardous undertaking, for the survival of creation is at stake, and whether this project succeeds or fails cannot be known in advance. It is only at some distant date that history will retrospectively 'consign us to ignominy or acknowledge our integrity' (ibid., p. 229).

None of the postmodern theologians examined in this chapter can be accused of offering fainthearted visions in respect to how theology might inform a technological transformation of nature and human nature. Whether their respective proposals can provide adequate guidance for an emerging technoculture and its posthuman inhabitants and to what extent their proposals are faithful to the Christian tradition they purport to represent are the chief issues that will be addressed in the remainder of this book.

Notes

1   The following section is adapted from my paper, 'Extending Human Life: to what end?', referenced in chapter three, note 6.
2   The *amor fati* in question is taken from Plato rather than Nietzsche.
3   Hence Kass's emphasis on developing moral habits and dispositions, particularly in regard to marriage and family (Kass, 2002, pp. 69–72).
4   In principle, Fukuyama must also be open to the possibility that a superior form of social and political association may emerge out of the evolutionary process.
5   See, for example, Bostrom, 'In Defense of Posthuman Dignity', at http://www.nickbostrom. com/ethics/dignity.html
6   See 'Pierre Teilhard de Chardin', at http://www.betterhumans.com/Resources/Encyclopedia/ article.aspx?articleID=2002-09-23-2, and 'Omega Point Theory', at http://www. betterhumans.com/Resources/Encyclopedia/article.aspx?articleID=2002-05-22-6; see also Moravec, 1999, pp. 201–202.
7   Chapters five and six.

CHAPTER FIVE

An Alternative Theological Framework

The purpose of this chapter is twofold. First, it aims to critically assess the principal linkages between posthuman discourse and postmodern theology. This critical task is undertaken by arguing that selected themes in postmodern theology, as examined in the previous chapter, dispense with the need of God as a creator or redeemer. What these postmodern theologians call 'God' is a compulsive and ubiquitous creativity that is itself an emergent feature of cultural evolution. Consequently, the particular strain of postmodern theology they represent can be construed as posthuman discourse with a pronounced Christian dialect. As such, it can only express emotive preferences regarding what kind of future humans should create, and what type of behavior is consonant in constructing such a fate, rather than making any normative claims about a given destiny that should in turn order human desire and conduct accordingly.

The second purpose of this chapter is to offer an alternative theological framework as a basis for a counter discourse regarding the normative ordering of human destiny and conduct. This constructive endeavor is pursued by contending that the principal weakness of postmodern theology, again as discussed in the previous chapter, is the absence of any compelling Christology. Given this absence, these postmodern theologians can, at best, blunt the sharp edges of the nihilistic underpinnings of posthuman discourse, but cannot offer an attractive, alternative moral vision. In response, I argue that Jesus Christ reveals the origin, temporal unfolding and destiny of the world as God's creation. This central contention is developed by a series of Christological themes on selected traditional Christian tenets regarding anthropology, providence and eschatology in light of the challenge posed by posthuman discourse. These themes are further developed in the final chapter, in which some alternative formative contours for an emerging technoculture are sketched out in opposition to those offered by posthuman discourse.

Creator, Creation and Creativity

Gordon Kaufman has written what he believes to be the definitive paraphrase of the opening lines to the Gospel according to John: 'In the beginning was creativity, and the creativity was with God, and the creativity was God. All things came into being through the mystery of creativity; apart from creativity nothing would have come into being' (Kaufman, 2004, p. ix). This revised version is needed because all 'theological ideas – including the idea of God' –

should 'be understood as products of the human imagination, when employed by men and women to orient themselves in life' (ibid., p. ix). Why is this reorienting rhetoric needed? When traditional or inherited understandings of 'God' no longer fit in a postmodern world, they must be radically reinterpreted.

In undertaking this interpretive task, postmodern theology must reject the biblically inspired anthropomorphic and anthropocentric images of God that have inspired the environmental and militaristic threats now endangering the earth's very survival. In overcoming this sad legacy, we may follow the lead of Fichte and Feuerbach in transforming God from a noun into a verb. By doing so we are enabled to radically critique and redirect inherited ideologies and institutions in 'more humanizing and humane directions' (ibid., p. 27). Radically reordering human life on a global scale is imperative for our very survival is at stake, and we, and we alone, are responsible for the decisions we make, or fail to make, that lead to a future we create or fail to create.

Yet if the burden of such responsibility rests on our shoulders, and our shoulders alone, why not dispense with God altogether? Kaufman admits that God may indeed be dead, but we nonetheless need to retain God as a powerful motivational symbol. It must, however, be a symbol that is palatable and relevant to a postmodern audience, and since this audience cannot conceive of a creation other than in human terms there is no sense in invoking a creator. Kaufman's task is to reinterpret the symbol of 'God', and its relationship to the concept of humanity, in light of our present threatening circumstances, especially the ecological crisis. His accompanying goal is to demonstrate that faith in 'God' can still help to solve our contemporary problems. The purpose of theology, therefore, is not to find meaning but to promote survival.

In undertaking this task, Kaufman disposes of any notion of a creator and creation in favor of a mysterious and serendipitous creativity. He does this to make theological discourse more compatible with the current transition from modern to postmodern thought. He contends that evolutionary categories are associated with modernity, while ecological thought is associated with postmodernity. Consequently, nature now competes with 'God' as the ultimate object of human attention. The theological challenge in response to this paradigmatic shift is to construct an intellectual and imaginative framework for relating 'God', humanity and the world within ecological categories. In order to successfully meet this challenge, we must construct a 'God' that is explicable within both an evolutionary and ecological worldview. Any concept of a creator God must therefore be rejected in favor of one that inspires serendipitous, rather than purposive, action.

According to Kaufman, creativity is admirably suited for satisfying this conceptual necessity. Creativity is a ubiquitous force that can be described in three modalities: (1) the coming into being of the universe; (2) evolutionary change; and (3) symbolic expression. The third modality is the linchpin of Kaufman's argument. It is through the power of symbolic expression that humans are able to order their lives in accordance with evolutionary and ecological trajectories. This capability is seen preeminently in the postmodern historicist construction of reality. Humans simultaneously record, construct and direct the future course of their own biohistory. By rejecting the primitive idea of God as a 'kind of cosmic person', humans become 'deeply embedded' in the 'creative activity in and through the web of life on planet Earth', which encourages them to 'develop attitudes and participate in activities that fit properly into this web of living creativity' (ibid., pp. 48–9).

Creativity serves as a 'God' which inspires the requisite awe as the basis of a transformative ethic, promoting the survival of celestial life. Kaufman believes such an ethic will be effective, because its grounding in evolution and ecology provides a compelling moral vision. 'We humans are being drawn beyond our present condition and order of life by creative impulses in our biohistorical trajectory suggesting decisions and movements now required of us' (ibid., p. 49). The dilemma facing us is a straightforward one: if we do not respond appropriately we will not survive, and if we do respond appropriately we will be rewarded by serendipitous creativity.

We will, no doubt, need to create new values to forge a favorable resolution to this dilemma. Fortunately, we do not need to create all these *ex nihilo*. The reservoir of our biohistory contains expressive symbols that we may revise in appropriate ways. We may, for instance, look to Jesus as a model of creativity. Kaufman warns, however, that in turning to Jesus the Christological images of the New Testament must be rejected, because they are either dangerous or useless. Rather, the models of reconciliation, love, peace and concern for enemies that Jesus displayed in his teaching and life must be emphasized, for they provide a pattern for how we may live lives that are more humane. Jesus, for example, demonstrates that we may consciously choose a morality of non-violence. Consequently, his teaching on love or *agape* may now be incorporated in a postmodern ethic grounded in evolution and ecology, for it provides a survival advantage given the destructive technological power at our disposal. The good example of Jesus inspires a creative response to our predicament of impending extinction. 'Thus our creativity will be serving – rather than restricting or otherwise countering – the forward movement into the open future on planet Earth of the cosmic serendipitous creativity to which we seek to be ultimately responsible' (ibid., p. 62).

Creativity itself is thereby the only appropriate object of postmodern worship and piety. Presumably such pious worship remains Christian, for the object is inspired by none other than Jesus. It is, of course, a Jesus liberated from the fetters of the Bible's primitive world, for we know that the God whom Jesus called Father is not a person to be proclaimed, but a concept to be invented. And it is a 'God' that must again be reinvented within the historicist, evolutionary and ecological categories that define our current reality. Unlike the naïve biblical writers, we know that 'God' came into 'being' as a new idea. Only humans, as far as we know, are in a position to discern and value – to give life to – this emergence. We should therefore give thanks for the random set of events and circumstances that brought us into existence, but for which we, and we alone, are now responsible for our future survival. Kaufman never specifies to whom we should express our gratitude, but he nonetheless assures us that we may bravely construct a future accompanied by a mysterious creativity which promises that our good efforts will be serendipitously blessed.

The purpose for interjecting Kaufman at this juncture is that his ubiquitous creativity demonstrates, in a clear and concise manner, the extent to which postmodern theology is a variant theme of posthuman discourse. He shares with posthumanists the postmodern belief that all horizons are historicist constructions, which in turn define reality. Humans now posses the power, primarily through technology, to shape themselves and their natural, social and political environments in accordance with this fabricated reality. Kaufman's re-creative emphasis should not be surprising for, as was discussed in the previous chapter, Christianity and posthumanism share certain affinities because they are both transformative religions. What is surprising, however, is the ease with which Kaufman discards a creator God in favor of the 'God' of creativity. Moreover, the 'God' he invokes as the inspiration of a moral vision that promotes the survival of life on earth is a self-aggrandizing demonstration of the extent to which humans have mastered the art of symbolic expression. Kaufman's 'God' is little different than the immortal posthuman, and in many respects pales in comparison because it is a 'God' that effectively can neither create nor redeem anything, for it is literally nothing more than the product of a creative imagination.

By invoking a 'God' who emerges in time as a symbolic expression of ultimate concern, Kaufman falls, along with his posthumanist companions, into the trap of attempting to transform necessity into goodness. Again as examined in the previous chapter, Christians (as explicated by Grant and Weil) can claim that the necessary and the good are separated by a gulf that can never be traversed from the temporal side, but only bridged from the eternal side by an incarnate reconciler. The evils stemming from necessity cannot be redeemed fully in time, and humans must therefore learn to love, or at least consent to, their fate as finite creatures, especially as exemplified in the suffering entailed in embodied existence. Posthumanists reject this premise, because they hold both the modern belief that necessity can be transformed into goodness through a mastery of nature and human nature, and the postmodern belief that all finite and temporal limits can be radically transcended and eventually negated.

In discarding a creator and creation, Kaufman also forecloses any possibility of bridging the gulf, because there is no eternity or infinity within which the temporal and finite are sustained and redeemed. In response, he proposes an infinite creativity that enables humans to construct their own good which they symbolically name 'God'. Yet like his historicist predecessors, Kaufman has not offered a program for constructing the good, but has exchanged one necessity for another. Exchanging creative necessity for that of natural or historical necessity does not guarantee any clearer moral vision. Are the faithfully married, for example, to be condemned because they refuse to experiment in more creative lifestyles, and are innovative tortures to be prized because their inventors have devised more creative methods for inflicting pain?

Kaufman may reply that his evolutionary and ecological criteria, in tandem with the examples of Jesus' life and ministry, set limits that prevent us from reaching such egregious conclusions. Yet if the creativity he invokes is as radically open and contingent as he claims, then no possible judgment or act can, in principle, be dismissed in advance, regardless of how offensive we find the prospect to be. Kaufman has created for himself two dilemmas similar to those of N. Katherine Hayles and Francis Fukuyama.[1] On the one hand, Hayles insists that we have become posthuman, because we think of ourselves in those terms. But in failing to admit that constructing the posthuman world requires technological transformation, her appeal to the finite and embodied limits have no critical purchase in formulating a counter moral vision; all she can offer is an alternative survival tactic. Similarly, Kaufman contends that we become creative beings by imagining ourselves in creatively new ways. He too fails to acknowledge that such imagining requires concrete implementation if creativity *per se* is to be efficacious, so his appeals to evolution, ecology and Jesus provide no basis for a counter moral vision. Again, all he can offer is a substitute survival strategy. On the other hand, Fukuyama invokes dignity as a normative objection against a posthuman world. Yet the dignity he invokes emerges from an underlying evolutionary process, and therefore cannot provide the stable moral criterion he craves. Similarly, Kaufman's creativity is also an emergent feature, and therefore also a moving target ill-equipped to provide the kind of moral trajectory he envisions.

Consequently, Kaufman's moral formula – modern evolution plus postmodern ecology flavored with the life and teachings of Jesus results in serendipitous beatitude – is more a wish than an ethic. On his own terms, none of the criteria he invokes can give the moral guidance he commends, for they cannot ultimately limit; and they cannot limit, because he has stripped them of any teleology. Teleology must be voided, because his criteria must also be subjected to radical transformation if creativity itself is to be honored, especially when survival is at stake. It is not inconceivable, for example, that Jesus' non-violence might have to be jettisoned for the sake of protecting evolutionary and ecological trajectories against life-threatening assaults. In effect, what Kaufman is offering is a kinder, gentler vision of a posthuman future. Yet it can only function as an emotive preference in contrast to, say, Hans Moravec's voraciously libertarian predilection (Moravec, 1999, pp. 163–89). Since Kaufman is merely stating a preference, it is puzzling why he retains any semblance of 'God' in his account of creativity, unless he believes it perhaps augments its evocative appeal. If so, it is an ineffectual tack to adopt since a creatively immortal posthuman is arguably a more intriguing symbolic expression to contemplate than that offered by an ephemeral 'God' of creativity. In its easy disposal of a creator and creation, postmodern theology effectively strips Christianity of any critical or constructive tools with which it may engage the emerging technoculture. Or in more provocative terms, Christian theology is mute when it has no prophetic judgment or Gospel of redemption to proclaim.

It may be objected that even if my critique of Kaufman is valid, and I admittedly have not yet proven my indictment, it is unfair to imply that he is an exemplary spokesman for postmodern theology, thereby tainting, through guilt by association, the postmodern theologians examined in the previous chapter. The revisionist theologies written by Arthur Peacocke, Pierre Teilhard de Chardin and Philip Hefner retain a functional role for a creator God. In briefly revisiting them, however, certain striking similarities with Kaufman can be inferred that render the Christian belief in a God who is both creator *and* redeemer highly problematic in these theologies purporting to be postmodern.

Peacocke's principal thesis is that God wants and needs fellowship with a being other than God. In order to satisfy this desire, God brings into being a creation that has the potential to produce a being with the capacity to enter freely into such fellowship. Hence the necessity of a radically open and contingent creation, for it is only through the interplay of chance and law that the kind of being God desires could evolve. With the emergence of *Homo sapiens*, God at last has a potential partner who may someday develop the talent to play the fugue God has composed. It must be underscored, however, that God is taking a genuine risk, for there is no guarantee that humans will ever fulfill this potential.

In rejecting any notion of teleology, Peacocke also makes his appeal to God superfluous to his argument. If humans emerged accidentally within the evolutionary process, then they also encounter God by accident. If this is true, then they also cannot discern any divine intentions for their subsequent evolutionary development embedded within nature, for this would be tantamount to reinserting a disguised teleological element that has already been expunged. Yet Peacocke insists that God is known predominantly through nature, seemingly unaware or unconcerned about the implications this unresolved contradiction entails. One may counter in Peacocke's defense that invoking the good example of Jesus' life and teaching resolves this contradiction without any recourse to an implicit teleology. But, as argued below, his appeal to Jesus is insufficiently Christological to overcome this dilemma.

Setting Jesus aside for the moment, we may return to the dilemma. In creating a universe in which a creature with a capacity for fellowship with God might evolve, God has seemingly taken a genuine risk, for the entire enterprise might fail. Yet this possibility of failure begs an important question: if the fugue God has composed is never played, is God's desire for fellowship ever fulfilled? If humans never develop the sufficient talent, or reject the art of the fugue in favor of jazz, how should God respond? Could God's desire be satisfied if God came to prefer jazz over baroque music? Peacocke's answer must presumably be *yes*, for he has written at length on divine being and becoming (Peacocke, 1993, pp. 99–134). Yet if God may be said to change over time, then is not God also an emergent feature of a contingent evolutionary process? And if this is the case, what does it imply about the reliability and goodness of God's initial desire for fellowship? Peacocke's God ends up looking very much like a human person writ large. In this respect, Kaufman offers a simpler explanation that 'God' is merely the symbol we have constructed to refer to an emergent and serendipitous creativity. God is the projection, not the source or object, of evolving creativity.

Determining whether Peacocke or Kaufman offers the more convincing argument is not at issue. Rather, we may make a more modest observation that despite their seemingly conflicting accounts of God, they both derive from evolutionary necessity an identical moral imperative: be creative, or perish! To do otherwise is to wage a futile struggle against the contingent nature of the universe. To resist this futility, it is, at best, far from clear why God, as either creator or symbol, is needed to embrace this imperative, for in either case the god invoked is little more than a mirror reflecting the image of the beholder.

Teilhard seemingly offers a way to preserve God's necessity as a cosmic creator. He accomplishes this by interjecting a teleological element that does not challenge creation's open and contingent future. Evolution is a process of constant change, but it is not a blind progression. Evolution is driven by an orientation toward greater complexity as witnessed by the emergence of life, followed by consciousness and culminating in humans as a species that is self-conscious. Through these self-conscious creatures, evolution continues its creative journey toward forming a universe that is self-conscious. Although evolution often gets sidetracked, it is nonetheless heading toward the Omega Point of a single cosmic being. Teilhard also appeals to Jesus Christ in making his case, but it is not confined to the salutary example of his teaching and ministry. Rather, the incarnation enables us to perceive creation's destiny which is already latent within the evolutionary process of ever greater complexity. Since all will be made one in Christ, diversity will be displaced by unity. Human self-transformation plays an obviously central role in attaining this end, thereby placing a heavy moral burden and obligation on the future course of cultural evolution. Consequently, Teilhard amends Peacocke's and Hefner's imperative to read: be Christologically creative!

Teilhard has rescued a peculiar God. It is a God dedicated to negating all distinctions and differences. A diverse creation must become a unity matching the singularity of its creator. In invoking Christ as the model of this unity, however, the triune God of Christian faith is either a horrible mistake or the three persons of the Trinity must also evolve into a God who is genuinely one. The first and third persons are collapsed into the second person or, in more traditional parlance, the Father and the Spirit must become the Son. For Teilhard, it is inconceivable that any genuine unity can be achieved so long as the One, the three, and the many may be said to exist. Consequently, creation's ubiquitous diversity is a problem to be solved, rather than an inherent feature to be affirmed.

To solve this problem, Teilhard has jettisoned the triune God in favor of a monadic deity. In doing so he has also embraced a violent ontology, for all distinction and difference must be ultimately negated in achieving a singular unity. He has embraced a false and deadly unity, however, for the diversity he decries is a pluriform manifestation of the triune God's singular act of creation. In this respect, Teilhard has fallen victim to the alluring modern slogan 'out of the many one', as opposed to the more salient Augustinian principle, 'from the one, many' (Augustine, 1984, pp. 547–94; Elshtain, 1995, pp. 101–5). Consequently, that which he wishes to annihilate is the very fruit of a true and life-giving unity that is inherently relational. To invoke a crude analogy, Teilhard is enamored with a God of fusion, complete with the energetic and highly destructive imagery that the violent collapsing of atoms suggests.

The moral imperative ensuing from this theological vision is, to use the most charitable term possible, blind. The particular must always be sacrificed for the sake of the universal; the interest of the individual is subsumed into the collective good. If the course of evolution is to have any meaning, then anything impeding its progression toward greater unity should be removed. The necessity to unify thereby justifies the destruction of recalcitrant elements that perpetuate divisiveness. In this respect, Teilhard shares with posthumanists the presumption that all so-called definitive boundaries are illusory, otherwise the singular destiny he champions cannot be obtained, thereby adding the normative principle of unity to Kaufman's nebulous creativity. One resulting ethical implication is, to say the least, chilling, for any closed relational categories are to be regarded as, at best, transitional, and, at worse, reactionary.

This judgment is seen in Teilhard's refusal to condemn Hitler's and Stalin's regimes as little more than failed experiments in social and political ordering, and his persistent condemnation of realists in their refusal to embrace the obvious benefits of a single world government and global society (Passmore, 1970, pp. 251–8). More telling is his reflection on the significance of the first atomic bomb (Teilhard de Chardin, 1964, pp. 140–48). Although a controlled nuclear chain reaction is employed for the purpose of developing a highly lethal weapon, Teilhard can only praise the event as a consummate display of human intelligence and cooperation. Whatever destruction may result from the use of this new technology does not detract from the grandeur of what has been achieved, for humankind has demonstrated that it now has the capability to direct its own evolution toward the Omega Point in a purposeful manner. In this respect, Grant's characterization of Teilhard as the 'flatterer to modernity' (Grant, 1969, p. 44) is correct, for a mushroom cloud is simply a symbolic expression of human mastery and creativity.

Hefner's created co-creator seemingly provides a corrective lens for Teilhard's impaired theological and moral vision. Created co-creators should not employ their scientific knowledge and technological skill to negate differences that presumably enable greater mastery and unity. Rather, such knowledge and skill should be used to promote natural, social and political ecologies that promote the flourishing of life in its multiple expressions. Teilhard is right in acknowledging the unity of creation, but it is an underlying feature, not a guiding force or principle. He is also right in commending social and political systems that seek to unify rather than divide, but this commendation does not justify the curt dismissal of atrocities as failed or misguided experiments. Although one can admire the scientific achievement and cooperation entailed in the Manhattan Project, one is properly appalled by its product given its power to decimate life-promoting ecologies. In short, the destiny of cosmic consciousness must not be an excuse to divert attention from the immediate concerns that created co-creators are called to address. Thus Hefner revises Teilhard's moral imperative, to read: be ecologically co-creative!

It is, however, a misty imperative. Since Hefner builds upon Peacocke's theological anthropology, it shares all the liabilities examined above. His creator God is, at the end of the day, Kaufman's symbolic 'God' of creativity. Hefner implicitly admits this by explaining that the appended adjective *created* refers simply to the 'conditionedness of the human being' (Hefner, 1993, p. 36).[2] And as Kaufman demonstrates, we can get along very nicely, indeed better, without a creator God posing as a cosmic being. This raises a perplexing dilemma for Hefner: with whom or what are we *co*-creating? Presumably it is with our own symbolic expression of the 'God' of creativity, and if this symbol is to have any content then it must refer to human *biocultural* history as the preeminent emergent feature of biological and cultural evolution.

In coining this neologism Hefner admits that nature and artifice are no longer distinguishable or definitive categories. The fate of life on earth depends increasingly on this bioculture, which, given its formative impetus in technology, is more aptly described as *biotechnoculture*. Consequently, Hefner's created co-creator is really the self-created creator; the being that is now transcending and directing the evolutionary processes from which it has emerged. Hefner can thereby celebrate that humans have already become cyborgs, but he cannot take the next step of affirming, because he fails to acknowledge, that the future belongs to the posthuman. Nor can his moral imperative offer any normative guidance regarding how we should undertake this self-transformation. For in appealing to the protection of various ecologies that promote the flourishing of life, he is attempting to somehow correlate the ever-changing manipulation of these ecologies with manipulators engaged in ongoing self-construction; he is simultaneously pursuing both a moving target and floating archer.

At best, Hefner offers some prudential considerations in constructing a posthuman world. In appealing to ecological 'wholesomeness' (ibid., p. 42) he is pleading that more, rather than less, emphasis be placed on the 'bio' dimension of the emerging technoculture. Furthermore, he appeals to the good example of Jesus' life and ministry as providing some useful guidance for morally and politically ordering the integral relationship among various natural and social ecologies. Yet it is a hard distinction to maintain since he has already collapsed nature and culture into a single category, subject to the willful control of the cyborgs we have already become. The good example of Jesus can therefore serve as nothing more than a rhetorical or emotive flourish, because he embodies no concrete *telos* other than the satiated desire of self-transformation. As Hefner readily concedes, our actions can be telemonic but never teleological (ibid., pp. 39–40), so there is no normative standard against which ecological ordering can be measured and assessed. This lack of any given standards is entailed by Hefner's weak Christology. The relationship between Jesus and God is one in which the second party is a symbolic projection of the first. And this 'God' points back relentlessly to its creator, disclosing that the so-called created co-creator is a self-creating artifact. The necessity to co-create is thereby little more than a disguised version of Kaufman's imperative to be creative, a value that can be easily absorbed into the posthuman lexicon, because its self-referential image is devoid of any objective content. Consequently, Hefner is reduced to pleading that some selected and sanitized traits of Jesus and the subsequent Christian tradition be included in the emerging posthuman, but he is hard pressed to explain what difference this genealogy – or better, genetic insertion – will make in forming a future whose only limits are an assertive imagination and expanding technological capability.

In sum, postmodern theology cannot provide an alternative mode of discourse to that inspired by posthuman discourse, because it has embedded itself deeply in the historicist presuppositions underlying the rhetoric. We create ourselves by creating our history, and in creating that history we recreate ourselves as well. In short, the posthuman is an artifact of its own fabricated horizons. Consequently, postmodernism does not invariably lead to posthuman discourse, but neither is it well equipped to resist it. In readily embracing the postmodern turn, theology enters the posthuman conversation with a few phrases to hock, but no alternative vocabulary and grammar to offer.

This means, however, that theology has also succumbed to the deceit underlying the postmodern world: there is, stated simply, no history to be created. The history late moderns (and presumably early postmoderns) so glibly invoke is itself a modern mythic invention to justify progressive convictions. Science and technology were the harbingers of a new enlightened era, because they enabled humans to form and master the accompanying mythical invention of nature. In this respect, a modern confidence in progress did not displace a belief in providence, but domesticated it by replacing an inscrutable God with rational inquiry and purposive application. The postmodern move entails the additional step of denying any given historical direction other than that willed by its constructors; history denotes a process of self-construction.

If this analysis is at all correct, then it is curious why Christian theology would be enamored with this strand of postmodernism. If history is a mythical invention, then, like any other myth (such as Kaufman's 'God'), it cannot be said to exist in an objective sense. And things that do not exist cannot be said to create, either alone or in partnership. Yet this is precisely the ideological mantel in which postmoderns wrap themselves in justifying their historicist projects. In this respect, Larry Schmidt offers the prescient observation that 'history-making must be viewed as a form of idolatry and loss of faith.' To paraphrase him further: when we die, we do not leave behind the lives we have made. When history comes to an end, humankind will not leave behind any history it has made. To which Schmidt adds the sobering admonition, 'Death is the irrevocable end of time and history' (Schmidt, 1978, p. 138). In embracing the postmodern turn, theology also enters a historicist project that cannot be genuinely creative, much less co-creative, for it joins the illusory undertaking of constructing an immortal history, culminating in the immortal posthuman.

How may we account for this curious embrace? What each of the authors we have surveyed have in common is the absence of a definitive Christology. This does not mean that the name of Jesus Christ is mentioned infrequently, but he is at the periphery rather than the center of their chief theological arguments. For Peacocke, Hefner and Kaufman, Jesus teaches and exemplifies how a good life should be lived. It is not a unique example, however, resulting in any objective theological or moral significance, for Jesus simply embodies a subjective potential that is latent in any other human being. As a result such doctrines as the incarnation, atonement, resurrection and especially the fall are either rejected or given short shrift as symbolic expressions stemming from an outdated worldview. Jesus Christ is thereby stripped of any redemptive significance, for if sin can be said to exist, it is a failure to realize one's potential (Peacocke), or to be creative (Kaufman) or co-creative (Hefner). These are conditions that, at least in principle, can be corrected without recourse to any divine aid. Jesus' death was certainly tragic, perchance heroic, but it (and perhaps the resurrection as well if it can be said to have in any sense occurred) has no salvific purchase other than inspiring humans in their process of historical self-construction. Teilhard's allusions to a cosmic Christ admittedly move us beyond this Jesuology. Yet even this image has no redemptive value, for sin is merely those divisive factors that resist greater unity. In this respect, Christ does not so much inspire as provide a target to aim at, and as such it magnifies latent creative potential that has always been present within the evolutionary process. Humans will become one with Christ through their own self-transformation; the new Adam is a highly enhanced version of the old one.

The rationale for these revisionist Christologies is purportedly to make Christian theology more intelligible in light of science. If this were merely the case, however, one wonders why any theology claiming to be postmodern has so easily granted this methodology such epistemological authority. Can we not also say that an attenuated Christology is the price that must be paid to make faith palatable to the postmodern project of constructing an immortal history? If there is no gulf separating the necessary and the good, and eternity does not define and delineate the temporal, then there is no need for a reconciler. Indeed, such a being could only engender hostility, because admitting any need for reconciliation would challenge the veracity and efficacy of endless self-creation. The price of admission into postmodernity is to replace the good and eternal God with a technical rationality that enframes a resulting ontology, for technology is the concrete means through which a history culminating in the immortal posthuman will be created (Heidegger, 1977, pp. 3–49).

The price extracted, however, is dear, for it robs Christian theology of any counter discourse with which to engage an emerging posthuman world in a critical and constructive manner. To mute, much less discard, the centrality of its salvific message is to also jettison its very *raison d'être*. For humans are in need of being saved from the tyranny of attempting to construct a destiny that can only be properly received as a gift; a good and eternal gift. Consequently, a redemptive Christology is central to any discourse on the present state and future prospects of the human condition, because it is commentary on the belief that 'time and history already participate in the eternity of God' (Schmidt, 1978, p. 138). Any effort to create something immortal, be it history or posthuman beings, serves only to distance ourselves further from the Word that was present when time began, and will also be there at the end when time is fulfilled. The revisionist Christologies proffer a half-truth: Peacocke, Hefner and Kaufman can only offer a Jesus whose good life ends in the agony of Golgotha, while Teilhard wants an ascended Christ without bothering to linger at Good Friday and Easter Sunday.

Can an alternative theological framework be developed that enables a more genuinely critical and constructive – and thereby, Christological – engagement with posthuman discourse? The remainder of this chapter, as well as the one following, attempts to answer that question.

Beginning with Christ ...

The Incarnation is the mainstay of Christology. As formulated at Nicaea, Jesus Christ is fully God and fully human. Jesus experienced the finite and mortal limits inherent to the human condition, yet in being raised from the dead into the eternal life of God these limits are transcended. Or employing terminology used in preceding discussions, necessity and temporality have been enframed and transformed in and through Christ. It is Easter Sunday that marks the destiny of creation and its creatures.

Given its underlying and formative philosophical categories, the Nicaean formula has been subjected to periodic revisions in response to changing intellectual milieus (Shults, 2003). In this respect, the theologians examined above and in the previous chapter stand within a tradition of doctrinal criticism and reformulation. In making the postmodern move, however, their subsequent and substantive revisions effectively dismantle the Nicaean formula. In the case of Peacocke, Hefner and Kaufman, Christology has been jettisoned in favor of a Jesuology. The good example of Jesus' life, teaching and ministry provides a model that can, in principle, be emulated by anyone, for there is no ontological difference between Jesus and any other human being. Since Jesus' story in effect ends with Good Friday, there is no resurrected and exalted Christ that serves as a normative *telos* for ordering the desires, aspirations and lives of believers. Jesus may be said to live on in the hearts of his followers as a creative source of inspiration for their self-transformation, a claim that is akin to the transhumanist goal of becoming posthuman. Teilhard certainly extends the story beyond Good Friday. His cosmic Christ is *the telos* drawing all of creation toward the Omega Point of complete, self-conscious unity. The extension is achieved, however, by severing any direct link with the story's preceding chapters. Christ is an abstract principle hovering above temporal necessity, but never quite touching it. The crucifixion and resurrection is a disappearing act, culminating in the mysterious appearance of an exalted Christ as a principle of universal union. At best Jesus is a kind of divine virus stimulating an inherent human potential to aspire toward self-divination, a goal quite at home within the confines of posthuman discourse.

The purpose of the following inquiry is to construct a rudimentary framework of an alternative Christology that endeavors to explicate the chief claim of the Nicaean formula in light of the postmodern distortions enumerated above. This limited objective is achieved by focusing on the death, resurrection and exaltation of Jesus Christ as the three-part culmination of the Incarnation.[3] In pursuing this inquiry I draw and expand upon the work of Oliver O'Donovan.

According to O'Donovan, the resurrection of Jesus Christ from the dead is the centerpiece of Christian moral deliberation and theological discourse. There are two reasons why this is the case. First, in raising Jesus from the dead, God vindicated Jesus' life and ministry. Moreover, since God is incarnate in this human life, the vindication extends to all of creation. Since humans were not 'allowed to uncreate what God created' (O'Donovan, 1986, p. 14), there is a created moral order that may be discerned because it has been vindicated by its creator. Consequently, the resurrection cannot be invoked as a theological claim and moral principle in isolation from the crucifixion, otherwise Easter Sunday is simply the validation of one man, and not the vindication of a creation that the incarnate one came to save. In keeping with apostolic teaching, the resurrection of Christ entails the resurrection of humankind and with it creation's renewal.

Second, Jesus' resurrection from the dead discloses creation's destiny. A vindicated creation does not imply that attention is fixated solely on origin and subsequent history. There is a proleptic trajectory revealed in the resurrection of the incarnate one, signifying creation's destiny in the exalted Christ. Consequently, the resulting ethic is teleological rather than restorationist, for God's vindicated creation is not headed toward a return to Eden, but toward a New Jerusalem. Creation and its creatures will be transformed over time, and human acts will contribute toward this transformation. Yet it is a transformation shaped by creation's *telos* in Christ, and not by attempts to overcome the limits of natural and historical necessities. The creator who vindicates a temporal creation will also redeem it in the fullness of time. Again, the resurrection cannot be invoked in isolation from the ascension, for otherwise Easter Sunday is merely an anomaly, and not *the* sign of a created order that has been redeemed by the incarnate one.

What exactly is this created order and destiny that Christ's resurrection has in the former instance vindicated, and in the latter vouchsafed? The concept of 'creation', as opposed to creativity, already implies an order rather than 'undifferentiated energy', for a creation *per se* does not refer to 'raw material out of which the world as we know it is composed, but as the order and coherence *in* which it is composed' (ibid., p. 31, emphasis original). In addition, a creation implies that it is ordered to its creator. Created order is thereby relational, reflecting its triune creator. More importantly, this relational quality is a crucial component of any objective order, for in its absence all we would have is a series of monadic, 'unconnected universes' rather than a single universe (ibid., p. 32). The parts comprising creation are related to each other, as well as to the whole of creation. O'Donovan characterizes this relational ordering as 'generic' and 'teleological' (ibid., pp. 32–5). Generic order denotes an equivalent derived from a shared status as creatures, whose relations are ordered within the confines of given purposes. Vegetables, for instance, may be said to be ordered as food for humans. These purposes, however, are not in turn generic, interchangeable or universal. There is no inherently teleological relation, for example, between fish and fire, nor are women naturally ordered to serve men.

It is not surprising that these generic and teleological relations differ within particular circumstances, and change over time. Rather, it would be alarming if these relations were identical and remained fixed, for they represent pluriform expressions of creation's underlying and vindicated order. The unity of created order that Christ both vindicates and fulfills does not negate difference; as Augustine insisted, women and men remain as such when they are joined with their Lord in their Sabbath rest (Augustine, 1984, pp. 1057–8). Consequently, the diversity Teilhard fears is not a threatening constraint to be overcome through self-transformation, nor is it a summons to impose evolutionary order through ongoing creativity or co-creativity. In this respect, the late modern 'belief in "continuous creation"' is merely the latest round in rejecting any prospect of a created order unfolding providently over time (O'Donovan, 1986, pp. 61–2). The task at hand is instead to order creation's pluriformity in accordance with its vindication and destiny in Christ.

What exactly is this destiny? No precise answer can be given, because no one, save God, has beheld the end of creation, but as the author of the Letter to the Hebrews reminds us, we have seen Jesus. We see in Christ the 'vindication and perfect manifestation of the created order which was always there but never fully expressed' (ibid., p. 53). Moreover, since it is through the same Christ that creation is created and redeemed, his victory over death and exaltation also discloses humankind as it is meant to be. The 'future age' will disclose a renewed 'created order as God intended it to be' (ibid., p. 54). Although we cannot perceive or imagine a renewed creation in its entirety, we can encounter a glorified Christ that anticipates this renewal. It is therefore crucial that theology speak about the redemption of creation as a whole instead of the salvation of humans, otherwise its hope is Gnostic rather than Christian. Specifically, this hope refers to a created order, and not just selected creatures, because it 'suggests the recovery of something given and lost' (ibid., p. 54). It is equally crucial to emphasize, however, that this redemptive hope is one of eschatological transformation, and not restoration; the new creation originates but does not return to Eden. As O'Donovan insists, 'The eschatological transformation of the world is neither the mere repetition of the created world nor its negation. It is its fulfilment, its *telos* or end' (ibid., p. 55). Genuine history, as opposed to late modern and postmodern historicism, has a given meaning and direction that can be understood and described as an overarching narrative, one that can be drawn toward its eschatological end rather than driven by its natural origins. Consequently, Christ's resurrection is the ground of Christian moral theology, because this event vindicates, redeems and transforms creation. The varying emphases of the Gospels suggest the central position of Easter Sunday between Good Friday and Ascension Day. Luke and John, for instance, look back from the resurrection and ascension, whereas Matthew and Mark look forward from the crucifixion and resurrection. These complementary emphases are needed because in Christ's vindication of created order, creation is both redeemed *and* transformed. In this respect, a theological understanding of destiny is more a matter of trust than a goal to be achieved (Pannenberg, 1994, pp. 228–9).

Consequently, the postmodern stress on emergent change and posthuman emphasis on transformation are correct but incomplete. Contrary to Teilhard, creation's unity will not be achieved through evolutionary engineering culminating in cosmic self-consciousness. Rather, given creation's origin in Christ, it unfolds over time and is enfolded in its *telos* that is also Christ. The necessity and temporality of creation which is inherently pluriform is made one in Christ's eternity and goodness. In this respect, Christ's resurrection simultaneously vindicates the crucifixion as an act of reconciliation, and anticipates the exaltation of creation's risen lord and savior. Contrary to Peacocke, Hefner and Kaufman, creation is not only contingent, open-ended and serendipitous, but also convergent. It is not surprising, given our temporal perspective, that a pluriform creation changes over time. Evolutionary change *per se*, however, does not exclude what may be characterized as a teleological influence of subsequent development. This is especially the case with the emergence of life in which the presumption of radical contingency and open-endedness is particularly vulnerable to critique on both scientific and philosophical grounds (Morris, 2003). The pathways open to the evolution of life are also convergent, thereby constraining the number and structure of future options open to future evolutionary development. Although the origins of life appear accidental, its subsequent evolutionary pathway is not a series of entirely chance accidents. Suspending teleology from scientific investigation is a proper methodological move, not a metaphysical imposition. The theological claim that the world is grounded in a vindicated created order being drawn toward its end in Christ is an arguable assertion that does not deny the evolutionary character of the unfolding creation over time.

Two salient strands of O'Donovan's theological framework lend themselves in particular to this inquiry. First, his 'natural ethic' (O'Donovan, 1986, pp. 16–21) overcomes the historicist presumptions of posthuman discourse. A created order encompassing creation provides an objective reference point for moral, social and political ordering. Contrary to posthuman discourse, moral judgments are not acts one is free to either perform or refrain from performing. Rather, one may choose to either conform to or rebel against an objective moral order. 'The way the universe *is*, determines how man *ought* to behave himself in it' (ibid., p. 17, emphasis original). Consequently, moral truth is not the exclusive possession of Christians, suggesting there are certain virtues that should be universally practiced. Human nature, malleable or otherwise, has no meaning if there is no larger nature within which it is embedded, and from which normative principles can be derived. In this respect, O'Donovan shares an affinity with natural law (ibid., pp. 85–6), but he does not believe that normative principles can be discerned and applied in the absence of revelation. It is in and through Christ that nature, which Christians properly name *creation*, discloses its vindicated order.

Such discernment enables humans to participate in created order, which is in turn grounded in and mediated through Jesus Christ. There is, then, no neutral explication of morality, for all inquiry is shaped by a series of overt or covert religious convictions. Theological inquiry in particular is cosmic in scope, because we can only gain some perspective of created order in the totality of relations among pluriform particulars, so we must also 'grasp the "shape" of the whole' in order to discern the moral meaning of the particulars (ibid., pp. 76–8). Yet given the finite and temporal limits of human existence, knowledge of the whole can only be obtained within it, and this knowledge in turn is gained only from participating in what is known. We can acquire some transcendent knowledge of the particulars in which we participate but not the whole of created order, except in partial terms through revelation. Specifically, it is by way of their position within creation that humans learn their proper role for participating in created order, and thus the normative location that has been assigned to humankind. Revelation is, therefore, the requisite starting-point for moral deliberation and discernment, for we can only 'understand the whole from a central point within it' (ibid., p. 85). Moreover, such revelatory knowledge discloses the goodness of the created order that cannot be displaced or destroyed by historicist construction, for it is a knowledge 'given to us as we participate in the life of Jesus Christ' (ibid., p. 85). Christ, in short, is *the* point of knowing the whole of created order from within the pluriform particulars of creation, so that true 'knowledge of the moral order is knowledge "in Christ"' (ibid., p. 85; cf Barth, 1958).

This revelatory prerequisite leads to O'Donovan's second strand of *obedient freedom* (O'Donovan, 1986, pp. 22–7). With Christ's resurrection 'we look not only back to the created order' but also 'forwards to our eschatological participation in that order' (ibid., p. 22). In the absence of this dual orientation, we become enslaved to a false perception of nature in which any natural moral order can only be perceived as threatening. Finite and temporal limits are thereby inimical to one's survival and flourishing; hence the posthuman imperative to overcome these limits through self-transformation (Pannenberg, 1994, p. 230). This process is based on the false assumption that freedom is expanded by transcending finite and temporal limits. The project is thereby enslaving for it leads to the 'incapacity to obey', and as incapacitated creatures, humans disfigure their proper dominion of creation into a domination of nature in encountering the threats of finitude and temporality (O'Donovan, 1986, p. 23). By participating in creation's eschatological destiny, however, these threats are exposed as given limits that define and order human lives; we are free to love our fate, because it has already been taken up into the eternity of our creator and redeemer. In this respect, true freedom is a gift of the Spirit that frees us to be obedient to the definitive limits which delineate our lives as finite creatures.

The temporal task of ordering creation's pluriform particulars must come to terms with these defining and formative limits, for they are either inherent aspects of created order and should be honored as such, or they are accidental features of an emergent evolutionary process and may be (dis)regarded as such. Opting for one alternative over the other is a crucial point of departure, for the decision shapes a subsequent pattern of moral deliberation leading, respectively, to obedient freedom or indulgent servitude. In the former instance, Christ's vindication of created order provides the foundation of a natural ethic in which these finite limits enjoy a presumptive normative status. In O'Donovan's words, 'Knowledge of the natural order *is moral knowledge*, and as such it is co-ordinated with *obedience*' (ibid., p. 87, emphasis added). Moreover, we come to know this order by participating in it, and ordering our lives in accordance with its structures and strictures. Our knowledge of natural order is admittedly imperfect and distorted by sin – and thus our obedient response is also imperfect and distorted – but we continue to know created moral order, for the 'image of God is "defaced" but not "lost"' (ibid., p. 87; cf Pannenberg, 1994, p. 228). Non-believers, for instance, are not ignorant of the veracity of such virtues as honesty and fidelity. This knowledge is incomplete, however, because created order cannot be discerned unless creation is grasped as a whole, and the efficacy of such a holistic vision requires acknowledgment of a creator. 'If the Creator is not known, then the creation is not known *as creation*, for the relation of the creation to its Creator is the ground of its intelligibility as a created universe' (O'Donovan, 1986, p. 88, emphasis original). Created order cannot be known in absence from its creator, otherwise idolatry, manifested as ideology, is the result (ibid., pp. 88–9; cf Ellul, 1985, pp. 172–81). Consequently, outside of Christ's revelation there is no genuine knowledge of reality, for a fragmentary knowledge of pluriform particulars has no moral meaning if they are not related to the whole of creation.

This knowledge of reality as the whole of creation is in stark contrast to the fragmentary knowledge presupposed by posthuman discourse. The posthumanist encounters a world of fragments, in which any appearance of order is tentative. These temporary patterns are imposed by a nexus of natural processes and technological manipulation; the difference between natural selection and willful construction is one of degree, not kind. The operative principle is that order is *always an imposed consequence* of perpetual change. This means that change itself is premised on a violent process of destroying antecedent patterns of order in constructing new ones. There is, however, no objective reference point, either natural or revealed, to judge the moral efficacy of new and emergent patterns. Consequently, the postmodern imperative of creativity is circular and self-referential, for we cannot judge the efficacy of an act until the deed has been done.

In contrast, the attempt to 'grasp the whole shape of things' presupposes a created order underlying a pluriform creation (O'Donovan, 1986, p. 91). Ethics, then, is not a process of accumulating moral insight or creating new values, but a matter of vision and changed perception of what is being envisioned. Moral truth is encountered, not constructed. 'One cannot *add* moral truth to moral truth; one can only *repent* false perceptions of the moral and turn to truer ones' (ibid., p. 92, emphasis original). When it is believed that moral truth can be accumulated, then artistic expressions and narrative accounts do not express and narrate the truth of an objective reality, which form and against which our acts should be conformed, but are attempts to impose order upon fragments comprising the world. It is the ability to repent that enables us to conform our lives to created order, and thereby to the one whose death and resurrection vindicated it. The conflict which led to Jesus' death and resurrection is not a mythical struggle between good and evil, but a conflict over true and false renderings of a single reality. The repentance entailed in following Christ signifies the acknowledgment of both truth and falsehood, and the subsequent commitment to discern the difference between true and false patterns of conduct. The cross and empty tomb indicate that obedience to God cannot ultimately coexist with disobedience.

Obedient freedom does not imply slavish conformity; to be conformed to Christ does not mean that all of Christ's followers are produced from a single template. Rather, the freedom to obey God is a gift of the Spirit who can be neither mastered nor manipulated. It is this formative life in the Spirit that discloses Good Friday, Easter Sunday and Ascension Day as the three-part culmination of the Incarnation that both shapes creation's unfolding history and enfolds it within God's eternal destiny. It is also in the life of the Spirit that past and future are at hand in each present moment. Christ's vindication of created order is a past event, but the fullness of creation's redemption lies in the future. As O'Donovan emphasizes, 'on these two points, the resurrection of Jesus Christ from the dead and his parousia, the whole of our life is made to depend even now, as each moment of it successively forms our present' (ibid., p. 102). The pattern of our life in Christ is formed between the polls of a 'remembered past' and 'unthinkable future' (ibid., pp. 102–3). It is this collapsing of time in the Spirit that frees the believer to both consent to and transcend the temporal and necessary constraints of finitude, for it is the eternal God that creates, enframes and redeems these limitations. Such freedom does not suggest a Gnostic escape or liberation from material constraints, for freedom implies the ability to act in ways that affirm the truth and goodness of a temporal and finite creation that has been vindicated by Christ. Yet neither do our free acts endorse the Pelagian conceit of an ability to perfect or transform ourselves, for this would mean that we, and not God, determine what is good and true about the world.

The practical import of obedient freedom is that it grants us genuine subjectivity. Since the Spirit evokes our free response to the reality of creation's vindication and redemption in Christ, then the Spirit also enables our willing and working in accordance with what is true. Freedom is thereby grounded in and manifested by the character of those participating in the temporal ordering of creation, particularly in respect to its underlying created order as revealed in Christ. Without the freedom of being conformed to Christ, moral ordering and action becomes an alienated enterprise of creating and selecting from a wide array of options. Freedom becomes a quantifiable possession that can be measured by the absence of external restrictions upon one's will. The freest person is ideally an autonomous monad. Freedom, however, is properly a descriptive statement about persons rather than a set of circumstances. To be free is not determined by the 'absence of limits,' because it refers to 'potency' instead of 'possibility' (ibid., pp. 107–8). Exercising one's freedom requires eliminating certain possibilities in favor of others, not creating more options. In this respect, freedom has more to do with foreclosing than pursuing possible courses of action. If an actualized possibility is to be, in any meaningful sense, freely chosen, then it must be defined and delineated by a sense of limits. In the absence of these limits, no genuinely free choice can be made. Consequently, creating a greater range of options or possibilities decreases the competency of the one choosing. The issue at stake, then, is not choosing *per se*. What is at stake is what is affirmed by the choice. Suicide, for instance, 'may be a free act, but it is not an act that affirms freedom' (ibid., p. 108). The endless options propounded by posthuman rhetoric for the sake of self-transformation do not result in freedom, but an indulgent servitude to pointless production and consumption.

What rescues our choices from such pointlessness and makes them genuinely free by being obedient is the reality of a vindicated created order that authorizes our moral agency. As O'Donovan has observed, 'Authority is the objective correlate of freedom' (ibid., p. 122). We cannot act without the commission *and* constraints of some authority, and such authority is not a theoretical construct, but embodies concrete structures instantiated in the reality of the world's created order. Otherwise, our moral choices would be neither obedient nor free. Moreover, 'since freedom is not indeterminacy or randomness but purposive action, that means describing the world as a place in which actions may have ends, that is to say, as a teleological system' (ibid., p. 122). It is the *telos* or end that determines whether a particular act is moral or immoral, because the *telos* or end authorizes that certain acts should be undertaken, necessitating in turn the foreclosure of other options. It is as a teleological system that the pluriform particulars of creation are ordered to each other over time in ways that provide continuity while accommodating change. Political action, for example, is ordered to justice, an enduring concept which instantiates the rule of law but has been expanded over time to embrace such excluded groups as women and slaves (ibid., pp. 127–30; see also O'Donovan, 1996, pp. 82–119; cf Arendt, 1998, pp. 22–78, Elshtain, 1981).

It is important to emphasize that a teleological system is *not* synonymous with a consequentialist ethic. Despite historicist presumptions to the contrary, it is not the consequences of an act alone that determines whether it is good or bad. If this were the case, then the *telos* or end of an act would be little more than an agent's projected goal, thereby reducing ethics to a self-referential will. Rather, the *telos* or end is a given that orders particular acts accordingly. A teleological system is an objective reality shaping subjectivity, not the result of subjective projection and construction.[4] The objective point of reference for the teleological system being explicated in this inquiry is creation and its vindicated created order. Consequently, the operational principle underlying the natural ethic is one of exercising authoritative judgment instead of asserting personal choice (O'Donovan, 1986, pp. 104–105). In short, we make judgments in regard to how patterns of moral, social and political ordering fit with the dictates of created order and creation's destiny in Christ. As sinners who cannot discern Christ's revelation with perfect clarity, our judgments will often be flawed, erroneous and subject to revision; hence the need for conversion and instruction. In implementing these judgments we also make choices, some we may come to affirm and others we may come to regret; hence the need for repentance, forgiveness and grace. The moral task at hand is not to create new values in response to changing historical horizons of our own making, but to conform our judgments to the vindicated created order in its temporal unfolding. Consequently, postmodern theology – at least the kind examined in this chapter and the preceding one – cannot provide a *telos* for posthuman discourse, because its implicit imperative is circular rather than teleological. To be creative or co-creative for the sake of creativity is, quite literally, pointless, for it directs moral action in no particular direction. Co-creators fashion a world to their liking, in the process recreating themselves as well. But when pressed to assert what end all this frenetic creativity will ultimately achieve or what purpose it serves, the best answer that can be offered is that no one, not even God, knows. In light of such a hollow theological answer, the posthuman goal of virtual immortality at least attempts to fill the void.

The chief benefit of this conceptual framework inspired by O'Donovan's account of Christ's vindication of created order is that it enables a critical recovery of traditional theological themes in developing a counter discourse to that offered by posthuman rhetoric. The operative principle in this process is that the recovery is *critical*. The goal is not to merely reassert traditional theological claims, but to amend them in light of the modern and postmodern critiques examined in the preceding chapters. The following inquiry initiates this critical recovery by examining briefly the theological themes of providence and anthropology.

Providence

Prior to the rise of modern science, the fate of humankind was seemingly at the mercy of natural and historical events, controlled by a capricious creator God. Modern science disclosed, however, that this perceived inscrutability was the result of ignorance, not divine whimsy. As knowledge about the laws governing nature and history increased, humans could assert greater mastery over their own fate. In this respect, progress displaced providence as the central principle of social and political ordering, and correspondingly, science displaced theology as the primary form of public moral discourse guiding this ordering.[5]

The postmodern move rejected this progressive impulse. The world really was a chaotic place, even more erratic than the champions of providence had dared to imagine. There are no ironclad laws governing either nature or history. Humans are the result of evolutionary accidents, and history is merely a subjective interpretation of past events and future aspirations. Whatever meaning human existence can be said to possess, it is severely constrained by temporal and finite limits. Consequently, the fate of humankind depends on its ability to overcome these limits by erasing and redrawing natural and historical boundaries. In the postmodern process of reconstructing nature and history, humans transform themselves as well, thereby providing a rationale for posthuman discourse. In this respect, progress has been jettisoned in favor of process as the operative principle of social construction and self-transformation, and correspondingly, technology is displacing science as the principal source of formative public discourse.[6]

If a critical recovery of providence is to succeed, then a satisfactory theological account of how change is to be interpreted and purposively enacted over time within a teleologically ordered creation must be undertaken. Such an account must, on the one hand, reject the postmodern presumption that the world is ultimately a product of historicist construction while, on the other hand, avoiding the modernist trap of achieving progressive change through the accumulative mastery of the laws governing nature and history. In other words, humans act in ways that shape the pattern of their individual and collective lives over time, but these acts are limited and delineated by the temporal constraints of finitude and necessity. Posed as a question: how may we account for a providential unfolding of created order over time in respect to human acts ordering nature and history that cannot be described as being entirely determined or entirely free?

Peacocke may seem to offer a satisfactory reply in his contention that order emerges out of the interplay between chance and law. His argument, however, leaves no room for providence, for the creator he invokes is not the eternal God. Peacocke's God transcends the future, but does so as an emergent symbol of this interplay which cannot know the future, or direct the world's eventual outcome. Consequently, finitude has no inherent normative value that can guide the construction of nature and history. All Peacocke has to offer is a pragmatic ethic that can only determine the efficacy of acts after the fact. It is only in retrospect, for instance, that we will be able to determine whether inoculations or splitting atoms prove to be good or bad. Consequently, he also has nothing to counter posthuman discourse. He cannot judge in advance whether such extensive self-transformation *in principle* is right or wrong, because he has no account of what humans are properly ordered to be, and to become. Other than perhaps a precautionary warning, he must reserve moral evaluation until after the enterprise has been undertaken. A commitment to an emergent and radically open future leads to an ethic in which a constantly changing future can only judge a constantly revised past, but has little to offer in guiding the course of future moral trajectories. It is, moreover, a frustrating and anemic ethic as demonstrated in Peacocke's unconvincing attempt to respect the integrity of natural ecologies, because they enable human survival and flourishing.[7] Such environmental valuing, however, may very well plummet as humans become posthuman, so that any so-called ecological integrity has no normative claim upon the present, because it is not grounded in any underlying order linking it teleologically with the future.

William G. Pollard's theological inquiry into providence offers a potentially more promising account of the relationship between law and chance. He rejects, on biblical grounds, the notion that God acts or intervenes in ways which violate scientific laws of nature (Pollard, 1958, pp. 25–34). Rather, it is within the realm of history that God may be said to act in ways that influence the course of human events over time (ibid., pp. 64–88). History, to a far greater extent than nature, is the product of chance and accident. Contrary to determinists who contend that history could only have occurred the way it did, Pollard insists that a wide range of alternative courses could have been taken. Each step in history faces innumerable choices. Once a choice is made other options are foreclosed, but then a new set of options are opened. History, therefore, is 'like a vast and intricate maze through which creation has threaded its way' (ibid., p. 67). Although there have been many possible histories, the existing pattern is the only one available to us, and since it is a non-repeatable process it cannot be subjected to experimental control. There are, in short, no laws governing history equivalent to those governing nature.

Pollard admits that his portrayal of history appears anarchical, but it is against this chaotic background that God may be said to act in a singular manner that directs the emergence of a particular historical pattern (ibid., pp. 94–5). This divine action cannot be discerned through scientific methodologies that are dedicated to identifying and charting statistical probabilities (ibid., pp. 39–60). God's singular act in a non-repeatable process is not subject to any statistical probability. Pollard's chief contention, in this respect, is that God's providential governance of history can only be revealed (ibid., pp. 85–6). Providence is not a template of history, but more akin to a lens through which believers perceive the historical unfolding of created order. Consequently, Christians see the 'chances and accidents of history as the very warp and woof of the fabric of providence which God is ever weaving' (ibid., p. 71). In the absence of revelation, history appears as little more than a chronology of anarchy. In Christ, however, a reliable historical trajectory is revealed which Christians may call providential.

Pollard takes us a long way in recovering a providential understanding of history as a viable alternative to the postmodern theological emphasis on a radically open and contingent world. He agrees with postmodern theologians that randomness and chance characterize biological and cultural evolution, but his construal of providence as singular acts of God in a non-repeatable historical process introduces the prospect of convergence. Because of these acts, human evolution and history are not as open and contingent as postmodern theologians claim, because certain possible destinies have already been foreclosed by antecedent choices and events. Moreover, the Incarnation is not confined to Jesus' exemplary teaching and behavior, but reveals God's providential care for creation and its salvific destiny. Consequently, history is not an artifact constructed by humans to impose evolutionary order, but a temporal realm in which humans, through their various choices and acts, respond to God's will as revealed by Christ.

Pollard, however, does not take us far enough in recovering providence as a cornerstone of a counter discourse, for he can only offer the foundation of a retrospective ethic: 'It is only in retrospect that the hand of God in the shaping of events is seen and responded to' (ibid., p. 64). The problem with an ethic that is entirely retrospective is that the morality of particular acts can be assessed only after they have been enacted, either materially or imaginatively. Whether creating and cloning human embryos for the purpose of harvesting their stem cells is right or wrong, for instance, can only be determined once a choice to either proceed or refrain from proceeding has been made or seriously contemplated. Only from a retrospective perspective, either actually or theoretically, can the relative merits or demerits of either choice be weighed in determining if a sin of commission or omission has been committed.

Yet if, as Pollard rightly contends, providence requires a response to God's will in making these choices, then it also implies a prospective and teleological ethic. Since God is directing creation toward a particular destiny, then this temporal trajectory should be discernible, albeit imperfectly, as revealed in Christ. Yet Pollard offers few clues as to how revelation might influence moral discernment in a prospective manner. O'Donovan's natural ethic helps correct this deficiency. In vindicating created order, Christ also discloses the teleological ordering of its pluriform aspects, although our temporal perception is again imperfect. Hence moral deliberation is not a process of assessing every possible outcome to every possible act or response, but a narrowing of moral vision within and aligning specific acts to the parameters of teleologically ordered relationships. It is important to stress, however, that this vindication does not constitute a radical alteration of creation, but a disclosure and fulfillment of its created order. The task is to align moral judgments and choices with what we may call providential patterns within the temporal unfolding of creation. Given this historical trajectory, the natural ethic can thereby account for changes in moral judgment over time as a consequence of corrected vision and reordering of desire, instead of creating and exercising new options; a result of new knowledge and insight gained through repentance and amendment, rather than responses *de novo* to emerging or novel circumstances.

In respect to the prospect of producing and cloning human embryos for the purpose of extracting their stem cells, for instance, the moral task is not to formulate new values and creatively novel responses to this technological potential. If this were the case, then the creation of every embryo would seemingly require an assessment of its every possible use and fate. Moral deliberation and discernment would effectively become an *ad hoc* process of isolated and inconsistent instances instead of a pattern of accumulated wisdom and judgment. Each particular embryo would be assessed in isolation from any normative framework, stripping it away from any generic ordering. The embryo is thereby effectively reduced to a commodity, whose use and value is assigned by its owner. Rather, the task at hand is to deliberate on human embryos as a generic kind which is ordered to a nexus of natural and cultural relationships. It is in deliberating upon the embryo within this given whole that we narrow our moral vision to a set of relevant considerations regarding its fitting use and fate. Only then can we make judgments of how certain proposed technological applications of embryos can be said to align with, or distort, the teleological ordering and providential trajectory of these relationships. Such deliberation may prompt repentance and amendment regarding previous perceptions of the embryo, and the choices made in light of the potential applications of cloning and stem cells will undoubtedly trigger subsequent reflection on the sins of commission and omission committed in applying, or refraining from applying, relevant technologies. The emphasis, however, is not on deciding and then assessing the consequences, either real or imagined, but making choices which conform, albeit in imperfect ways, to the providential trajectory of created order as it is being drawn toward its destiny in Christ.

Yet who are these human creatures who make these deliberative choices, and by what authority do they deliberate and choose?

Anthropology

A comprehensive theological anthropology is beyond the scope of this book, but we may explore some suggestive themes that are pertinent to our inquiry. Given the preceding discussion on providence, we may begin by saying that humans are the creatures that God has elected to oversee the providential unfolding of God's creation (Barth, 1960, pp. 3–57; cf Pannenberg, 1994, pp. 35–59). This does not imply that God has authorized humans to master and shape creation in whatever form they might desire. Since they are creatures and not the creator, their oversight is limited; they have been chosen by God to be the agents that align creation to its created order. Humans are not called to be co-creators, for this suggests that creation, and by implication its creator, are dependent upon an autonomous human creativity that is independent of God's providential care. Co-creators too easily distort their rightful dominion that accompanies their election into hubristic domination. Adam and Eve were, after all, created by God to tend Eden, not to co-create it.

Human election is compatible with the principles of biological and cultural evolution. The fact that *Homo sapiens* emerged from antecedent species does not call into question that this species is the one that God has called to order and direct creation toward its appointed destiny. Indeed, since creation is a unified act by an eternal creator who transcends time, human evolution tends to confirm creation's pluriform character, and its redemptive destiny as a whole (Pannenberg, 1994, pp. 112–14). Moreover, cultural evolution serves to clarify what human election means in light of creation's temporal and providential unfolding. We may say that it is with the emergence of differentiated cultures that humans simultaneously embrace their election, while disclosing the world's underlying created order. It is within the integral nexus of nature *and* history that humans assume and perform their providential calling of ordering creation to its vindicated order. It is precisely in and through culture that humans, as natural creatures, become aware of and embedded in a created history, as opposed to a historicist construction, in which past and future are made objectively real and present.

Consequently, late modern and postmodern accounts of the relation between nature and history are to be rejected, because both attempt to negate the former by asserting the primacy of the latter. Late moderns attempt to master nature in order to gain as much advantage as possible over the constraints of finite and temporal necessity, while postmoderns are dedicated to eventually eliminating these constraints by absorbing nature into a comprehensive project of historicist construction. In both cases, culture becomes a convenient shorthand signifying on the one hand, mastery gained through an expanding knowledge and application of the laws of nature, and on the other hand, a limitless creativity achieved through the elimination of all natural boundaries and historical borders. In both instances, humans are reduced to assertive and fabricated wills that are separated by degree rather than kind. For late moderns, a human person is a cultural artifact produced by various associations and institutions enabling a progressive mastery over natural limitations, while for postmoderns a personality is a self-constructed artifact in which cultural resources are plundered to negate and eliminate natural constraints.

Both late moderns and postmoderns share a fear of finitude, especially as manifested in the inherent limits of being embodied creatures. The body symbolizes the enemy of the will, for its finite and temporal necessity resists all attempts at mastery or negation. Hence finitude can only be encountered as an adversary that can only be overcome, or at least kept at bay, by either mastering or transcending it. Yet to regard finitude as an enemy is to void human volition of any normative content, for it ignores the eternal origin and destiny that enframes temporal existence and thereby bestows it with its meaning and direction over time. If finitude is nothing other than a threat, then all humans can do, in both their late modern and postmodern ideological expressions, is to launch futile sorties against an unconquerable foe.

This endless war implies that finitude is somehow inherently evil. This is a curious assumption. Since evolution can presumably produce only finite creatures, it must itself be terribly flawed. Hence humans must take control of their own evolution in order to correct an inept process of natural selection. This strategy, however, begs the question, is there any reason to assume that the creatures produced by evolution can perfect a process that seemingly can only produce finite, and therefore imperfect, creatures? Or, following Wolfhart Pannenberg along a theological line of argument, if finitude is inherently evil, then humans are the product of an inferior creator God (ibid., pp. 161–74). This conclusion is the result of faulty definition, for it is not that finitude is evil, but that evil originates in rebelling against finite limits. It is not because finitude is evil that humans suffer, but rather in fighting against finite limits that humans suffer the evil effects of their rebellious acts. This suffering is especially pronounced in desperate attempts to establish self-sufficient autonomy through mastering nature or self-transformation. Or, in Pannenberg's words, the 'source of suffering and evil lies in the transition from God-given independence to self-independence' (ibid., p. 172). The strategies adopted respectively by late moderns and postmoderns (especially posthumanists) can only exacerbate the scope of suffering, because they reject the very source of dependence upon God, that in turn grants them the independence they rightfully seek. It is only in accepting their finite limits that humans may encounter and have fellowship with the eternal God.

It is in consenting to their finitude, then, that humans also embrace their election. God has chosen humans *as creatures* who derive their being from, and are sustained by, God's good creation and its created order. As creatures their lives are delineated by finite and temporal limitations that, to reinforce Pannenberg's salient point, are not to be regarded as imperfections that God has elected humans to correct. Humans do not experience evil and suffering because they are imperfect beings; evil and suffering result from dealing with the necessity inherent to their finitude and temporality as creatures. Specifically, much of the evil and suffering endured is a consequence of humans rightfully attempting to differentiate themselves from other creatures and their creator as would be expected in a pluriform creation. This differentiation requires both cooperation and competition over time, again as would be expected given the emergent and convergent qualities of biological and cultural evolution. This differentiated pluriformity is not morally problematic, unless one is prepared to somehow indict natural selection for producing a diverse range of living creatures which are necessarily finite and temporal. Rather, again following Pannenberg, evil and suffering result – or better, sins are committed – when the balance between cooperation and competition is disordered through self-assertion. This self-assertion is, in effect, an aggressive assertiveness against other creatures and ultimately their creator, for what is denied is any limit or dependence on anything greater than the act of self-assertion itself (ibid., pp. 173–4). Practically, this assertive will is expressed through technological development enabling greater mastery over, if not radical transformation of, nature and human nature. Instead of coming to terms with the strictures of necessity, moral, social and political ordering mutates into a technique for converting the necessary into the good, thereby denying or attempting to negate the finite and temporal limits which delineate the form and *telos* of human life within a created order. In this respect, technology becomes an instrument for recreating or uncreating created order, and a striking symbol of rebellion against the creator.

In embracing their divine election humans are liberated to be obedient rather than rebellious. In obedience they consent to their finite and temporal limits as creatures, and order their lives accordingly within the strictures these limits necessitate. Such consent entails the recognition that these limits pose a normative standard rather than arbitrary barriers to be overcome, or imperfections in need of repair. Christ has not rescued human creatures from their finitude and temporality, but has vindicated and redeemed a finite and temporal creation. The normative import of finite and temporal constraints is especially prescient in respect to the body. Since 'flesh and blood' is the object rather than the means of salvation, the creatures being saved are necessarily embodied, and thereby necessarily finite and temporal. Consequently, to deny or disregard the limits imposed by these defining features is also to foreclose the possibility of redemption. The posthuman dream of rescuing the personality (read information) from its embodied captivity is little more than a high-tech Manichean fantasy.

The obedient freedom ensuing from election suggests a dual, though not dualistic, ethic for ordering human acts and aspirations within creation's historical and providential unfolding. These two aspects are complementary while also in tension. On the one hand, there is an impetus to *preserve*. Since Christ's death and resurrection have vindicated created order, there are inherent teleological relationships within the fabric of creation that should be safeguarded. In the absence of any strong commitment to preserve these relationships, the world is reduced to a storehouse of raw resources, rather than a temporal and material outcome of an underlying created order; humans have been appointed by God to preserve creation's pluriformity. Hence Teilhard's distress with a diverse universe is misplaced, for he has mistakenly assumed that it is only through human ingenuity and technological prowess that order can be imposed on an anarchical universe; the challenge is to make the many one. Yet since the universe is the result of created order, then its pluriformity is an expression of its creator's love and providential care; the challenge is to preserve the one so the many can thrive. Moreover, the impetus to preserve is performed by ordering our desires and acts to the mandates of created order, as discerned through the lens of a natural ethic that discloses patterns of generic and teleological ordering. The tasks of moral, social and political ordering entail safeguarding *and* amending institutional embodiments of created order, as opposed to co-creating novel patterns of power and control. Procreation, for example, is properly ordered to such institutions as marriage and family which preserve the integral relationships among spouses, parents and children in stark contrast to co-creative reproduction in which the resulting child (or embryo to be used for non-reproductive purposes) is the outcome of a collaborative reproductive will. The practical issue at stake is not to create or co-create new values justifying the restructuring of reproduction in accordance with the growing technological potential to manipulate human biology, but to evaluate potential technological applications in light of their tendencies to either uphold or weaken the nexus of familial relationships that order procreation.

On the other hand, there is a need to be *prospective*. Safeguarding does not imply a steadfast resistance to change and amendment. The impetus to preserve is tempered and complemented by a need for completion and fulfillment. In Christ's resurrection and ascension, the vindicated created order is fully redeemed; made whole and complete. The very notion of providence requires that created order be headed toward a particular destination. The generic ordering of a pluriform creation derives its meaning and rationale from its *telos* in the exalted Christ. In short, the necessity of finite and temporal limits is stripped of their normative import in the absence of any operative eschatology. Consequently, moral, social and political ordering must also be prospective tasks, seeking to align our acts and desires in accordance with the destiny toward which creation is being drawn. In this respect, Teilhard is right in insisting that Christ is *the* end of the universe, but he is wrong in assuming that this fate is the result of humans asserting ever greater mastery over nature and their own fate. The resurrected Christ is not an artifact of his disciples' creative hopes, but the One who has been vindicated and exalted by the Father. The need to be prospective, then, is not a license for unfettered expression, but a summons to amendment. Although creation is not inherently flawed, neither is it perfect. Hence our election by God to prepare creation for its perfection in Christ. Technology, for instance, can be used prospectively to align creation toward its appointed destiny. It is important to emphasize, however, that we are called to prepare creation for its perfection by Christ, and not to perfect it for Christ's sake. Technologies may be used in ways that transform nature and culture, thereby also transforming their inhabitants. There can be little quarrel, for example, in using genetics and nanotechnology to develop more effective therapies and prosthetics. Yet there are limits to the extent of these transformations if election is not to be voided of any meaningful content, and reduced to a religious cipher blessing creativity for its own sake. Consequently, it is a quarrelsome religious proposition to propose using genetics and nanotechnology to create posthumans. This is an especially pressing issue if Christian theology is to provide a genuinely counter discourse to that offered by posthumanism. Contrary to Hefner, our self-transformation into androgynous cyborgs is not a prospect to be celebrated and blessed, for it marks a callous disregard for the embodied particularity that defines us as finite and temporal creatures, created in the image and likeness of God (Herzfeld, 2002). The disappearance of the particularity that Hefner celebrates is what God wills to redeem and perfect, but *not* negate.

The preceding discussion is admittedly skeletal. Adding flesh and muscle requires that we spend some time examining how eschatology is related to providence and anthropology, and more importantly, how this relation informs an operative ethic that is simultaneously preservationist and prospective. These tasks are undertaken in the final chapter by focusing on the themes of destiny and dominion.

Notes

1 See the previous chapter.
2 For incisive criticisms of the concept of co-creatorship, see Cole-Turner, 1993, pp. 98–103; Deane-Drummond, 2001, pp. 97–101; and Hauerwas, 1995, pp. 109–24.
3 The limited scope and nature of this argument needs to be emphasized. I am using the three-part sequence of death, resurrection and exaltation, for example, for the purpose of inquiry rather than demonstrating its veracity. Consequently, my argument is dogmatic rather than apologetic.
4 A teleological system is admittedly a construct, but it is a construct which seeks to interpret an objective reality that is independent of the interpreter. See McGrath, 2002.
5 See chapter one.
6 See chapter two.
7 Similar attempts by Kaufman and Hefner also suffer this weakness.

CHAPTER SIX

Remaining Creaturely

This concluding chapter has three goals. The first of these is to develop further the theological framework sketched out in the preceding chapter by examining how eschatology is related to the themes of providence and anthropology. This is accomplished in the following section by explicating the concept of *destiny*. Drawing on this theological framework, the second goal is to coin a rudimentary vocabulary and grammar for a counter discourse to that of posthumanism. This task is undertaken in section two by examining selected moral implications of the biblical mandate for humans to exercise *dominion* over creation. The third goal is to demonstrate what practical difference this counter discourse might make in respect to the formation and performance of Christian convictions within an emerging technoculture. This objective is completed in the final section by focusing on the central role of formative *practices*.

... Ending with Christ

It was argued in the previous chapter that Christian theological claims about providence and anthropology are devoid of any meaningful content in the absence of eschatology. If there is no given *telos*, as opposed to a projected goal or objective, then the temporal acts of ordering creation are literally pointless meanderings, because they lack any point of reference for determining a direction over time. There is no eventual destination beyond the horizon, only infinitely more horizons. If there is no given end, then providence is a vacuous doctrine, for there is no created order that can be said to unfold over time, and human acts are reduced to creative self-assertion, because there are no temporal trajectories with which humans may align their desires and will. Without an operative destiny, we remain enslaved to an infinite regress of historicist cultural construction and posthuman self-creation. The postmodern world is headed nowhere because it simply has no place to go; it is not coincidental that 'destination' and 'destiny' are derived from the same root.

It is also not surprising that 'destiny' has been largely expunged from posthuman discourse. Its deletion stems from a presumed dichotomy between openness and determinism. The future is radically contingent, open and indeterminate, or, to the contrary, it is the inevitable outcome of predetermined events and inexorable processes. Given this stark choice, postmoderns and posthumanists have opted for the former.

Postmodern theology has largely endorsed and embraced this choice. The principal reason for this alliance is that a radically open and contingent universe is the final nail in the coffin of a dreadful monster that has haunted

Christian theology, namely, the doctrine of predestination. To speak of providence seemingly requires that one must also invoke this damnable denial of human freedom within an evolving universe. If creation is nothing more than a mechanical playing out of a program that allows no deviation, then novel innovation and freedom are illusory, and creativity is nothing but an empty gesture. Fortunately late modern inquiries into nature and history disclosed a deity that is far less controlling, unfettering postmoderns to pursue their historicist construction of a future of their choosing.

The cost of discovering a more agreeably indulgent 'God' is the effective ejection of providence from the Christian theological lexicon; a bargain given the consequential unleashing of human creativity. The price, however, is higher than it first appears to be, for expunging providence requires an eviscerated eschatology, since postmodern theology does not refute the doctrine of predestination, but sequesters it as an irrelevancy. Rather than attempting to reconcile the eternal with the temporal, the former is summarily dismissed allowing the latter to be dispersed as an endlessly expanding horizon of novel possibilities. Eschatology is reduced to a goal whose pursuit exerts an influence over current perceptions and courses of events. There is no eschaton toward which creation is heading; only fleeting visions of alternative futures. Even Pierre Teilhard de Chardin's breathtaking account of the cosmic Christ is not so much a treatise on destiny as it is an epic poem in praise of evolution's creative power. The Omega Point is a mirror whose refraction enlarges the reflected image of its maker. Postmodern eschatology is, at best, a parody of Paul's puzzling reflections of the future *as if* in a mirror (1 Corinthians 13:12). This mirror, however, is not a medium disclosing tantalizing, but imprecise, images of an eternal destiny. Postmoderns transform Paul's simile into a principle of creative expression in which images are bounced back and forth between the constructed poles of present and future, leading to a process in which the beholder, and simultaneously maker, of both mirrors becomes subsumed into an abyss of infinite regress.

Discarding providence and embracing an eviscerated eschatology is seemingly the price that must be paid to rid the world of the appalling doctrine of predestination. Yet in neglecting eternity as an operative category, postmodern theologians have slain a caricature, for the doctrine of providence never affirmed the strict determinism that its supposedly underlying dependence on predestination implied. Rather, the central teaching of this doctrine is that there are recognizable and reliable patterns governing a created order over time which nonetheless admit unexpected and inscrutable changes. If there were never any variations from established patterns, then there would be no pluriform or differentiated temporal expressions of created order, resulting in a static artifact of divine creativity rather than a genuine creation that is other than its creator. And if there were no recognizable and reliable patterns but only change, then it would be impossible to speak about a creation, much less created order, in any meaningful manner. Even Gordon Kaufman's expansive creativity would have no import unless a series of creative events are instantiated in an ordered pattern over time. Consequently, to portray providence, and its accompanying eschatology, as a strictly deterministic option is to fabricate a false dichotomy and counterfeit choice. The issue at hand is both/and, not either/or.

The central contention of reliability *and* inscrutability is not unlike the evolutionary principle that postmodern theology purportedly seeks to honor, for, as Arthur Peacocke argues, the universe is an outcome of the interplay between law and chance. Biological evolution is neither entirely open-ended nor determined, for emergence is tempered and complemented by convergence. The emergence of life was dependent on previous chance mutations within relatively static chemical processes, but subsequent evolutionary development did not occur within a matrix of infinite possibilities. The emergence of life admittedly created new evolutionary possibilities, but subsequent development necessitated the foreclosure of many options in order to sustain this development.

An analogous pattern is repeated in cultural evolution. The evolution of a culture is neither entirely determined nor open-ended, given the tension between tradition and the non-repeatable character of historical events. The formation of culture depends on the emergence of certain capabilities, such as a capacity to invent and use tools. The development of these capabilities converges over time, forming patterns which may be called cultural traditions; tools are used to build towns and cities. Tradition is a formative factor in subsequent cultural evolution, but it is not determinative given history's non-repeatable characteristic. Constantine's edict of toleration, for example, was a singular event that altered extensively the future development of the Roman Empire. The edict opened certain possibilities that heretofore had not existed, but in doing so it foreclosed other options, thereby narrowing the scope of subsequent development.

There is nothing inherent to the evolutionary principles of emergence *and* convergence that contradicts or confirms a theological account of a pluriform creation being drawn providentially toward its end in Christ. Consequently, the radically revisionist accounts proffered by the postmodern theologians surveyed in the previous chapters are unwarranted. Presumably they are attempting to reformulate theological convictions in light of science, a profitable enterprise that has often been undertaken within the Christian tradition. Yet rather than plundering science to enrich and amend the principal tenets of the tradition, they use it as a scalpel to excise central doctrines, such as the Incarnation, providence and eschatology. The principal motivation for this extensive revision is presumably the conviction that theologians and scientists are ultimately recounting the same reality, albeit with differing vocabularies and grammars. The relationship, however, is not one between equals, for science is effectively privileged in determining what constitutes valid theological discourse. If science, for example, cannot discover a creator, then theologians must confine themselves to speaking about divine and human co-creators, or creativity.

The denuded quality of postmodern theological discourse is, at least partly, a consequence of elevating a sound methodological limitation to an interpretive and discursive principle which is ill-equipped to sustain these tasks. Scientific inquiry rightfully suspends teleological principles, for instance, for good methodological reasons. There is no inherent reason, however, why this suspension must be carried over into theological discourse. In assuming that science and theology describe the same reality, postmodern theologians have, ironically, failed to honor their own operative presupposition that discourse is both descriptive *and* formative. Various disciplinary and interdisciplinary inquiries are conducted for the sake of enriching a range of particular descriptive perspectives which in their totality are formative; the goal is to order and enrich layers of discourse, not concoct a bland Esperanto. In carrying over the methodological limitations of scientific inquiry, theology, as one of the two disciplines seeking to give a normative account of this totality,[1] cannot be formative by suspending any operative teleology and accompanying doctrinal categories such as created order, providence and eschatology. Science can inform theological inquiry, but it should not dictate the content of its vocabulary or the structure of its grammar.

We may speak theologically, then, of a *destiny* that may be said to be both emergent and convergent. George Grant provides a philosophical account of destiny for explicating these emergent and convergent qualities that are particularly pertinent to the context of a late liberal technoculture. Grant's account presupposes late liberalism's endemic historicism and nihilism, which was examined in chapter two. Late liberals use technology to assert their will by mastering nature and human nature. In gaining such mastery, it is largely assumed that technology consists of a set of neutral instruments that can be used for good or evil purposes (Grant, 1985, pp. 1–12).

Grant contends that this neutrality is illusory, for technological development and application accords with its accompanying destiny. Destiny is *not* synonymous with fate. Grant is not arguing in favor of a strict determinism in which the introduction of a technology leads inevitably to a prescribed set of consequences and circumstances. Rather, the technology in question produces, defines and constrains an ensuing range of options that can be selected by the user, and the selection of these options is shaped, in turn, in terms of more expansive technological application. In short, we are not free to use various technologies in any manner we choose, and the chooser in turn becomes shaped by the choices being made and contemplated. Moral vision, and therefore assessment as well, become enveloped in a set of values that are imposed by technological potential instead of vice versa. Consequently, when 'we are deliberating in any practical situation our judgment acts rather like a mirror, which throws back the very metaphysic of the technology which we are supposed to be deliberating about in detail. The outcome is almost inevitably a decision for further technological development' (Grant, 1986, p. 33). As we grow more deeply embedded within a technological metaphysic, there is no outside perspective from which we can deliberate and judge.

We may speak, then, about emergent possibilities within technoculture which when implemented converge to form a pattern of moral choices and acts, and this convergence, in turn, defines and delineates further emergent possibilities. Or using Grant's terms, we may speak of an *unfolding* and *enfolding* destiny. He uses two examples to explicate these characteristics.

First, Grant quotes a leading computer scientist of his day that the '"computer does not impose on us the ways it should be used"' (ibid., p. 19). The adage is meant to reassure the scientist's audience that computers are merely instruments over which we assert our control. The reassuring rhetoric is misleading, however, for it reflects late liberalism's 'common sense' view of rationality, and this ideological blinder does not allow us to perceive computers for what they really are (ibid., pp. 20–21). What are computers? According to Grant, they are physical representations of a particular paradigm of knowledge and tradition of mastery. The computer embodies late modern 'reason' as the 'summoning of anything before a subject and putting it to the question, so that it gives us its reasons for being the way it is as an object' (ibid., p. 21). External objects simply have no objective or inherent claims upon the subjective observer and manipulator. Consequently, the computer marks the latest step in gaining greater mastery over nature and human nature, further liberating the human will by enabling it to create more favorable social and political environments, while also improving or recreating the will's biological host. Grant does not challenge the veracity or adequacy of these underlying beliefs, but he insists that 'without this destiny computers would not exist. And *like all destinies*, they "impose"' (ibid., p. 22, emphasis added).

The adage that computers do not impose their ways upon their users is misleading, because it hides an imposing destiny in a guise of instrumental neutrality. By reassuring ourselves that the computer does not impose its ways upon us, we have already succumbed to the imposition of its destiny. The computer, for example, promises greater freedom in creating and organizing data in accordance with our goals and purposes. Yet computers can only be used in a limited number of ways for creating, storing and classifying this information, thereby forming the goals and purposes that it purportedly serves in an instrumental manner. The resulting 'freedom' is illusory, because the computer, like any technology, constrains the range of choices its users can make within the limited parameters of its imposed destiny. More broadly, particular technological developments and applications permit certain forms of civil society and political community while excluding others (Ellul, 1964, pp. 148–318). The ubiquitous automobile, for instance, has required the construction of a particular infrastructure and investment schemes enabling the late modern urban and suburban complexes, replete with their accompanying mobile lifestyles, to the exclusion of other possible configurations.

For Grant, the most troubling consequence of this technological destiny is its distortion of what justice, goodness and freedom have come to mean. Following Nietzsche, there are no objective standards of justice outside of a particular destiny against which certain acts are measured and assessed. Hence technology cannot be a set of neutral instruments, because their 'neutrality' is defined within the imposed ways it *should* be used. What has 'should' come to mean in a late modern technoculture? According to Grant, the word originally expressed a notion of indebtedness (Grant, 1986, pp. 28–9). Justice, then, is rendering what is rightfully due to others, such as neighbors, citizens and God. There are objective goods that form and constrain one's acts, and order one's desires, because of the debt one owes to them. As late modern and postmodern modes of thought eroded any objective foundation for various goods, the debt has not so much been forgiven as transferred to the self. Justice is thereby rendered by paying the debt we owe ourselves, and is expressed through nihilistic self-assertion, or in kinder and gentler forms of creative expression.

Paying off this debt to ourselves requires that goodness be reduced to the ability to create one's own life, and there are no standards to determine whether what is created is good or bad, and therefore whether or not the debt has been paid, for there are no other debtors who have a claim on us. At most, what we owe others is a bill for services rendered in assisting us in pursuing our self-interests and fulfilling our idiosyncratic purposes. The greatest injustice that can be committed against a postmodern is to be denied the means for pursuing one's self-creation. Or, in Grant's words, 'The modern conception of goodness does not include the assertion of a claim upon us which properly orders our desires in terms of owing, and which is itself the route and fulfilment for desire. In the prevalent modern view, owing is always provisional upon what we desire to create' (ibid., p. 30). The technology used to liberate us from the constraints of nature and human nature is the flip side of a late modern and postmodern ideology that we are free to create ourselves, our associations and political communities, and most importantly, free to construct our own destinies.

This attenuated understanding of freedom is again misleading, as indicated by Grant's second example. Since late moderns and postmoderns have asserted the right to freely construct themselves and their destinies, they must have readily available raw materials required to complete these tasks. Technology is the most effective means of undertaking these construction projects. Late moderns and postmoderns, then, must be proficient and voracious consumers of the materials at their disposal, requiring an expanding range of options from which to choose if their freedom is to remain unfettered, and their work creative. Goodness and justice are diminished in the absence of free choice. Consequently, 'when we represent technology to ourselves through its own common sense we think of ourselves as picking and choosing in a supermarket, rather than within the analogy of the package deal' (ibid., p. 32).

Presumably the supermarket is neutral space where consumers select the products they need in line with their respective goals and purposes. To paraphrase the cheerful adage of Grant's computer scientist, the supermarket does not impose upon us the ways it should be used. Yet it does impose its ways upon consumers, for its illusion of enhanced freedom gained through more choices masks its destiny of picking and choosing, and it is a destiny that enslaves rather than liberates because it defines and constricts by reducing those selecting to nothing more than consumers. The supermarket, for instance, does not disclose any difference between a good and bad diet, or how such a determination might be related to conceptions of goodness, justice and freedom, for this determination has no normative reference point. Rather, all the supermarket can disclose is the preferences of its consumers, and those preferences, in turn, are shaped and manipulated by the dictates of offering more choices. To cross the threshold of the supermarket is to enter a formative space. Contrary to its late modern and postmodern champions, the freedom purportedly enhanced by greater choice deceives, for consumers are not liberated in their acts of selecting, but constrained by the terms of the package deal of picking and choosing.

Moreover, it is a package deal whose destiny unfolds in the process of picking and choosing, enfolding its adherents 'in its own conceptions of instrumentality, neutrality and purposiveness' (ibid., p. 32). As Grant contends, these conceptions shape, or better misshape, our operative values, in turn distorting our ensuing moral vision, for the price of becoming enfolded in this destiny of picking and choosing requires 'changes in what we think is good, what we think good is, how we conceive sanity and madness, justice and injustice, rationality and irrationality, beauty and ugliness' (ibid., p. 32). If the 'good' is nothing other than a process of historicist self-construction, then the resulting 'freedom' can be nothing more than an expressive and assertive will that makes its choices for the sake of choosing; even a decision not to choose is a choice. What does constant choosing mean in respect to paying the debt of justice? In fulfilling our duties whatever is not forbidden is permitted. Yet if the debt is owed almost exclusively to oneself, then what is permitted is virtually unrestrained, for what is forbidden is the result of contractual agreement and expedient calculation incurred in our various construction projects, for there are no given qualities, roles or relationships that have an inherent claim upon us. Hence the last remaining late liberal imperative: that we should be free to pursue our respective interests so long as we do not intentionally harm any other person in the process. It is an innocuous imperative, however, for the 'should' has been stripped of normative content and reduced to a procedural principle, since it has been torn from any binding obligation to anything other than an insubstantial and fabricated self. To know oneself now requires that one must also make the self that is known. The maker and made meld into a single reality in which the debt can never be paid, because what is owed to this new creation is infinite.

Although Grant's account of destiny is critical of late modern modes of thought, particularly in respect to its distortions of such moral and political concepts as goodness, justice and freedom, his objective is to ascribe rather than condemn. It is only in coming to terms with late modernity that a genuine counter discourse can be coined. Grant is convinced that we must turn to antiquity, especially Greek philosophy and Christian theology, to recover a basic vocabulary and grammar, for the late modern paradigm lacks a capacity to be self-critical.[2] He is not proposing a naïve recovery, but an appropriation of antique philosophical and theological categories that have been refined in the fire of late modern thought, and for the purpose of this inquiry, we should add the fires of postmodern and posthuman discourse.

Undertaking this recovery leads Grant inevitably back to the problem of the relation between the good and the necessary. Countering late modern distortions of goodness, justice and freedom as nihilistic assertions of the will requires a reference to the eternal which enframes, and thereby provides, these moral and political categories with their normative content. In the absence of the eternal, which defines and delineates the temporal and finite, we cannot determine what humans are fitted for, or describe what being a good human might entail in anything other than emotive terms. When the eternal is dismissed or excised, there is no *telos* against which moral and political values are formed and measured, thereby promoting measured moral and political acts. Late modern social and political ordering, in both its liberal and Marxist manifestations, has simply become one more attempt at transforming the necessary into the good, replete with all the thin justifications for the suffering inflicted in the name of necessity. Goodness, justice and freedom become weapons employed by the powerful to assert their will over the weak, rather than boundaries limiting the abuse of such power. History, as fashioned in the image of the historicist, is its own self-appointed judge and moral arbiter. Choice, hailed as the linchpin of historicist construction, then, is really nothing more than a fig leaf hiding late modernity's and postmodernism's naked aggression in the name of freedom. Consequently, a supposed choice between antiquity's closed or postmodernity's open-ended narrative is a false dilemma, for the issue at stake is between their competing destinies, and therefore determining which one is true, and which one is false.

In meditating upon destiny, Grant fashioned an able scalpel enabling him to expose late modernity's lethal tumors. The surgery he performs, however, offers no cure. For instance, in his devastating critique of North America as the world's first and most advanced technological civilization, Grant exposes a culture fading into 'the winter of nihilism' (Grant, 1969, pp. 15–40). A novel civilization is taking shape that is addicted to a mind-numbing materialism and consumerism, disfiguring truth and beauty as a side effect. Yet he is either unable or unwilling to offer an alternative destiny, seemingly content with diagnosing the disease. In the end, Grant is a vivisectionist rather than a surgeon. He identifies the cancerous effects of historicist rhetoric, but he offers no alternative discourse to effect a cure. Why the reticence? Although Grant deliberates a great deal on the problem of goodness and necessity, he never proposes a tentative resolution, and therefore can offer no moral, social and political applications.

One possible reason for his reluctance is Grant's plea that he lacks the ability to think through the issue of the good and the necessary as formulated by Plato and Simone Weil. All he can do is admit the importance of the task but no more. It is arguable, however, that Grant's reticence reflects a tacit acknowledgment that he has reached the limits of philosophy as a predominantly diagnostic discipline. To effect a cure would require recourse to theology (Heaven and Heaven, 1978). It is important to remember in this regard that although Grant's career was that of a philosopher, his formal academic training was in theology. He was aware of the respective scope and limits of these two disciplines, and may have simply honored the proper constraints imposed by his inquiry as a philosopher. This meant that he could enucleate, but not rectify, the plight of late modernity. By refraining from invoking such theological themes as incarnation, providence and eschatology, for instance, Grant can really offer no alternative destiny to the technological destiny of North America that he decries. In the absence of these theological themes, he cannot point to any revealed reference points and their corresponding trajectories regarding the world's unfolding and enfolding destiny over time, and what the ultimate destination of this temporal process might entail. Consequently, Grant can also offer no effective counter discourse to the historicism he repudiates, other than falling into the postmodern trap of asserting an alternative narrative devoid of any objective canons of veracity and rationality. It is somewhat like trying to overlay Augustine's *City of God* on the postmodern world in which any references to divine providence, Christ's divinity and the eighth day of creation have been removed. The resulting 'history' is a denuded account of the Christians' surprising prowess in out-narrating their pagan opponents.

Grant, however, is first and foremost a Christian, and he realizes that his critical appropriation of antiquity's vision of the true, the good and the beautiful requires both philosophy *and* theology; the vocabularies of Athens *and* Jerusalem. Although he has restricted himself to the discourse of the former city, he is acutely cognizant of the need for that of the latter. Although Grant does not undertake this theological task, he does suggest a promising avenue this inquiry might pursue in his lectures on Augustine (Grant, 2002, pp. 476–90). According to Grant's explication of Augustine, in Christ's crucifixion we see that the necessary and the good 'are at an infinite distance' (ibid., p. 483). No justice whatsoever is seemingly present in this brutal execution of a good and innocent man. Yet the crucifixion expresses a supernatural justice, because it entails a form of suffering that as humans we cannot choose. It is a suffering that only the purely just can undertake: at Golgotha, Jesus Christ consents to necessity in an act devoid of goodness. The Passion, therefore, reveals the internal and eternal life of the triune God; a life we cannot imitate. Moreover, since it is a life that cannot be imitated by creatures, then only the creator can save us, but we cannot be saved without our consent.

Augustine insists that this consent is a redemptive prerequisite, for we must love only that which is worthy in every respect, namely, God alone. One, then, can become a martyr for the sake of Christ, but no one can take up Christ's cross. Only the One who is purely good can consent to this cross and what it represents: an 'absolute love which somehow bridges for us the infinite distance between the necessary and the good' (ibid., p. 485). This is why a liberal understanding of redemption as the basis of a sacrificial ethic fails, because it turns the cross into a repeatable act of martyrdom. The crucifixion, however, is a providential and non-repeatable event in which the eternal and infinite becomes incarnate in the temporal and finite. Any attempt at replication denotes an utter failure to discern the chasm separating goodness and necessity, so any reenactment of Good Friday becomes a tawdry simulacrum stripped of any redemptive significance; the only roles that humans can play are those of Pilate and the two thieves. In the absence of a savior who has consented to necessity, the only justice to be rendered is one of accusation, judgment and execution. Ultimately the necessary and the good can only be reconciled by an initiative originating in, and returning to, the eternal, for all temporal efforts end up being little more than thinly veiled attempts to justify evil.

Once again, Grant does not develop a systematic theology of the cross to enable further reflection on the necessary and the good which could be used to explicate a richer account of destiny. Yet his insight that recovering the discourse of Athens in tandem with that of Jerusalem offers a genuine alternative to postmodern and posthuman rhetoric is on target. Consequently, to speak of destiny requires that we also say something about eschatology.

Eschatology is inquiry into the *eschaton*. Whatever claims theology makes about the end of creation, then, are obviously tentative and speculative. No one, save God, knows the day or hour. For the purpose of this inquiry, eschatology must be differentiated from the apocalyptic, for the latter contends that the road leading to the end can be plotted like a map. The challenge is to break the code by discerning the signs of the time, thereby enabling precise navigation. Yet this is to speak more about fate than destiny (Waters, 1992). To speak of the end of creation in terms of a theological vocabulary and grammar is to engage in disciplined reflection on, to use Grant's terminology, an unfolding creation and its enfolding destiny. Such eschatological reflection, however, is not an esoteric exercise, but a central practice in forming a moral vision that claims to be Christian.

As was noted in the previous chapter, postmodern theology dismisses any prospective understanding of providence, because it also rejects an operative eschatology that can be revealed in temporal terms. If God 'knows' the future, then any semblance of human freedom is shattered. Humans are merely programmed automatons rather than creative agents. Moreover, any notion that the world might have a given destiny must also be rejected, because of its incompatibility with a radically open-ended future. Eschatology flies in the face of solid scientific evidence, and must therefore be discarded as a useless doctrine, or reinterpreted in realized terms as a motivational guide to prudential judgment.

This curt dismissal of eschatology, however, is unwarranted. To assert that God's 'knowledge' of the future somehow voids human freedom is to impose categories upon the eternal that do not apply. To claim that an eternal perspective of the temporal results in an ironclad determinism is a conclusion based on a false premise. To claim there is an 'eternal perspective' is absurd, for the temporal does not exist in parallel with the eternal, but within it; the eternal may be said to frame the temporal. This does not imply that God has the kind of knowledge enabling perfect prediction of future events, for this is to impose temporal categories that again are not applicable. Rather, God can be said to 'know' what we call past, present and future in a singular manner, and such singular knowledge is unavailable to temporal creatures. To claim that the end of creation is 'known' by the eternal God does not thereby negate human freedom, particularly when such freedom is expressed through willful choices. Such freedom is itself a product of emergent and convergent processes that form and constrain free choices in a determinative manner.

Rejecting eschatological claims because they seemingly defy scientific evidence fails to take into account this interplay between emergence *and* convergence. To invoke the eternal is not to possess an infallible guide predicting future events, but to acknowledge that the world has an end, and is therefore necessarily temporal and finite. This acknowledgment suggests two interpretive principles that are germane to this theological inquiry. First, the destiny of creation is continuous with the antecedent events through which it is formed and shaped. Unlike the first creation, the new creation will not be brought into being *ex nihilo*. Thus, we may speak about a providential unfolding of created order being drawn toward its end over time. A destiny may be said to emerge out from antecedent convergent processes, a claim that is not incompatible with evolutionary theory. Second, the destiny of creation is also discontinuous with antecedent events through which it is formed and shaped. Unlike the first creation, the new creation has no end. The old may be said to perish, but it is raised into the eternal life of its creator. To speak of such a destiny is to expect the unexpected; to anticipate the genuinely novel rather than to pursue novel creativity. We may also speak, then, however warily, about emergent possibilities being enfolded into a converging destiny, a claim that science, *as science*, can neither confirm nor refute.

To ponder the end of creation, and what it might mean in terms of its formative influence on the present, requires that we also speculate on the end of time and finitude, an admittedly daunting task to be taken on by temporal and finite creatures. Moreover, if this speculation is to be theological, then we must also contemplate the prospect of the necessary and the good being reconciled in a manner that does not merely negate the temporal and finite. How can we, as temporal and finite creatures, say anything meaningful about a reconciliation that is initiated on the eternal side of the chasm separating the necessary and the good? If our inquiry were confined to philosophy or science there is little we could say, and eschatology, as well as providence, would rightfully have no place within the vocabulary and grammar of Christian faith. The proper methodological constraints of these respective disciplines, however, need not prove fatal, for if theology is nothing else it is at least discourse on *revealed knowledge*.

For the purpose of this inquiry, the Incarnation is a pivotal revelatory reference point enabling Christian theological discourse on creation's destiny (Pannenberg, 1994, pp. 218–31). This is especially the case in regard to the Incarnation's threefold culmination discussed in greater detail in the preceding chapter. In his crucifixion, Jesus Christ consents to creation's necessity. It is through his suffering and death that a bridge between the necessary and the good, the temporal and eternal, and the finite and the infinite has been erected. The world is not an adversary that must be either dominated or escaped. In his resurrection, Christ vindicates created order. The realm of necessity is not godless or godforsaken, implying a fundamental dualism between an evil materiality and good spirituality. Since creation manifests God's created order, temporality and finitude are not evils inimical to human flourishing. In consenting to necessity *and* a vindicated created order, Christ also blesses the temporal and the finite. In his exaltation, Christ redeems creation. Temporal and finite necessity is transformed by being raised, in and through Christ, into the good, eternal and infinite life of God. To consent to finite and temporal necessity, and affirm a vindicated created order, is also to embrace an eschatological hope. Yet the promised redemption is more akin, following Augustine, to a slow healing process than instant or abrupt transformation, requiring on our part a response of patient anticipation (Brown, 2000, pp. 367–70). When Christians speak about the end of creation they refer to its destiny in Christ, for he embodies the triune God who creates, sustains and redeems creation; the origin and end of created order who creates, sustains and redeems out of a plentiful and gratuitous love rather than in response to any necessity, because such love knows no temporal or finite limits. It is in and through this love that creation may be said to be fulfilled and perfected as a gift of God's grace, and not an artifact of human creativity.

If the origin and end of creation is love, then the Christian moral life entails an ordering of desire in accordance with what this love requires. In this respect, postmodern theology is correct in insisting that ethics consists of making choices. Yet it is not a matter of creating the options from which we select, for the choice subsequently made is a self-referential assertion of the will against external constraints. The resulting ethic is founded on disordered desire, for in the absence of an operative eschatological hope, every moral choice becomes a kind of final judgment that rightfully belongs to God alone, instead of a patient act of hope in anticipation of eternity's verdict. The freedom of postmodernity's endlessly expanding array of choices is in the end enslavement, because it fails to recognize the destiny enfolding and warping the moral vision of what constitutes choosing. Every so-called free act serves to constrain rather than to liberate the chooser.

The prerequisite of genuine freedom is obedience, and obedience in turn is the expression of properly ordered desire. Since Christ is *the* object of our desire, we should order our lives accordingly to the love that creates, sustains and redeems us. Consequently, the moral life entails making choices, but they are not selections from a set of alternatives of our making. Rather, following O'Donovan, our choices are replies to a single and simple question posed to us by God: what do our choices 'constitute for eternity'? (O'Donovan, 1986, p. 259) This eschatological question can only be answered in 'relation to Christ in whom all the transformed world is already present to us' (ibid., p. 260). The moral life is, therefore, properly distilled to the stark simplicity of choosing for or against God. Without this eschatological orientation, Christian ethics is little more than a peculiar collection of the world's ambiguous platitudes, hidden behind a thin veneer of religious rhetoric; ambiguities produced by a world that believes it has no future other than what it creates. Yet abiding with Christ is not passing time, creatively or otherwise, but participating in an unfolding created order. It is also through this participation that the stark, simple question is posed to us by God that moral language is built on a series of opposing terms, 'good and bad, right and wrong, noble and base' (ibid., p. 261). Consequently, morality is a practice of ordering our desire, and an exercise in choosing, for every act is a choice between good and evil. And since every choice is a reply to the question of eternity, Christians are cognizant that their replies are judged by Christ, the vindicator of creation. Christ renders a judgment on all human acts, but it is a verdict accompanied by the promise of a destiny that depends on God's grace and not our deeds. God's final word at the end of a creation is one of grace as a 'work of love which will abide for eternity' (ibid., p. 264).

Accepting our election by God constitutes a fitting response to this anticipated final word. Yet how do we embody this response in respect to the necessary task of ordering a temporal creation before this final word is uttered?

Dominion

Exercising dominion over creation is the practical and effective embodiment of human election. Humans are the finite creatures God has ordained to order the temporal unfolding of a vindicated creation in accordance with its destiny in Christ. The most explicit formulation of this divine mandate comes from the opening chapter of Genesis (1:26–31). Humankind is created in God's image and likeness for the purpose of subduing the earth and exerting dominion over its creatures. In these lines from scripture, we encounter a theological rationale for the preeminent role human culture plays in God's creation.

There are seemingly two competing conclusions that can be extrapolated from this rationale. God's handiwork is incomplete in the absence of beings with a capacity to make the earth a paradise. Humans are thereby co-creators, working with God in continuing to extract an orderly cosmos out from a formless chaos, and in their creativity the divine image they bear burns ever brighter. The fate of creation depends as much on the work of the co-creator as it does on the creator. Although there is no guarantee this fate will prove pleasant, there are reasonable grounds to be optimistic given the nearly infinite creative potential that humans possess. Or to the contrary, some insist that this infamous biblical mandate offers little more than a thin rationalization to plunder and exploit the earth. 'Dominion' is read 'domination', so the earth and its creatures are little more than a treasure trove of raw resources to satisfy every human want and longing. The adage to do as you will is shouted, while the preceding qualifier of loving God is barely whispered. Given the avaricious and insatiable nature of human desire, the fate of the earth and its creatures is grim since the resources it has to surrender are not infinite.

Neither of these extrapolations is warranted, however, for both fail to recognize that dominion is the application of an ethic that is *simultaneously* providential and eschatological. Exercising dominion is to pursue, in obedient freedom, a course of moral, social and political ordering that is both limited and teleological. Since Christ's resurrection has vindicated created order, we may speak of certain objects, processes and relationships as possessing natural or inherent limits and borders which, in obedience to Christ, should be honored. These limits or borders, however, may not prove to be as permanent or inflexible as once assumed, so in freedom they may be adjusted or reconfigured. One reason why our initial setting of limits or borders proves to be wrong is that due to the distorting influence of sin we do not perceive correctly, requiring in turn a response of repentance and amendment. More importantly, however, is the eschatological qualification that all objects, processes and relationships are subject to transformation, given Christ's lordship of creation, beyond our imaginative capabilities to comprehend. In this respect, subduing the earth is neither creative license nor a permit to exploit, but entails the ordering of a temporal and finite creation in accordance with its created order and aligning it with its destiny. Admittedly such ordering is imperfect, imprecise and subject to revision, but what dominion seeks to instantiate is that in principle there are limits to be honored, and the task of moral deliberation is to discern what honoring those limits might mean in the ordering of our individual lives and corporate life as God's elected creatures. Consequently, the optimism of the co-creator is misplaced, because the task at hand is not to impose order on a chaotic universe, but to conform our lives to an underlying order that already exists and has been vindicated by Christ. A pessimistic assumption regarding the inevitable fate of creation is equally misguided, for it fails to admit the possibility of repentance and amendment, as well as the world's transformed destiny in Christ. Humans are not called by God to be either co-creators or exploiters, but have been elected by God to assert a *limited* dominion over a finite and temporal creation in the name of the One whose image and likeness they bear.

It may be asked what effective difference an ethic derived from limited dominion might make in respect to moral, social and political ordering? The question is a legitimate one, especially if Christian theology is to offer a genuine alternative to postmodern and posthuman forms of discourse. In addressing this question, I will demonstrate, in a rudimentary rather than exhaustive manner, that an operative mandate of limited dominion provides a stimulus for purposeful human action, while also imposing limits upon those actions in line with the temporality and finitude that characterize both the purposive actors *and* the objects of their purposeful actions. The derivative ethic thereby provides an intermediate position between the extremes of a naïve romantic idealism on the one hand, and a reductionistic expediency on the other. In this respect, limited dominion elaborates the natural ethic examined in the previous chapter by seeking to identify a teleological relation between the providential unfolding of created order and creation's eschatological destiny as revealed in the death, resurrection and exaltation of Jesus Christ.

We may begin this discussion by contending that the biblical mandate authorizes humans to use *natural* resources, objects and processes for the purpose of enriching their lives. Specifically, humans are given dominion over plants and animals in order that they may be 'fruitful and multiply', thereby enabling them to subdue the earth. What this subjection refers to is not willful domination, but a generic and teleological ordering that God pronounces, on this penultimate day of creation, as being 'very good'. The creation of humans, however, does not indicate that they represent the apex of creation. Humankind is not the crowning glory of creation, but the creatures elected by God to bear witness to creation's sovereign creator and redeemer. The climax of created order is not the sixth day's mandate of dominion, but the Sabbath rest of the following day. What the emergence of humans represents is part of an integral and cumulative order running as a thread throughout each day of creation that God speaks into being, an image reinforced in the opening lines of John's Gospel (1:1–5). It is in and through the Word that the creator creates, a theological claim that does not denote a vague creative principle, but an affirmation of order. Moreover, this order is affirmed by the incarnate Word, and vindicated by Christ's resurrection from the dead; in the reconciler's death, God does not allow creation to collapse back into the formless void from whence it came. A vindicated created order sustains creation as its temporal unfolding becomes enfolded in Christ's destiny.

This temporal unfolding does not suggest a static universe. Nature and history are rife with change, particularly in respect to purposeful human action. Yet neither is this change necessarily random and radically open-ended, again especially in respect to human acts that may be said to align this temporal unfolding with the teleological relationships of created order *and* eschatological destiny. Dominion is not the foundation of a preservationist ethic, but requires action shaped and limited by a prospective moral vision. Consequently, we may say that creation is incomplete in the absence of a properly administered human dominion. In O'Donovan's words, the 'redemption of the world ... does not serve only to put us back in the Garden of Eden where we began', because 'the outcome of the world's story cannot be cyclical return to the beginnings, but must fulfil that purpose in the freeing of creation from its "futility" (Rom. 8:2)' (O'Donovan, 1986, p. 55).

A properly administered dominion – one which simultaneously endeavors to conform the temporal unfolding of a finite creation with its vindicated created order and destiny – prevents either an unwarranted romanticizing or exploitation of nature. In the former instance, nature is a realm of exquisite beauty and sustenance. In nature we encounter those processes that both sustain and enrich human life, rightfully inspiring a response of awe and gratitude. Yet any caricature of nature as a nurturing parent or friend is unwarranted, for the same forces that sustain and enrich our lives also bear down on us, destroying our aspirations and subjecting us to futility. Nature is also a prevalent source of suffering, pain and death as witnessed by such natural phenomena as famines, earthquakes and disease (Gustafson, 1981). In the latter instance, nature is a collection of raw resources to be exploited. In nature we encounter processes and forces that are inimical to human flourishing, thereby inspiring a defensive response of mastery and domination. Yet perceiving nature as a relentless foe that can be conquered or held at bay is a deception. Although human mastery and domination may ameliorate the pain and suffering resulting from natural necessity, it can only delay death's eventual victory. In technologically advanced cultures, for instance, the ten leading causes of death have changed dramatically over the past century, but there are still ten leading causes of death. For all its bravado, a domineering strategy is little more than a delaying tactic that does little to alleviate, much less remove, a sense of futility.

Postmodern rhetoric incorporates both of these approaches, while doing little to resolve their inherent tension. This irresolution is most apparent in Hefner's and Kaufman's respective attempts to somehow preserve pristine ecologies while also maximizing creative expression. For Hefner, the task is to preserve the environment's 'wholesome' integrity which in turn is replicated in a more wholesome social ecology, while for Kaufman the challenge is to pursue a serendipitous creativity in a manner that does not compromise the earth's capacity to sustain human life, and by implication further creativity. For both, technology represents the gravest threat to preserving the natural environment. Toxic pollution and weapons of mass destruction threaten the earth's capacity to sustain life in general, and human life in particular. Yet technology is arguably the supreme expression of human creativity, a claim that neither deny. Why, then, do they draw inflexible boundaries around the natural environment that should not be transgressed? The short answer is, because survival is at stake. If the natural processes sustaining human life become severely degraded or extinguished, then human creativity also becomes impoverished, or worse, extinct. Hefner's and Kaufman's plea on behalf of natural ecologies is certainly prudential, but in drawing a protective boundary they also undermine their core imperative, namely, that creativity is not, after all, infinite. Humans may be creative until they hit the hard wall of necessity. Consequently, the creativity they espouse incorporates an implicitly sullen resignation to their own finite and temporal limits. This means also that the natural environment they champion has no inherent but only an instrumental value, for it reinforces stifling limits against the infinite creativity they wish to pursue. The natural environment is not good *per se*, but is only good in respect to its limited capacity to sustain life. The so-called creativity they invoke, then, is rendered vacuous when it hits the limits of necessity, for the prudential consideration of survival requires that any creative options considered or pursued conform ultimately to finite and temporal strictures. To invoke Grant's analogy, the best Hefner and Kaufman can offer is a greener supermarket, but it remains a supermarket nonetheless, for necessity dictates that there really is no other alternative that can be created.

By invoking the prudential consideration of survival, however, postmodern theology, as represented by Hefner and Kaufman, throws open the gate to an alternative, posthuman solution. If the problem is that human creativity is blocked by its dependence on natural ecologies, then engineer human life to be less dependent. This solution incorporates a twofold strategy of radically transforming both natural ecologies and human individuals. The objective is to make human flourishing, both individually and corporately, progressively less dependent on natural processes that are not subject to purposeful control. The overriding goal is to use technology to push back the limits necessitated by finitude and temporality, culminating in humans merging with artificial life forms to achieve virtual immortality. This strategy removes the urgency for preserving the so-called integrity of the natural environment, for if certain ecologies are deemed worthy of protection the reason justifying that decision is that they enhance (post)human flourishing rather than mere survival. The boundary drawn around the natural is, after all, neither necessary nor inviolable. Such radical transformation greatly expands the range of (post)human creativity, a value which such postmodern theologians as Hefner and Kaufman would presumably endorse.

Even if we grant that the posthuman dream of virtual immortality is feasible rather than fanciful, its twofold strategy of radical transformation fails, for the problem of finite and temporal necessity is not overcome, but merely displaced and denied. In the first instance, independence from ecological processes is achieved by shifting human dependence from nature to artifice. In deploying technology to become progressively less dependent on natural processes, humans will be using artifacts of their own design, and therefore subject to their control. Yet the eventual success of the posthuman project is predicated on the evolution of artificial life that is superior to humans, and therefore not under their control. Dependence is not so much overcome as displaced; natural necessity is exchanged for an artificial counterpart. In the second instance, assuming that no border or boundary is inviolate strips the creative imperative of posthuman discourse of any moral content. If there are no limits to be honored in principle, then there are also no standards to differentiate good creative acts from evil destructive ones. The emergent posthuman, whatever it might prove to be, will be said to be 'good' because it simply exists. Despite pleas to the contrary, creative transformation serves to bless the posthuman project as a nihilistic will to power; a will, it might be said, on high-tech steroids. Necessity in this instance is simply denied as an unsolvable problem, because finitude and temporality are not definitive limits to be honored, but irksome obstacles to be overcome.

The problem that the postmodern and posthuman approaches outlined above share is that neither provides a normative framework for making provisional distinctions that are required in an imperfect and amendable process of moral deliberation and discernment. Consequently, a proximate value is elevated as an ultimate good. The good of 'survival' or 'transformation' serves as an overriding consideration, skewing subsequent moral reflection. This distorting effect is seen in a postmodern romanticism that sees nature as a fragile vessel that must be protected, and in the posthumanist view of nature as a treasure chest resisting the plundering of its contents. The price of elevating the proximate goods of survival or transformation to that of ultimate goods is ignoring finitude and temporality as defining features of the very agents engaged in moral deliberation and discernment. The result of this willful ignorance is the Good as a projection of the desire to overcome finitude and temporality, rather than an imposed standard against which finite and temporal desires are shaped and measured.

How might exercising limited dominion correct these postmodern and posthuman distortions? Its theological grounding in both providence and eschatology provides a critical and constructive framework in which the values of survival and transformation are given their due without granting them an unwarranted ultimacy. This is achieved by consenting, in obedient freedom, to finitude and temporality that are inherent to finite and temporal creatures. This consent does not entail an affirmation that finite and temporal necessity is good, but it does affirm that the vindicated created order underlying the temporal unfolding of a finite creation is good. Moreover, since created order is enframed by eternity, consenting to finitude is also to embrace an eschatological hope that the necessary will be integrated into the Good in the final redemption of creation.

Although the postmodern counsel to preserve the integrity of the natural environmental is well taken, the admonition can only be prudential, rather than normative, so long as survival is the overriding issue at stake. Presumably, if humans were to evolve, either through natural selection or technological modification, to a point where their survival required radically new ecologies, either natural or artificial, then there would no longer be any compelling reason to value, and thereby preserve, such things as rain forests or endangered species. By implicitly elevating survival as an ultimate concern, postmoderns have impaled themselves on both horns of a dilemma. On the one horn, they cannot grant any enduring value to the natural environment they wish to preserve, because in their commitment to a radically open-ended creativity they have denied any teleological and generic ordering that would enable them to make a stronger normative claim. If a case cannot be made that humans are creatures that are properly ordered to certain given natural objects, processes and therefore limits, then the natural environment cannot be said to be good other than in its instrumental and temporary utility to enable survival. Indeed, it is ultimately nature that impedes human creativity; preserving rain forests and endangered species may in time prove to be little more than a distraction. This impediment leads to the second horn of the dilemma: since postmoderns have no operative destiny, then they also have no prospective ethic allowing them to make moral, rather than instrumental, distinctions. If no normative claims about an imposed destiny can be made, and these claims are admittedly based on imperfect interpretations of revealed knowledge, then we have no binding standard with which to endorse one particular proposed course of action as opposed to another. When in principle there is no destiny to limit or channel an infinite creativity, then no possible courses of action can, in principle, be foreclosed in advance. The integrity of natural ecologies, for instance, exerts no moral claim upon humans other than in terms of their instrumental value for enabling their survival. In this respect, postmoderns are hard pressed to argue for the preservation of rain forests and endangered species if genetically modified trees and animals should prove superior alternatives in enabling human survival.

In the absence of any operative notion of providence and eschatology, posthuman discourse can only fabricate a highly impoverished understanding of 'transformation'. The transhumanist cannot envision, and therefore produce through technology, a destiny that is both continuous and discontinuous with what has preceded it. Limits must be honored if *both* continuity over time *and* the possibility for transformation are to be maintained. When all borders or boundaries are provisional, then there are no generic and teleological standards governing the ordering of various relationships. As a result, novel configurations must be constantly fabricated to satiate what proves to be an insatiable appetite for novelty. There are no given or natural purposes to these reconfigured relationships, only those defined and imposed provisionally by the fabricator. The purpose of a forest, for example, may change from a game preserve to providing lumber, or a pig may be transformed from a pet to meat for dinner. None of these purposes may be said to be inherent to a forest or a pig, but are imposed by those having the power to do so. The so-called 'transformation' derived from these imposed purposes is a thin rationalization justifying a willful power under the banner of improvement or enhancement; a forest providing lumber offers greater economic opportunities than preserving it for hunters, and using pigs as a source of meat, rather than pets, is more profitable. Yet if the consumption of these commodities (lumber and meat) cannot satiate an insatiable desire, then further 'transformation' is warranted. Genetically altering trees with perfectly dimensioned and identically square trunks, for instance, would enhance the quality of lumber, and using nanotechnology to transform inert matter into material with the consistency and taste identical to that of pork but without fat and cholesterol would improve one's diet. Yet to what extent the 'trees' and 'pork' resulting from these transformations can be said to be continuous with forests and pigs is highly tendentious, especially if technology is developed to produce edible 'trees' and 'pork' as a building material. It is precisely this radical and shifting imposition of purposes that underlies posthuman discourse, for continuity is reduced to little more than semantic convention while discontinuity becomes the norm, for there are no given, normative ends to be honored in ordering a temporal and finite creation. Lest the preceding examples of trees and pigs appear too fanciful, may we not say already that in joining human gametes in a laboratory the resulting 'embryo' may have purposes, and therefore differing destinies, imposed upon it ranging from developing into a baby to being a source of stem cells? (Waters and Cole-Turner, 2003)

It may be objected that the ethic of limited dominion outlined above does not achieve its goal of clarifying a moral vision as opposed to postmodern and posthuman alternatives. The 'natural ethic' embodying conformity to created order and aligning ethical judgments prospectively to creation's destiny in Christ is no more a reliable guide for moral, social and political ordering than that afforded by postmodern creativity or posthuman transformation. At least the respective principles of survival and willful power offer more concrete reference points for directing creative or transformative acts than the emotive preferences derived from religious beliefs. In an ongoing process of moral deliberation and discernment, limited dominion does not provide a promising foundation for a counter discourse, because it is more vague and arbitrary than its postmodern and posthuman counterparts.

In response, moral, social and political ordering should be subjected to periodic amendment and revision. This is to be expected in exercising limited dominion over the temporal and pluriform unfolding of created order. These amendments and revisions are, at least in principle, no less vague or arbitrary because they are based on theological convictions, and reinforced through religious practices. Indeed, it is arguable that they are, again in principle, less vague and arbitrary because the amendments and revisions are derived from the requisite practice of *repentance*. Repentance does not entail an idiosyncratic expression of regret, but is a formal practice defined and refined within a theological tradition and community of ritual enactment. This enfolded position in tradition and community serves as a check and balance against vague revisions and arbitrary amendments. Repentance promotes the freedom to revise and amend the moral, social and political ordering of creation as needed in an obedient manner. In this respect, the postmodern emphasis on survival and posthuman fixation on willful power serve as *a priori* commitments that occlude, rather than clarify, the respective moral visions of assertive creativity and radical transformation. We may expand the formative role repentance plays in moral deliberation and discernment by examining briefly two additional aspects of limited dominion.

First, exercising limited dominion incorporates what may be ascribed as a *cultural* mandate (Bonhoeffer, 1955, pp. 179–83). In electing humans, God has authorized them to use plants and animals to fulfill the command to be fruitful and multiply. Thus, we may say that trees and pigs, for example, are ordered to satisfy the human needs of shelter and food. Fulfilling this mandate necessitates the creation of various social, economic and political institutions. These institutions have changed dramatically over time, often in response to technological innovations. These changes require a process of moral deliberation to discern their efficacy. For instance, it is arguable that lumber mills have enabled the construction of relatively comfortable and affordable housing, and hog farms have provided relatively inexpensive and plentiful meat. Moral deliberation, however, may also result in condemnation, repentance and amendment, leading to policies preventing deforestation and inhumane treatment of animals. Prospectively, we will need to deliberate on whether or not trees should be genetically modified to make them more resistant to disease, or the immune system of pigs enhanced to make them less dependent on antibiotics.

In order to exercise a dominion that is truly limited, however, requires a moral vision that does not see trees and pigs solely as lumber and pork. Although humans have been authorized by God to use plants and animals in meeting their needs of shelter and food, they are not ordered solely for this end or purpose. If the world is the finite and temporal embodiment of a vindicated created order enframed by an eternal destiny, then the generic and teleological ordering of its pluriform particulars must necessarily defy any total comprehension, much less mastery. Consenting to necessity is thereby acknowledging that the details of providence remain unsearchable and inscrutable, and eschatology is disciplined preparation for a surprise ending. Admittedly the kind of moral deliberation and discernment I am proposing here offers no obvious solutions to a host of contentious issues. It is debatable, for instance, whether exercising limited dominion is more compatible with centralized or free-market economies, or with socialist or democratic regimes; and neither does it easily resolve whether or not animals should be eaten, or if stem cells should be extracted from human embryos. Its principal value is that in the midst of such contentions, it keeps in the forefront a widening rather than constricting and reductive moral vision, a prospective vision of ordering an unfolding creation within its enfolding destiny. In its absence the 'other' can never be truly other, but only an object to be redefined and consumed in line with the beholder's creative or transformative purposes. Postmoderns reduce a tree to a source of lumber, or a precious ornament to be protected against the lumberjack, but in either case it ceases to be a tree. More expansively, trees become something other than trees if transformed into food. The posthuman moral vision literally misses the forest for the atoms comprising its trees.

Second, there is no mandate to exercise dominion over *oneself or other humans*. Although God's command to subdue the earth is sweeping, there is no mention of including humans in this decree. Dominion reinforces a repetitive biblical theme that since humans are creatures bearing the divine image, they share a fundamental equality. This does not imply that such equality can or should be instantiated within social structures and political institutions, for necessity requires certain distinctions, divisions of labor, and hierarchical relations. These differences, however, are functional rather than ontological. In this respect, human life is more akin to a gift and loan entrusted to the care of its recipients, than a possession to be used at the discretion of its owner. Our lives are not our own, nor can we own the life of another. The divine image borne by humans is not a permit to engage in godlike creativity, but an emblem of the One to whom they belong.

Posthuman discourse confuses functionality with ontology, and in doing so pursues a salvific course that can only lead to annihilating what it seeks to save. Humans must be saved from their finitude and temporality. Consequently, their flesh, to invoke a biblical concept, must be transformed into information that can be organized into more enduring patterns. It is not the Word made flesh that redeems, but flesh made data which enables survival. Therefore, necessity is not to be consented to but negated, for there is no created order which in obedient freedom forms our lives, but only raw material to be conformed to our will. We bear no image other than our own. This means, however, that the posthuman project of radical self-transformation is founded on a contradiction and hubristic deceit. The contradiction is that the virtual immortality it seeks is not eternity, but endless temporality. The eternal has neither a beginning nor an end, whereas the immortal has a beginning but presumably no end. Consequently, the former enframes and delineates the temporal, thereby bridging the gulf separating the necessary and the good, whereas the latter remains embedded in the necessity it wishes to negate and therefore has no ultimate good to pursue. The posthuman project is self-annihilating in its pursuit of endless transformation. The deceit is that in negating necessity, finitude will be overcome. If virtual immortality is extended temporality, however, then finite limits are not overcome but extended, at least in principle, indefinitely. This means, however, that posthumans are ultimately not the masters of their own fate, but only proficient delayers. Even in Greek mythology the immortals are not eternal, and therefore remain subject to a fate they cannot control (Arendt, 1998, pp. 18–20). Moreover, postmodern theology can offer no substantive alternative, for its appeal to any limits on creativity is derived from prudential concerns for survival. If future technological development eases these concerns, then presumably these limits will need to be redefined in order to promote greater creativity. The cyborg Hefner celebrates is little more than a cautious, liberal version of an audaciously libertine posthuman.

Once again, the prohibition on exercising dominion over oneself or other humans does not offer any easy solutions to many troubling and contentious concerns posed by the advent of a late modern technoculture. Exercising limited dominion over creation entails what may be described as creative acts and self-transformation in which technology plays a central and efficacious role. Consequently, there is no obvious Christian position on such issues as embryonic stem cell research, enhanced human longevity and performance, or germline modification. What limited dominion offers, however, is a counter discourse of honoring, in principle, given temporal and finite limits as suggested by the related considerations of a vindicated created order and creation's destiny in Christ. What is important to emphasize in this regard is that these limits do not direct attention exclusively on prudential considerations, for if that were the case then Christian theology would not coin a genuinely counter discourse, but would simply be a more conservative version of postmodern and posthuman rhetoric. Rather, limited dominion offers a counter discourse for moral deliberation and discernment by insisting that their execution is a functional task, not an ontological enactment. To state the matter tersely, human nature does not entail self-creation or transformation. Rather, humans find their fulfillment, or in more traditional terms become sanctified, in an obediently free embrace of their election. The limits derived from the prohibition of exercising dominion over oneself and others do not appeal to any so-called biological essentialism. As was argued above, Christianity is *not* a preservationist faith. The issue at stake is not that in pursuing the postmodern or posthuman projects humans may cease to be human, but that they will cease to be creatures bearing the *imago dei* in effectively rejecting their election.

Yet how do humans concretely and effectively exercise a limited dominion? Any answer to this question cannot avoid the question of technology, especially any answer which claims to be Christian.

Christian Technologies?

The question this section attempts to answer is admittedly an odd one. Technologies are usually associated with specific goals or tasks. Transportation technologies, for instance, are manufactured to transport freight and passengers. Or technologies may refer to underlying processes having an expansive range of applications. Digital technology, for example, enables the development of products that are applied to other clustered technologies involving such purposes as transportation, information and weaponry. Normally, we do not associate technologies with particular cultures or religions. There are, to the best of my knowledge, no English or Anglican technologies.

Yet technology has become a formative cultural force. It is now commonplace to invoke a technological society or technoculture to describe our contemporary circumstances. Jacques Ellul and other critics contend that technological development represents a ubiquitous and irresistible force that is destroying the particularity of local societies in favor of a homogenous global culture (Ellul, 1964). As more and more individuals use similar technologies they come to share nearly identical values, promoting in turn further technological development. The airplanes, computers and mobile telephones used in Dallas are the same as those in Tehran. More importantly, they are used for the identical purposes of transportation and communication.

Although it is undeniable that technology plays a formative role in shaping the social and economic structures of late modern societies, its homogenizing influence is overstated. Form and use are *not* synonymous with purpose and content. For example, there are two commercial airline pilots, one living in Dallas and the other in Tehran. Both fly identical aircraft, and own the same laptop computers and mobile telephones. The pilot living in Dallas is a fundamentalist Christian, while the one in Tehran is a devout Muslim. The former believes that transporting fellow Christians around the globe to spread the gospel is a divine calling, regularly surfs the Internet to keep apprised of events leading to Armageddon, and uses the mobile telephone to hear a daily reading from the Bible. The latter believes that transporting Muslims on pilgrimage to religious shrines is serving Allah, regularly surfs the Internet to keep apprised of Western threats against Islam, and uses the mobile telephone to listen to a daily reading from the Koran. Both value the mobility and easy availability of information afforded by these technologies, but the purposes they serve remain distinct. It is the valuation of form, not content, that becomes homogenized.

In separating form from content, however, have I not contradicted my previous repudiation of an instrumental understanding of technology? No, for the preceding discussion discloses that the determinative and instrumental models offer heuristic paradigms that are, respectively, too sweeping and too narrow to promote a sufficiently critical engagement with the role that technology plays in late modern moral, social and political ordering. Both capture an element of truth, but not the whole truth. The determinative model is correct in identifying the homogenizing influence that technological design and application exerts on shaping the fabric of daily life, but this influence does not necessarily extend to the creation of new or synthetic values. This limitation can be seen by revisiting the two pilots. If the determinative paradigm were correct, then their use of identical technologies should promote a revision of the content of their respective religious beliefs in ways that more closely resemble each other, or perhaps inspire both to reject their religious faith in favor of profane values. Yet this is clearly not the case; both use these technologies to practice their respective faiths. If the instrumental model were correct, then the two pilots should be using their technologies in radically different ways that are commensurate with their disparate purposes. Yet again, this is not true; both use their technologies in identical ways to fulfill differing purposes.

It is only by holding in tension the determinative *and* instrumental aspects of technology that we gain some clarity on the formative, yet seemingly paradoxical, role technology plays in shaping the late modern world. On the one hand, the determinative influence of technology cannot be denied, but its homogenizing influence is not total. There are only a limited number of ways that airplanes, computers and mobile telephones can be designed and used, thereby requiring that common skills must be learned. Yet these uses may not inevitably transform the users to any significant extent. Christians can remain Christians and Muslims remain Muslims while flying an airplane, surfing the web, or listening to the reading of a sacred text on a mobile telephone. On the other hand, instrumental flexibility cannot be denied, but this malleability is not infinite. Using a technology requires some adaptation on the part of the user that to some extent also transforms the user. Christians and Muslims use the same airplanes, computers and mobile telephones rather than developing different devices that are uniquely Christian or Muslim – there are no such things as Christian airplanes or Muslim computers. In holding the determinative and instrumental poles in tension, the principal issue at stake is to identify and assess the extent to which the adaptation required by the use of various technologies exerts a corrosive influence on prior religious convictions. Is adapting to rapid advances in transportation and information technologies, for instance, subtly transforming Christians and Muslims into consumers of religious commodities instead of believers formed by particular religious practices? And in turn, what kinds of practices are needed to prevent such adaptation from becoming malformation?

In respect to the purpose of this inquiry, we may ask specifically: what practices are needed to develop and use technologies that enable a faithful exercising of limited dominion? And more importantly, what practices are required to resist behavioral adaptations promoting malformation? Or more tersely, how should Christian faith be performed and enacted in an emerging technoculture as portrayed in postmodern rhetoric and posthuman discourse? Answering these questions requires a counter form of discourse, one which is theological, and therefore formative of both a moral vision and particular acts of social and political ordering. Moreover, there is no foregone conclusion that technology assists or distracts in forming this vision and performing these acts. The issue at stake is not merely to critique the development and application of technology, but to assess the underlying paradigms driving this development and application, so that discriminating choices can be made in respect to its influence on Christian formation or malformation. Consequently, *practice* bears a heavy weight in performing and enacting Christian faith, for the right ordering and amendment of love, hope and desire are accomplished through specific practices.

The concept of focal things and practices developed by Albert Borgmann offers a fruitful conceptual framework.[3] According to Borgmann, technology dominates both the foreground and background of contemporary culture. This domination does not merely reflect the ubiquity of machines, gadgets and artifacts in the fabric of daily life. Rather, technology represents both the means and ends of what is valued, and, perhaps more importantly, technological potential is the premier force in forming social mores and individual values. What Borgmann calls the *device paradigm* promotes wide-ranging 'commodification and mechanization', leading to 'cultural displacement', distraction and diminished engagement (Borgmann, 2003, pp. 122–3 and 1984, pp. 76–88). Various technologies have helped make food more affordable and readily available; fast food and frozen dinners are cheap and easily consumed. In valuing cost, availability and ease of preparation, however, food is reduced to a commodity to be consumed rather than the means through which a meal serves as an occasion for social interaction and exchange. Dining is exchanged for munching and eating on the run.

Borgmann is not a technological determinist. He is not arguing that technology inevitably transforms dining into grazing. Individuals with sufficient time are free to prepare and share leisurely meals. Rather, he is contending that the values of cost, availability and easy preparation exert strong pressures to transform dining into consuming commodities. The result is that dining becomes increasingly difficult to practice, and is thereby devalued due to inattention. A similar pattern is repeated in respect to a wide range of habits and activities. When work and leisure are reduced to primarily producing and consuming commodities respectively, the fabric of daily life is subtly, yet substantially, altered. Moreover, the enfolding and enveloping character of this alteration is exacerbated by the atomizing tendencies of postmodern rhetoric which presumes that human life and the lives of humans must necessarily grow increasingly fragmented (Borgmann, 2000, pp. 353–4).

In response to these commodifying and fragmenting tendencies, Borgmann contends that the 'counterforce to the rule of technology is the dedication to focal things and practices' (ibid., p. 356). What are focal things and practices? Defined succinctly, 'Generally, a focal thing is concrete and of a commanding presence. A focal practice is the decided, regular, and normally communal devotion to a focal thing' (Borgmann, 2003, p. 22). A focal thing is not an artifact and therefore a commodity to be consumed, but an objective reality that shapes the values and behavior of those whose attention is seized by its presence. A focal practice consists of acts that express and perform the values and behavior that are formed by those devoted to the focal thing. Although a focal thing commands the attention of its devotees it is not self-sufficient, requiring the care and attentiveness of practitioners. Focal things and practices thereby embody a formative tradition against which the character and virtues of its adherents are conformed. In this respect, Borgmann's account of focal things and practices is similar to Alasdair MacIntyre's exposition of internal goods and practices, in that both are attempting to explicate a normative structure of what constitutes a good life (Borgmann, 1984, pp. 206–7; MacIntyre, 1985).

Borgmann uses a family meal to illustrate the formative influence of focal things and practices. 'The great meal of the day, be it at noon or in the evening, is a focal event par excellence. It gathers the scattered family around the table' (Borgmann, 1984, p. 204). Those gathered at the table, however, are not present merely to consume food. Rather, the meal itself becomes a focal point of activity, binding the family together through common traditions and practices. Ingredients are carefully chosen and prepared in following favorite recipes. The table must be properly set, and later the tableware washed and stored. Family members must also adjust their schedules to be present at the prescribed time, and focus their attention in order to participate in the conversation around the table. Moreover, the meal links the family to a larger network of social relationships. When guests are present there are rules of hospitality to follow, and the meal itself should inspire a sense of thanksgiving for the efforts of farmers, cooks, dishwashers and crafters who make the meal possible. As a focal activity, such a meal is the 'enactment of generosity and gratitude, the affirmation of mutual and perhaps religious obligations', a far cry from the 'social and cultural anonymity of a fast-food outlet' (ibid., p. 205). Most importantly, the meal as a focal thing reinforces the fact that those formed by the practices of the dinner table are finite and temporal creatures. They are dependent upon bountiful harvests, and unlike the easy and incessant consumption of packaged commodities, the communal meal is bracketed by time; it has a designated beginning, middle and end.

The 'culture of the table' (Borgmann, 2003, pp. 117–28) is emblematic of a larger form of 'deictic discourse' (Borgmann, 1984, pp. 169–80) that provides a potent counterforce to an emerging technoculture. Why is such counterforce needed? In answering this question it is important to emphasize that Borgmann is not anti-technology. By invoking the culture of the table he is *not* grasping for a nostalgic fantasy of a bygone, less frenetic age. Rather, the deictic discourse generated by focal things and practices is needed to bring about a 'principled and fruitful reform of technology' (Borgmann, 2003, p. 22). This reform is especially urgent as we cross the postmodern divide (Borgmann, 1992). According to Borgmann, we are crossing over, or have already entered, a postmodern world. As described in chapter two, the postmodern terrain is one without permanent borders and boundaries, subject to endless and temporary construction of this malleable material in respect to intellectual paradigms, moral values, social relationships and political structures. In this respect, postmodernism is, ironically, an effective critical tool, but an ineffective constructive instrument. Technology is the principal tool that is used in asserting contending and temporary patterns of order. Yet in the process of constructing these various realities, the creators construct themselves as well. There is nothing in postmodern discourse, then, that would preclude the prospect of humans recreating or transforming themselves into posthumans.

In order to navigate postmodernity's perilous and chaotic terrain, liberals propose social engineering, while conservatives try to recover a natural order. Borgmann insists that neither option is tenable, because we 'live in self-imposed exile from communal conversation and action' (ibid., p. 3). The devastating consequences include a naked public square, soulless procedural politics, cancerous individualism and a narcissistic pursuit of loneliness. Although various technologies have significantly improved the physical well-being of many people, Borgmann concludes that the emerging, postmodern technoculture is accompanied by declining happiness and shabby standards of excellence (Borgmann, 2000, pp. 356–60). Consequently, he fears that the postmodern world may simply become a hypermodern and hyperactive realm of sullen resentment (Borgmann, 1992, pp. 5–19). The problem with such a world is not that it is overtly wicked, but rather, its pervading shallowness and banality slowly drains the vitality of its inhabitants.

Borgmann believes, however, that such a sullen fate is not inevitable. As an alternative he proposes a 'postmodern realism' that is characterized by 'patient vigor' and 'communal celebration' (ibid., pp. 110–47). The limits of this inquiry do not permit a detailed and critical exposition of Borgmann's postmodern realism, but it suffices to note that the principal challenge at hand is to establish genuine communities which, through the emergence of festive cities and communal politics, can resist the commodification of postmodernity's hyperactivity. The goal is to establish a culture and polity that is a 'community of communities rather than a society of sects' (ibid., p. 141). Focal things and practices play a pivotal role in achieving this goal, for communities cannot be manufactured; they can only be encouraged to grow through focal activities. These focal communities serve as pockets of resistance to the emerging postmodern technoculture, for in contrast to its pervading banality, shallowness, individualism and consumerism, they offer a commitment to excellence, depth and celebratory communalism (Borgmann, 2003, p. 33). It is these communities that will be the vanguard for reforming technology. Borgmann uses a wide variety of focal activities such as sports, crafts, music and art to illustrate the parameters of his proposal, and it is significant that many connote implicitly religious, and in some instances explicitly Christian, dimensions. He admits, for instance, that for Christians it is but a 'short step' from the culture of the table to the sacrament of the Lord's Table (ibid., pp. 125–8).

I will take that short step to suggest that the Eucharist may serve Christians as a focal thing and practice to form and sustain a counter theological discourse to that offered by posthuman discourse. For Christians, the Eucharist is a commanding presence that captures their attentiveness and engagement. Through the requisite practices of confession, repentance and amendment of life, the Lord's Table becomes the centerpiece of celebrative community. The requisite practices are also formative, shaping the church as a repentant, forgiven and sanctified community. Moreover, the materially ordinary bread and wine affirm the finite and temporal nature of creaturely existence; it is in partaking of Christ's body and blood that we consent to the limits of necessity. Yet the Lord's Table is also an eschatological banquet, anticipating an eternal fellowship in the fullness of time; at this table we receive a foretaste of creation's good destiny in Christ. It is in and through lives formed by the Eucharist that Christians, in obedient freedom, assert a limited dominion over an unfolding creation. Or in less prosaic terms, the Eucharist provides Christians with a focal point for discerning how their finite lives may be conformed over time to the contours of a vindicated creation being drawn toward its destiny in Christ.

More broadly, I am suggesting that the Eucharist may, like Borgmann's culture of the table, serve an emblematic function for inspiring a decidedly Christian theological form of deictic discourse to counter that of posthuman discourse. Such theological discourse may provide the narrative and normative base to form communities that effectively resist a pervasively sullen and banal postmodern hyperactivity, and such resistance may help promote the kind of extensive reform of technology envisioned by Borgmann. What might these Christian communities look like, and what kind of ethic would ensue in promoting such extensive reform? That is the question this book begs, but it must wait to be answered. Answering that question would move this inquiry well beyond its limited scope, for it would require a detailed theological account of a fuller range of Christian focal things and practices, a more in-depth and critical assessment of postmodern realism, and the development of a proposed program of moral, social and political ordering. The more modest purpose of this book has been to offer a critical account of postmodern rhetoric and posthuman discourse from an overtly Christian theological perspective, and to suggest some rough outlines of an alternative form of moral discourse. I hope that my effort will inspire others to begin answering the question posed above, and more importantly, that it might prompt Christians when gathered at the Lord's Table to reflect on how their lives may be shaped in accordance with the commanding presence of this centrally focal sacrament of their faith.

Notes

1 Philosophy is the other discipline.
2 Grant undertakes this recovery of Greek philosophy and Christian theology, as represented by the symbols of Athens and Jerusalem, in his essay 'Two theological languages' (Grant, 2002, pp. 49–65). For a critical assessment of this attempt, see Hall, 1978.
3 This brief summary does not do justice to the scope and depth of Borgmann's critical and constructive analysis, and the reader is referred to his works in the bibliography.

Bibliography

Arendt, Hannah (1968), *The Origins of Totalitarianism*, San Diego, CA, and London: Harcourt.

Arendt, Hannah (1998), *The Human Condition*, Chicago and London: University of Chicago Press.

Athanasiadis, Harris (2001), *George Grant and the Theology of the Cross: The Christian foundations of his thought*, Toronto and London: University of Toronto Press.

Augustine (1984), *Concerning the City of God against the Pagans*, trans. Henry Bettenson, London: Penguin Books.

Barth, Karl (1958), *Church Dogmatics, Vol. III, Part 1: The doctrine of creation*, Edinburgh: T & T Clark.

Barth, Karl (1960), *Church Dogmatics, Vol. III, Part 3: The doctrine of creation*, Edinburgh: T & T Clark.

Basalla, George (1988), *The Evolution of Technology*, Cambridge, UK, and New York: Cambridge University Press.

Begley, Sharon (2004), 'New ethical minefield: Drugs to boost memory and sharpen attention', *The Wall Street Journal*, 1 October.

Bernstein, Richard J. (1991), *The New Constellation: The ethical–political horizons of modernity/postmodernity*, Cambridge, MA: MIT Press.

Bonhoeffer, Dietrich (1955), *Ethics*, trans. Neville Horton Smith, London: SCM Press.

Borgmann, Albert (1984), *Technology and the Character of Contemporary Life: A philosophical inquiry*, Chicago and London: University of Chicago Press.

Borgmann, Albert (1992), *Crossing the Postmodern Divide*, Chicago and London: University of Chicago Press.

Borgmann, Albert (1999), *Holding on to Reality: The nature of information at the turn of the millennium*, Chicago and London: University of Chicago Press.

Borgmann, Albert (2000), 'Reply to my critics', in Eric Higgs, Andrew Light and David Strong (eds), *Technology and the Good Life?*, Chicago and London: University of Chicago Press, pp. 341–70.

Borgmann, Albert (2003), *Power Failure: Christianity in the culture of technology*, Grand Rapids, MI: Brazos Press.

Bostrom, Nick (n.d.), *Transhumanist Values*, http://www.nickbostrom.com/ethics/values.html

Bostrom, Nick (2003), *In Defense of Posthuman Dignity*, http://www.nickbostrom.com/ethics/dignity.html

Brooke, John Hedley (1991), *Science and Religion: Some historical perspectives*, Cambridge, UK, and New York: Cambridge University Press.

Brooks, Rodney A. (2002), *Flesh and Machines: How robots will change us*, New York: Pantheon Books.

Brown, Peter (1996), *The Rise of Western Christendom: Triumph and diversity AD 200–1000*, Oxford and Malden, MA: Blackwell.

Brown, Peter (2000), *Augustine of Hippo: A biography*, Berkeley and Los Angeles, CA: University of California Press.

Brunner, Emil (1949), *Christianity and Civilisation: Second part: Specific problems*, New York: Charles Scribner's Sons.

Bushnell, Horace (1849), *God in Christ: Three discourses, delivered at New Haven, Cambridge, and Andover, with a preliminary dissertation on language*, Hartford, CT: Brown and Parsons.

Bushnell, Horace (1960), *Christian Nurture*, New Haven, CT: Yale University Press.

Cole-Turner, Ronald (1993), *The New Genesis: Theology and the genetic revolution*, Louisville, KY: Westminster/John Knox Press.

Deane-Drummond, Celia E. (2001), *Biology and Theology Today: Exploring the Boundaries*, London: SCM Press.

Edwards, Jonathan (1974), *The Works of Jonathan Edwards, Vol. I*, Edinburgh and Carlisle, PA: Banner of Truth Trust.

Ellul, Jacques (1964), *The Technological Society*, trans. John Wilkinson, New York: Vintage Books.

Ellul, Jacques (1985), *The Humiliation of the Word*, trans. Joyce Main Hanks, Grand Rapids, MI: Eerdmans.

Elshtain, Jean Bethke (1981), *Public Man, Private Woman: Women in social and political thought*, Princeton, NJ: Princeton University Press.

Elshtain, Jean Bethke (1995), *Augustine and the Limits of Politics*, Notre Dame, IN: University of Notre Dame Press.

Engelhardt, H. Tristram, Jr. (1996), *The Foundations of Bioethics*, 2nd edn, New York and Oxford: Oxford University Press.

Ferkiss, Victor C. (1969), *Technological Man: The myth and the reality*, New York: Mentor Book.

Fukuyama, Francis (2002), *Our Posthuman Future: Consequences of the biotechnology revolution*, New York: Farrar, Straus and Giroux.

Gay, Peter (1966), *The Enlightenment: An interpretation – the rise of modern paganism*, New York and London: Norton & Co.

Gay, Peter (1969), *The Enlightenment: An interpretation – the science of freedom*, New York and London: Norton & Co.

Graham, Elaine L. (2002), *Representations of the Post/Human: Monsters, aliens and others in popular culture*, New Brunswick, NJ: Rutgers University Press; Manchester, UK: Manchester University Press.

Grant, Edward (1996), *The Foundations of Modern Science in the Middle Ages: Their religious, institutional, and intellectual contexts*, Cambridge, UK, and New York: Cambridge University Press.

Grant, George (1969), *Technology and Empire: Perspectives on North America*, Toronto: House of Anansi.

Grant, George (1985), *English-Speaking Justice*, Notre Dame, IN: University of Notre Dame Press.

Grant, George (1986), *Technology and Justice*, Notre Dame, IN: University of Notre Dame Press.

Grant, George (1995a), *Philosophy in the Mass Age*, ed. William Christian, Toronto and London: University of Toronto Press.

Grant, George (1995b), *Time as History*, ed. William Christian, Toronto and London: University of Toronto Press.

Grant, George (2000), *Lament for a Nation: The defeat of Canadian nationalism*, Montreal and London: McGill-Queen's University Press.

Grant, George (2002), *Collected Works of George Grant, Vol. 2: 1951–1959*, ed. Arthur Davis, Toronto and London: University of Toronto Press.

de Grey, Aubrey, ed. (2004), *Strategies for Engineered Negligible Senescence: Why genuine control of aging may be foreseeable*, New York: New York Academy of Sciences.

Gunton, Colin E. (1993), *The One, the Three, and the Many: God, creation and the culture of modernity, the Bampton Lectures 1992*, Cambridge, UK, and New York: Cambridge University Press.

Gustafson, James (1981), *Ethics from a Theocentric Perspective: Vol. 1: Theology and ethics*, Chicago: University of Chicago Press; Oxford: Basil Blackwell.

Habermas, Jürgen (2003), *The Future of Human Nature*, Cambridge, UK: Polity Press.

Hall, Douglas John (1978), 'The significance of Grant's cultural analysis for Christian theology in North America', in Larry Schmidt (ed.), *George Grant in Process: Essays and conversations*, Toronto: Anansi Press, pp. 120–29.

Hall, Stephen S. (2003), *Merchants of Immortality: Chasing the dream of human life extension*, Boston, MA, and New York: Houghton Mifflin Co.

Haraway, Donna J. (1991), *Simians, Cyborgs, and Women: The reinvention of nature*, London: Free Association Books; New York: Routledge.

Hayles, M. Katherine (1999), *How we became Posthuman: Virtual bodies in cybernetics, literature, and informatics*, Chicago and London: University of Chicago Press.

Haseltine, William A. (2003), 'Regenerative medicine: A future healing art', *The Brookings Review*, **21**(1), Winter, 38–43.

Hauerwas, Stanley (1995), *In Good Company: The church as polis*, Notre Dame, IN, and London: University of Notre Dame Press.

Heaven, Edwin B., and David R. Heaven (1978), 'Some influences of Simone Weil on George Grant's silence', in Larry Schmidt (ed.), *George Grant in Process: Essays and conversations*, Toronto: Anansi Press, pp. 68–78.

Hefner, Philip (1993), *The Human Factor: Evolution, culture, and religion*, Minneapolis, MN: Fortress Press.

Hefner, Philip (2003), *Technology and Human Becoming*, Minneapolis, MN: Fortress Press.

Heidegger, Martin (1977), *The Question Concerning Technology and Other Essays*, trans. William Lovitt, New York and London: Harper & Row.

Heidelberg Catechism (1962), trans. Allen O. Miller and M. Eugene Osterhaven, Philadelphia: United Church Press.

Heim, Michael (1993), *The Metaphysics of Virtual Reality*, Oxford and New York: Oxford University Press.

Herzfeld, Noreen L. (2002), *In Our Image: Artificial intelligence and the human spirit*, Minneapolis, MN: Fortress Press.

Hobbes, Thomas (1996), *Leviathan*, ed. J. C. A. Gaskin, Oxford and New York: Oxford University Press.

Hogue, David A. (2003), *Remembering the Future Imagining the Past: Story, ritual, and the human brain*, Cleveland, OH: Pilgrim Press.

Houston, Graham (1998), *Virtual Morality: Christian ethics in the computer age*, Leicester, UK: Apollos.

Jeeves, Malcolm, ed. (2004), *From Cells to Souls – and Beyond: Changing portraits of human nature*, Grand Rapids, MI, and Cambridge, UK: Eerdmans.

Joy, Bill (2000), 'Why the future doesn't need us', *Wired*, **8**.04, April.

Kant, Immanuel (1991), *Political Writings*, ed. Hans Reiss and trans. H. B. Nisbet, Cambridge, UK, and New York: Cambridge University Press.

Kass, Leon R. (1985), *Toward a More Natural Science: Biology and human affairs*, New York and London: Free Press.

Kass, Leon R. (2002), *Life, Liberty and the Defense of Dignity: The challenge for bioethics*, San Francisco, CA: Encounter Books.

Kass, Leon R. (2004/2005), 'On human frailty and human dignity', *The New Atlantis*, **7**, Fall/Winter.

Kasson, John F. (1976), *Civilizing the Machine: Technology and republican values in America 1776–1900*, Harmondsworth, UK, and New York: Penguin Books.

Kaufman, Gordon D. (2004), *In the Beginning ... Creativity*, Minneapolis, MN: Fortress Press.

Kuhn, Thomas S. (1970), *The Structure of Scientific Revolutions*, 2nd edn, Chicago: University of Chicago Press.

Kurzweil, Ray (2000), *The Age of Spiritual Machines: When computers exceed human intelligence*, New York and London: Penguin Books.

LaFee, Scott (2004), 'Blanks for the memories', *The San Diego Union-Tribune*, 11 February.

Lamb, Gregory M. (2004), 'Strange food for thought', *The Christian Science Monitor*, 17 June.

Lasch, Christopher (1991), *The True and Only Heaven: Progress and its critics*, New York and London: Norton & Co.

Latourette, Kenneth Scott (1975), *A History of Christianity, Vol. I: to A.D. 1500*, New York and London: Harper & Row.

Lindberg, David C. and Ronald L. Numbers, eds (1986), *God and Nature: Historical essays on the encounter between Christianity and science*, Berkeley, CA, and London: University of California Press.

McCosh, James (1882), *The Method of Divine Government, Physical and Moral*, London: Macmillan and Co.

McGrath, Alister E. (2002), *A Scientific Theology, Vol. 2: Reality*, Edinburgh: T & T Clark; Grand Rapids, MI: Eerdmans.

MacIntyre, Alasdair (1985), *After Virtue: A study in moral theory*, London: Duckworth.

MacKay, Donald M. (1991), *Behind the Eye*, Oxford and Cambridge, MA: Basil Blackwell.

McKenny, Gerald P. (1997), *To Relieve the Human Condition: Bioethics, technology, and the body*, Albany, NY: State University of New York Press.

Meilaender, Gilbert C. (1995), *Body, Soul, and Bioethics*, Notre Dame, IN, and London: University of Notre Dame Press.

Meilaender, Gilbert (1996), *Bioethics: A primer for Christians*, Grand Rapids, MI: Eerdmans.

Mitchell, Robert and Phillip Thurtle, eds (2004), *Data Made Flesh: Embodying information*, New York and London: Routledge.

Moravec, Hans (1988), *Mind Children: The future of robot and human intelligence*, Cambridge, MA, and London: Harvard University Press.

Moravec, Hans (1999), *Robot: Mere machines to transcendent mind*, Oxford and New York: Oxford University Press.

Morris, Simon Conway (2003), *Life's Solution: Inevitable humans in a lonely universe*, Cambridge, UK, and New York: Cambridge University Press.

Niebuhr, H. Richard (1951), *Christ and Culture*, New York and London: Harper & Row.

Niebuhr, H. Richard (1960), *Radical Monotheism and Western Culture*, New York and London: Harper & Row.

Nisbet, Robert A. (1980), *History of the Idea of Progress*, New York: Basic Books.

Noble, David F. (1999), *The Religion of Technology: The divinity of man and the spirit of invention*, New York and London: Penguin Books.

O'Connor, Anahad (2004), 'Wakefulness finds a powerful ally', *The New York Times*, 29 June.

O'Donovan, Joan E. (1984), *George Grant and the Twilight of Justice*, Toronto and London: University of Toronto Press.

O'Donovan, Oliver (1986), *Resurrection and Moral Order: An outline for evangelical ethics*, Leicester, UK: Inter-Varsity Press; Grand Rapids, MI: Eerdmans.

O'Donovan, Oliver (1996), *The Desire of the Nations: Rediscovering the roots of political theology*, Cambridge, UK, and New York: Cambridge University Press.

Paley, William (1820), *Natural Theology: Or, evidences of the existence and attributes of the deity, collected from the appearance of nature*, New York: Evert Duychinck.

Pannenberg, Wolfhart (1994), *Systematic Theology, Vol. 2*, trans. Geoffrey W. Bromiley, Grand Rapids, MI: Eerdmans; Edinburgh: T & T Clark.

Passmore, John (1970), *The Perfectibility of Man*, New York: Charles Scribner's Sons.

Peacocke, A. R. (1979), *Creation and the World of Science: The Bampton Lectures, 1978*, Oxford: Clarendon Press.

Peacocke, Arthur (1986), *God and the New Biology*, San Francisco, CA, and London: Harper & Row.

Peacocke, Arthur (1993), *Theology for a Scientific Age: Being and becoming – natural, divine and human*, London: SCM.

Pollard, William G. (1958), *Chance and Providence: God's action in a world governed by scientific law*, London: Faber and Faber.

President's Council on Bioethics (2003), *Beyond Therapy: Biotechnology and the Pursuit of Happiness*, Washington, DC: A Report of the President's Council on Bioethics.

Pullinger, David (2001), *Information Technology and Cyberspace: Extra-connected living*, London: Darton, Longman and Todd; Cleveland, OH: Pilgrim Press.

Ramsey, Paul (1970), *The Patient as Person: Exploration in medical ethics*, New Haven, CT and London: Yale University Press.

Rauschenbusch, Walter (1991), *Christianity and the Social Crisis*, Louisville, KY: Westminster/John Knox Press.

Rauschenbusch, Walter (1997), *A Theology for the Social Gospel*, Louisville, KY: Westminster/John Knox Press.

Rawls, John (1972), *A Theory of Justice*, Oxford and New York: Oxford University Press.

Rawls, John (1996), *Political Liberalism*, New York: Columbia University Press.

Rist, John M. (1994), *Augustine: Ancient thought baptized*, Cambridge, UK, and New York: Cambridge University Press.

Robertson, John A. (1994), *Children of Choice: Freedom and the new reproductive technologies*, Princeton, NJ: Princeton University Press.

Schmidt, Larry (1978), 'George Grant and the problem of history', in Larry Schmidt (ed.), *George Grant in Process: Essays and conversations*, Toronto: Anansi Press, pp. 130–38.

Schultze, Quentin J. (2002), *Habits of the High-Tech Heart: Living virtuously in the information age*, Grand Rapids, MI: Baker Academic.

Shults, F. LeRon (2003), *Reforming Theological Anthropology: After the philosophical turn to relationality*, Grand Rapids, MI, and Cambridge, UK: Eerdmans.

Song, Robert (1997), *Christianity and Liberal Society*, Oxford: Clarendon Press.

Springsted, Eric O., ed. (1998), *Simone Weil*, Maryknoll, NY: Orbis Books.

Stein, Rob (2004), 'Is every memory worth keeping?', *Washington Post*, 19 October.

Suchocki, Marjorie Hewitt (1988), *The End of Evil: Process eschatology in historical context*, Albany, NY: State University of New York Press.

Teilhard de Chardin, Pierre (1964), *The Future of Man*, trans. Norman Denny, London: Collins.

Teilhard de Chardin, Pierre (1965), *The Phenomenon of Man*, New York and London: Harper & Row.

Turner, James (1985), *Without God, Without Creed: The origins of unbelief in America*, Baltimore, MD, and London: Johns Hopkins University Press.

Verhey, Allen (2002), *Remembering Jesus: Christian community, scripture, and the moral life*, Grand Rapids, MI, and Cambridge, UK: Eerdmans.

Waters, Brent (1992), 'A meditation on fate and destiny in a technological age', *Bulletin of Science, Technology and Society*, **12** (4 & 5).

Waters, Brent (2001), *Reproductive Technology: Towards a theology of procreative stewardship*, London: Darton, Longman and Todd; Cleveland, OH: Pilgrim Press.

Waters, Brent, and Ronald Cole-Turner, eds (2003), *God and the Embryo: Religious voices on stem cells and cloning*, Washington, DC: Georgetown University Press.

Index